THE SUN SHINES AT MIDNIGHT TOO

J. Lamarr Cox, Ph.D.

Aurole Publishing
P.O. Box 52292
Raleigh, NC 27612

Cover Design by Suzanne H. Holt

Sketches by Marie Turner

Publisher's Cataloging in Publication

Cox, J. Lamarr.
    The sun shines at midnight too / J. Lamarr Cox
    p.cm.
    ISBN 0-9646440-0-2

    1. Life. 2.Philosophy. 3.Happiness. I. Title.
BD431.C69 1995   128
                   QBI95-20222

ISBN 0-9646440-0-2

Library of Congress Catalog Card Number 95-76784

Aureole Publishing
P.O. Box 52292
Raleigh, NC 27612

To
Julie, the love of my life;
and to my friends,
they know who they are.

Contents

Contents

Contents

I. Starting Where I Am

The last of earth's brash Gobblegales,
In seeking something he could munch,
Caught just a glimpse of shiny scales
And craved their owner for his lunch,
In circles tight, at speeds unknown,
Around and round he sought his goal,
And grabbed a tail—it was his own—
And swallowed himself whole.

1

"Good afternoon!" Or, "Good morning," if you are one of those nuts who read before noon. My day began as usual. I awoke early, about six o'clock, I suppose. I lay in bed a while longer, partly because the bed was warm and the morning air cool, and partly to listen to the cooing of the doves. If doves were more aggressive with their coos, I thought, their calls would not differ greatly from the call of the owl I heard during the night. And I was glad they were not more aggressive. I liked them the way they were. While the cooing of the doves was a restful, peaceful sound, I had found the distant "Whoo? Whoo? Whoo?" of the owl to be mildly disturbing. Whoo, indeed! I already knew "whoo"; what I wanted to know was why, what, and how! I wanted to know, for example, why I should get out of bed, what I wished to do with the day, and how I could know for sure it made any difference. On a larger scale, I wanted to know why the busy, busy years of my life had passed so swiftly, what I wanted to do with the balance of my life, and how I would ever find the answers.

The mental search for a rough draft of reasonably satisfactory answers shook the last traces of drowsiness from my foggy brain. I sat on the side of the bed and stretched. The thin sliver of daylight that had found its way through the gap between the panels of the not-quite-closed drapes provided just enough light for me to see to dress without stumbling over something and disturbing my wife, who was still asleep. I touched Cleopatra the Cat gently between her ears. She half-opened her eyes, purred softly, and settled a bit more firmly into the upholstery on top of the back of the bedroom chair. I moved quietly down the hall to the back door. It was the beginning of a new day in the journey from HERE to THERE.

I opened the door to the back porch, stepped out into the cool, quiet morning air, and eased the door shut behind me. As is my custom, I walked down the covered walkway to my workshop and scooped up one coffee can of bird seeds and another of sunflower seeds. I took these to the spot just beyond the walkway where the ground has been pecked and scratched bare. There I scattered the bird seeds on the ground for my chickadees, titmice, wrens, doves, and other bird types. Squeaks the Squirrel was up early and was sitting on one of the fence posts beside the gate that opened into the small, winter-idled vegetable garden. She was waiting for first pick of the sunflower seeds. She jumped to the ground and stood facing me with one small, grey paw folded across her snowy-white chest.

I said my usual, "Good morning, Squeaks," as I stood over her with the can of sunflower seeds in my hand.

Squeaks stared me in the eye and said, "A seed in my craw is worth ten in your paw, you know. Are you going to put 'em down here or just stand there and hold on to 'em 'till I starve to death?"

I spread the seeds on the ground for her and the other squirrels who had not yet arrived and replied, "There you are, thank you. It is a beautiful morning, isn't it?"

She bounced over, began an eager inspection of my offering and, finally, paused from her munching long enough to respond with, "Well, it could be if you would kind of keep your voice down. I don't 'xactly want to share these munchies with nine zillion other squirrels."

I stepped over her, picked up the garden hose, turned on the yard faucet, and refilled the bird bath that stood at the end of the feeding area next to the woods. I left Squeaks to her breakfast, walked down the gravel driveway to the street, and picked up the newspaper. On my way back, I used the toe of my shoe to smooth out the gravel the deer had kicked up on their nightly trips through the yard. I slipped the rubber band off the newspaper and tossed it into the trash bin. I also paused to pick up and toss back in the few scraps of trash that had been removed during a raccoon's or opossum's nightly raid. I paused to chide myself briefly for forgetting to latch the trash bin the previous evening and, then, I left the still-shadowy yard for the cheerful lights of the kitchen. With my first cup of instant decaf steaming in one hand, I fumbled the newspaper open on the kitchen table and began to read what someone, somewhere thought was important. Cleopatra jumped onto the seat of the chair next to me and, using the chair arm as a step, eased herself onto the table and curled up on top of my newspaper, completely covering the article I had been reading.

I said, "Well, thank you!"

She half-opened one eye and grumbled, "Keep it down, please. I am still mostly asleep."

And, so, I kept it down. But this interference didn't really matter; I wasn't all that interested in the newspaper or talking with cats anyway. I love to sit at the window in the quiet of the dawn's half-light and watch the first streaks of orange appear on the eastern horizon. This is my favorite time for reviewing my schedule for the day and trying to note where there might be an empty minute here or there into which I might squeeze some additional activity. Finally, satisfied that I had my priorities for the day reasonably straight, I popped a frozen bagel into the microwave, punched a few random buttons to start it growling, pulled a container of cream cheese from the refrigerator, and ate my bit of breakfast. The smell of food roused Cleopatra from her sleep, and she closed her teeth gently on my hand as a reminder of what might happen to me if she were not fed immediately. I got up, reached into the pantry, pulled down a new can of minced mouse or whatever, opened it, and fed Cleopatra. I then was free to start my day's work.

While waiting for the grass to give up its cool, dewy dampness, I cleared a flower bed of the first green weeds of spring, cleaned the automobile windshields, pumped up one of the tires on my bicycle, picked up sticks and leaves from the driveway, and checked the spark plug, oil, and gasoline in the lawn mower. After considerable difficulty, I got the lawn mower engine started. It always is difficult to start after sitting idle all winter.

3

I spent most of the remainder of the morning mowing grass and trimming around trees, fences, and flower beds. Before I realized it, the morning was gone. I ate lunch, cleared the table, fixed myself another cup of decaf, and retired to the porch chair to take a few minutes to catch my breath.

Cleopatra, pleased that the outdoors finally was free of the growling of the lawn mower, climbed up my leg, jumped to the table next to me, eased herself into a reclining position, and instantly fell asleep. Casey the Canine bounced over from next door, said his hellos, and stretched out on the bricks of the porch floor.

2

So, there I sat in the cool quiet of a spring afternoon with only the sounds of Cleopatra's low purrs, the peeping and chirping of the birds, the chattering of the squirrels, and the soft thump thump of Casey's tail on the floor. Times like those are conducive to sitting, absorbing the stillness, and thinking. Several months had passed since I stopped going to the office every day, and I had not quite adjusted to the resultant momentous changes in my life. Retirement, some call it. For me, it was more a case of shifting gears and starting up a steep hill in a new direction. And, while I still seemed to be fully occupied, I must not have been quite as busy as before because I seemed to have a bit of time, every now and then, to THINK. And THINKING can be ever so much bother! It is much easier and less painful to stay so busy that one doesn't have time to think. But thinking seemed to be an appropriate occupation while sitting there in my chair with Cleopatra the Cat curled up beside me. Besides, I dared not move. She had reached over with one paw and had her claws dug lightly into my leg. This was her involuntary response to my attention to Casey the Canine—for whom she has an intense innate disdain.

I have what I suppose is an advantage over many people in that I can do pretty much anything I please with each day. This is considerably more the result, of course, of what pleases me than it is of what I can do. But, one of the things I have learned in life is that the only sure way to get what you want is to want what you get. And, that afternoon, what I was getting was the opportunity to sit there in my chair for a while, sip my decaf, rub Cleopatra's ears, watch Casey's eyes slowly close as sleep overtook him, and think a bit about my yesterdays, todays, and tomorrows.

One of my more mundane thoughts was about the previous day's trip to the neighborhood library. There, I had searched through past copies of the Home Whodunit magazine for an article I remembered seeing earlier in my own copy of the magazine. I had, of course, discarded my copy, thinking, as I often do when I get rid of something I am certain to need later, that I can't keep everything. The article was about how to clean a VCR. I found the article in the library, photocopied it, brought the copy home, and put it on top of our VCR to remind me to read it again to see if I thought the instructions were clear and simple enough for me to follow. So, the previous evening, I read the article. It was clear and straightforward enough. I was reasonably certain I could follow the instructions and clean the VCR.

And, so, this afternoon I was thinking about all the clear, straightforward instructions I have seen and heard in my lifetime. There have been instructions on almost every conceivable subject: how to tune your automobile engine, how to make a million dollars, how to lose weight, how to get a wife, how to get the cheapest airline tickets, how to make Christmas decorations out of colored popcorn, and a million other things both useful and ridiculous. Also, there has been endless advice: try McDuck's grease biscuits, buy a cemetery plot today, use Scratcho toothpaste, drive a Mammoth automobile, recognize that nine doctors out of ten recommend Pinky Winky Pills, and drink Burpo to be a part of the "in" crowd. Added to this, the ministers, priests, rabbis, psychologists, sociologists, economists, politicians, bartenders, hairdressers, and others have constantly offered instructions and advice on all aspects of life. We perhaps have good reason to call this the information age. With my computer-to-telephone connection, I literally am able to access mountains of information. The local library, as well as the shelves of my own study, is filled with more information than I will ever be able to use. Virtually everything the human animal has ever put into thoughts is available from one information source or another. If all the world's instructions and advice were laid end to end, they would reach from here to eternity and back.

But, I wondered, why is it, that even with all these instructions, all this information, and all this advice, we seem to have so much difficulty keeping our directions straight? I remembered an experience I had some years ago flying in a small plane through a stormy night between Denver and some obscure town in western Kansas. The pilot remarked to the six or eight passengers that we had a strong tail wind and, thus, were making excellent time. And then he added, "Unfortunately, we also are lost!"

I remembered that night, and I wondered about the wisdom of hurrying through life without having our directions straight. Why, I wondered, do most of us, if we ever stop running long enough to think about it, have such an empty, sinking feeling that we don't quite understand what is going on with us and the world around us? And it occurred to me that most of the instructions, information, and advice available to us deal with the trivial incidents of life, but not with life itself. Each of us is traveling through a strange land without a map, without a compass, and with only a few hints as to where and why we are traveling. We see the bits and pieces of life but fail to see the whole of it. Seeing the whole of life requires, perhaps, the courage to be fully aware and the discipline to act on our awareness. And this can be a difficult, painful, and risky thing. It is not surprising, I suppose, that we hide from ourselves in the humdrum of daily activities. But even the pilot who is making good time needs occasionally to rise above the clouds and get his directions straight. That is, unless he is willing to let the fates determine where he will land when he can soar no more.

I realized, as I sat there thinking, that the instructions on how to clean my VCR were not particularly important. In fact, I could easily get along with neither VCR nor television. More important is to have a reasonable understanding of life—and death. I have seen and felt, so it seemed to me, in my relatively short life, an eternity of unbearable suffering, sorrow, misery, and pain. I have seen and felt desolation, loneliness, fear of the known, and even greater fear of the unknown. I have, of course, also known and seen such wondrous things as joy, happiness, kindness, caring, sharing, and love. But, often, even in the midst of the goodness of life, I have seen lost souls searching vainly for meaning in a life that seems to them to have no meaning, and for direction in a world where the darkness obscures the few guideposts that might have helped mark their way.

And I, too, am not always certain of my way. I wish to be fully aware not only of each detail of my journey through life but also of why I am traveling and what destination I am attempting to reach. I want life to make sense to me. I want the pain, suffering, and despair to make sense to me. I want to know how the glad, secure, growing times fit in with the sad, scary, stagnant times. I want to know why the world is the way it is and how I fit into it. If I can't know all of this, I at least want to know as much as I can. And I want these things badly enough to be willing to work for them.

3

A pair of blue jays flew in and their raucous cries aroused Casey from his sleep. He raised his head, yawned mightily, and began again the thump thumping of his tail on the floor. I looked down at him and said, "Casey, you always look so contented and happy."

"Of course," he responded. "Aren't—woof—you?"

"Well," I admitted, "no, not always. I have my ups and downs."

"Woof," said Casey. "Happiness is a big bone with some meat still on it. Happiness is a bounce ball to bounce. Happiness is... woof, why aren't you always happy?"

"Well," I said, "I think it has to do with sometimes having difficulty finding meaning in life."

"No—woof—meaning?" asked Casey. "Where have you looked for meaning?"

I decided to tell him the truth, even though I doubted he would understand. "I have tried looking outward at the larger universe," I said. "But mostly all I saw was uncountable lights twinkling in endless darkness. And I already knew the lights, and I already knew the darkness. To get a better perspective of what planet Earth is like, I also have, in my fancy, often traveled to the moon and, a few times, to Mars and looked back on Earth for hints of things I might have missed from my usual close-up view. This, I regret to say, has not been particularly productive. While this showed Earth to be a relatively tiny and, perhaps, insignificant part of the whole, I think I already knew that.

Backing up and getting an even longer view from a distant star also seemed only to confirm what most of us already have gathered from other sources."

"Woof," said Casey. "No meat bones or bounce balls there? Woof! Where else have you looked?"

"I have, in an attempt to gain a different perspective, used a microscope to explore the tiny worlds that make up worlds," I said. "But, looking inward, I see only an infinity of the same things I see when I look outward. Also, I have used my mental time machine to try to shift into a different time perspective and look at life from the past and from the future. From both, I see mostly the same things I see through the telescope and microscope, countless lights twinkling in endless darkness."

A wee "meorl" came from Cleopatra who supposedly was asleep. I looked over and saw one eyelid ease open about an eighth of an inch. "You will not find it that way," she murmured.

"So, I suppose you have all the answers," I said.

"Don't bother me when I am sleeping," she said. "Try the obvious. Look, with greater awareness, at the place and time where you happen to be." And she was asleep again.

All was quiet for a minute and, then, Casey spoke up on a completely different subject. "I have—woof—been wondering," he said. "Where did you come from?"

Again, though sure he would not understand, I answered. "I am an alien here," I said. "Are not we all? I am a stranger in a strange land. Are not we all? We are merely passing through this time and place. We UNDERSTAND that we came from the dust of the earth and, inevitably, return to the earth. But, we do NOT believe that is all there is to it. We don't really know from where we came. We don't really know where we are. We don't really know why we are here. We don't really know where we are going. And we are not really sure how to find out."

"Is that really where you came from?" asked Casey, shaking his head in bewilderment. "I—woof—came from a kennel."

He was quiet for a minute and then apparently worked up enough courage to ask another question. "What did you mean back there when you said you—woof—have ups and downs?" he asked. "Do you mean you get—woof—bounced around a lot?"

"Something like that," I answered. "Sometimes, when the sun is shining, everything seems bright and happy. But, then, the sun goes down, and darkness and despair move in."

"Shortsighted!" snorted Cleopatra. "The sun shines at midnight too. But you let commonplace things stand in your way of seeing it. If you would just be aware and patient, you would see that what goes down comes around."

Casey stood up, stretched, yawned, scratched, and said, "At times like these—woof—dogged if I'm not simply delighted to be simply a delightful dog. Got to go home now and—woof—chew bones and bounce balls."

I patted him on the head and told him he was welcome over any time. Casey was off. Cleopatra scowled after him, grumbled to herself, jumped down from the table, and scratched on the door to be let into the house. I let her in and returned to my chair. I wanted to be alone with my thoughts.

Why, I wondered, was finding meaning in this alien world so difficult? Could it be that many of us refuse to search for eternal truths for fear of what we might find? And do others of us expect ready-made, easy, simple truths to be handed to us without effort on our part? Is truth "out there" somewhere waiting to be pounced upon, or are the pieces all about and within us waiting for conditions to be right for them to come together and be known?

Cleopatra probably was right; she usually is. Perhaps the dark times in life really are the results of our individual distorted perceptions. Perhaps, if we could rise above our doubts and fears, we could know a truer vision of life. Perhaps this new, more objective vision WOULD show the sun always shining, eternal promises always kept, and a life and death that have deep meaning and eternal significance. What new truths, I wondered, might we discover if we had the courage to be aware, the will to work, and the patience to wait?

I promised myself that I would begin at the time and place where I happened to be and that I would invite the pieces of truth to come together and be known. I promised to pay keener attention to my observations, thoughts, and feelings, to seek understanding, and to find the patience to wait.

II. Cleopatra, Queen of the Nile

I think I chose imprudently
The day I judged that she
Had choices, too, and callously
Chose to misjudge me.

4

There are days when I wander and days when I wonder; this had been one of the latter. I had been thinking about my decision to be more aware of the world within and without, and I was wondering if that decision would actually have any impact on my level of awareness. Did I MAKE a decision or was I simply doing what I had to do? Do we really have choices in life or are our destinies sealed by the fates? If we do have choices, why do we seem sometimes to choose to be less than fully aware? Thinking such long thoughts was beginning to make my head hurt, so I decided to get up from my favorite chair, stop thinking so hard, and go out on the porch and read the newspaper.

I started up from my chair and then stopped to reconsider. Did I HAVE to go sit on the porch and read the newspaper, or did I have choices? I could think of at least fifty things I could NOT do right then, even if I were to decide they were the things I wished to do. I could not, for example, flap my arms and fly; my arms are too small and my body too heavy. I could not rob the neighborhood bank; I was not sure why I could not, but it was just one of those things I could never bring myself to do. But, also, I could think of at least fifty things I COULD do if I wished. I really did have SOME choices. I might be a puppet in some ways, but in other ways I could pull my own strings. I did not even have to take the easy way out. I could choose to do certain things even when part of my data said it was not the thing I wished to do. To prove this to myself, I determined to stay in my chair and keep on thinking long thoughts, even if it did make my head hurt.

As I continued to puzzle over the degree to which we have choices and over the factors that seem to impact on our awareness, I looked down at Cleopatra the Cat who lay sleeping at my feet and my thoughts drifted back to a time sixteen years ago when she made some decisions that I still did not understand.

5

Her screams were heartbreaking, but we had done everything we knew to do. She had been high in the huge poplar tree for two days and obviously was growing weak from hunger, thirst, and exposure. She was just a kitten. She had been only six weeks old when we first got her, and she had lived with us for less than a year. We had named her Cleopatra, Queen of the Nile, after her predecessor who had died peacefully in her old age. Cleopatra, from the beginning, had been a great climber, but never before had she climbed such a large tree. The trunk of the poplar was about two feet in diameter, and Cleopatra was stuck on a limb fifty or sixty feet up. Something drastic had to be done that day, but we had no idea what to do.

I reviewed what we had tried thus far. We had spent endless hours trying to call her down. I had leaned a ladder against the tree trunk, climbed the sixteen feet to the top, and tried to coax her into "meeting me half way." Our teenage son had used pure logic and veiled threats in a vain attempt to talk her down. Our daughter, who was nine years old, had wept dramatic tears and promised the cat virtually everything we owned if she would just please, please come down. Some of our neighbors had tried tying a string to a stone, throwing the stone over a limb, and using the string to pull a rope over the limb. The string kept slipping off the stone. They substituted a golf ball in a sock but none of them could throw hard enough to get the ball over. They tried a bow and arrow, with a string tied to the arrow. They had only two arrows. These got hung up in the tree and likely are still there. The neighbors gave up and went home.

My wife talked to the vet who said cats usually come down on their own if you leave them alone. But, after two days and a cold, rainy night, he did not seem quite so confident. He suggested another vet who specialized in wild animals. My wife phoned the new vet but was told we would have to bring the cat to his office; he did not make house calls.

Next, we called the police. They could do nothing because the cat had broken no laws. They said cats in trees was what fire departments were for. We phoned the fire department and were told they did not do cats. We asked them what they thought we should do. Their advice was to get a long ladder and ropes and go up after her. I asked where I might get such a long ladder. They said the only place was the fire department. I thanked them for their advice and asked when they could bring a ladder. They asked if my house was on fire. I said I did not think so. They said I should call back if the house caught fire and then they would bring a ladder. I phoned a tree service and asked them if they did cats. They said they would be glad to cut down the tree so I could retrieve the cat myself. I said I was afraid the tree's crashing down would kill the cat. They said they would guarantee their method would kill the tree but their guarantee did not cover cats in any shape, form, or fashion, and that if I wanted a guarantee on a cat, I should phone a pet shop or a vet.

I phoned the power company and asked if they climbed trees. They said they only climbed poles and, if I could get the cat to come down from the tree and climb a pole instead, they would be happy to come out and rescue her. I phoned the telephone company. They asked if my phone was working. I replied that it seemed to be working fine. They said, in that case, I should not bother them but should phone somebody to come get the cat down. They recommended that I use the yellow pages to locate an appropriate rescue organization. I looked under "cats," but all I could find was "catalog showrooms," "caterers," and "cattle guards." I tried "climbing," but found only "clergy," "clinics," and "see mountain climbing equipment." I turned to "mountain climbing equipment," but found only a reference that said "see climbing." I already had tried "trees," but decided to try again. I selected several tree services that had impressive advertisements in the yellow pages. I phoned them and received several offers to take down the tree and grind up the stump but none to rescue the cat. I went out and called "here, kitty, kitty" until my throat was sore. Cleopatra's throat must have been sore too; her screams had changed to low croaks.

I phoned the fire department again and asked what they could do for me if the tree happened to, accidentally-like, catch fire. This would be a small fire, of course, down around the base of the trunk where the smoke would not hurt the cat. They said something about the stiff penalty for arson and reminded me that, even if they came to put out a tree fire, they might have to bulldoze my house out of the way to get to the tree. I hung up on them, but they had given me a new idea. I went to the hardware store and bought a special nozzle for the garden hose. This nozzle made a fine, strong stream of water. Maybe I could climb the sixteen-foot ladder, aim the hose at the limb where Cleopatra sat, and scare her into coming down. After all, she hated water. I climbed and I squirted. Cleopatra found her lost voice, let out a shriek, and climbed another twenty feet up the tree. I gave up. I was out of ideas. She would just have to stay up there and starve to death.

My neighbor dropped by to see what was causing all the commotion. He seemed not to appreciate the seriousness of the situation. He said there was a firm rule concerning cats in trees: if they did not come down within twenty-four hours, they never came down at all. So, he said, I might just as well forget about her and go buy a new cat. My daughter heard this, let out a bloodcurdling scream, and did a dramatic death scene that would have made Romeo and Juliet look like rank amateurs. I asked him how he knew this about cats. He said he read it somewhere, so it had to be true. He asked if I had phoned Pets Are Us. I told him I had never heard of them. He said they were who people called to have cats snatched out of a tree. I asked him why he had not told me this earlier. He said I had not asked.

I went in and phoned Pets Are Us. A nice young man named Ned answered the phone and promised to came out immediately. And he did. He got out of his little red pickup truck, put on his climbing spurs, galloped up the tree, grabbed the cat, stuck her under his shirt, climbed down, and handed little Cleopatra to me.

This was hard to believe, but he said he did it all the time. I thanked him, paid him, tossed in a generous gratuity, and took my poor kitten in for water, food, and rest. I don't remember the details, but the possibility exists that I might also have heaped a few soft, delicate, disparaging words of ridicule upon her tender head.

Our son watched the rescue operation with great interest. He said, "I could have done that if you had let me and if I had a pair of climbing spurs. And, for the money you gave him, I could have bought his climbing spurs and made a down payment on his truck."

Our daughter showered Cleopatra with pity and nurturing—for about twenty seconds. And then she was hard at work making plans for a fabulous welcome-home party. All her friends were invited. Refreshments and door prizes were selected. Decorations were hurriedly hung. Gifts, including a dead mouse, were wrapped in bright paper and bound with colorful ribbons. And she had her speech of welcome to the guest of honor planned down to the last dramatic detail.

Cleopatra revived quickly. Within ten minutes, she had her voice back and was on the porch playing with our porch toad. She worked on flipping him onto his back and spinning him around until he was dizzy. She has a short attention span, however, and quickly tired of this.

And then she went over and climbed right back up the very same tree!

I was appalled. I told her to come down immediately. She was screaming. She was scared. She was afraid she would fall. She didn't know what to do. She pleaded with me to please, please get her down. I asked her why she climbed up there again. She poised daintily on a tiny limb, spent several minutes giving a thorough cleaning to her two front paws, and said, "That is just one of the things cats do, you know. Whoever heard of a cat that does not climb trees?" I went in the house, slammed the door, sat down, and read three days' worth of neglected newspapers.

Again, Cleopatra stayed in the tree for two days and two nights and grew weak from hunger, thirst, and exposure. Again, I phoned Pets Are Us, stood under the tree while Ned repeated his rescue act, thanked him, paid him, gratuitied him, and listened to his offer for a discount if I hired him by the week. I took Cleopatra inside, tossed her none too gently on the floor, and informed her that she now was a full-time house cat.

Since that time over sixteen years ago, we have built a new home near a state park where Cleopatra is free to coerce me into letting her in and out of the house as she pleases. But she has gotten stuck in a tree only once since that time so long ago when she did it twice in a row. The last time, she climbed a smaller tree and our son was able to climb up after her. However, he was not as proficient as Ned at stashing a cat under his shirt. Cleopatra antiqued his chest with her claws and then slipped out from under his shirt. She fell twenty feet to the ground, bounced twice, ran into the house, and hid under the bed. She stayed there for two days and two nights.

6

As far as we know, cats first began to tolerate humans somewhere between 2000 and 1600 B.C. This apparently happened first in Egypt about the time Egyptians began to store grain. The stored grain attracted rats, and the rats attracted cats. These first cats were a species of the small African wild cat, *Felis sylvestris libyca*.

My understanding of the beginning of the era of the domestic cat is based on a story told to me some years ago by a black, one-eyed, scar-faced, ragged-eared, lop-tailed, alley cat of questionable reputation.

The era began, so the story goes, one morning just as the sun rose over the river Nile and brightened the shadows in the elaborate gardens of a splendid Egyptian prince. A young princess, just six years old, laughed to herself as she ran across the lawn and shrewdly hid behind a bush to escape the doubtful eye of the elderly nursemaid assigned to watch over her. The nursemaid's eyesight had failed in recent years, so she focused her attention on a nearby shrub that had blossoms of exactly the same color as the princess' gown. The shrub trembled in the morning breeze just enough to convince the nurse that the princess was right there in front of her. The young princess, still wearing her mischievous smile, ran through the garden to explore a forbidden edge that was close to the forested area next to the river. Just as she arrived at the line of trees, there was a minute movement of one branch of a shrub and a slight rustle in the grass. Something was there! The little princess stopped and gazed in wonder to see what would emerge. She had waited for only a second when, from behind the shrub, appeared the nose, eyes, and ears of a tiny wild kitten.

The kitten saw the princess and froze into a perfect stillness. Its tiny brain rippled with excitement and fear. What should it do? It could remain still and hope this strange creature would go away, it could turn immediately and try to escape, or it could take the offensive and attack. The latter possibility was immediately rejected; cats usually play it safe, and this colorful, two-legged creature was much too large to attack. And, somehow, the kitten was in no mood to run away. This was an exciting new world and the kitten wanted to see what it was like. Unfortunately, its mother, an African wild cat, had been killed the day before by a crocodile. The kitten was hungry and lonely.

As the kitten paused, wondering what to do, the princess dropped to her hands and knees and crept up close. The two looked into each other's eyes and wondered. The princess reached out her small hand to rub the kitten's head. This startled the kitten. It arched its back, puffed up it hair, and gave out a short, low hiss. The small hand hesitated for a moment and then moved closer. The kitten drew back one paw, claws fully extended, and prepared to strike. The princess talked softly to the kitten and moved even closer. The kitten knew it must strike then or never. It stood still with paw poised. And it thought long thoughts. Who knows exactly what those thoughts were? Do all of us have times when we must make choices that will determine not only our own destiny but also the destiny of those who will come after us? Can we really decide our fate; or is our fate always out of our control? Do the gods direct and we follow? Or, do the gods offer and we choose? What would the kitten do?

The princess' hand now was poised just above the kitten's nose. The kitten paused a second longer and then slowly but imperceptibly dropped its raised paw back to the ground. It purred softly and stood its ground. It shuddered slightly at the light touch of the princess' hand, moved out a few inches from the shrub that hid it, and then thrust its head forward to receive the full effect of the caress. Its purrs grew louder as it permitted the princess to move closer and stroke its neck, shoulders, and back. The kitten hesitated and almost panicked when the princess cradled it gently in her arms and, while talking softly in its ear, walked slowly back to the nursemaid and then on to the house of the kings.

The full story is lost in antiquity, but it is known that the kitten became a favorite of the royal family. It was named Amenamhettie after one of the pharaohs and was the ancestor of the domestic cats that have been with us for four thousand years and still remain as inquisitive, precocious, and loving as was this distant ancestor. Amenamhettie lived a long and eventful life and died peacefully in her sleep in her old age. A bronze statuette of her can still be seen in a Cairo museum. At least that is what was told to me by the black, one-eyed, scar-faced, ragged-eared, lop-tailed, alley tramp of doubtful reputation as he concluded his story of the first domestic cat.

Although the Egyptians found adult wild cats to be fierce and unmanageable, they discovered that young cats sometimes could be socialized by gentle, patient handling. After the Egyptian grain keepers tamed a few wild kittens and watched them grow up, they began selectively breeding them to reinforce the traits they desired. The result was the beginning of an entirely new species, *Felis catus*, our modern domestic cat.

The Egyptians sometimes made the cat a god. They had a cat-headed goddess named Pasht, a name that evolved into today's "puss." Cats sometimes were mummified and buried along with mummified mice and a saucer of milk to see them through to the next world.

Phoenicians carried cats to sea, probably to keep their ships free of rats. They sometimes traded their cats for tin, spices, and silk, thus spreading domestic cats over the then known world. In Europe, during the Middle Ages, people believed witches talked with cats and, sometimes, turned into cats. For this reason, suspected witches and cats sometimes were burned together. In our day, cats have reached a new high in popularity. This is partly due to the lifestyle of the modern human which makes it awkward to keep horses and elephants in studio apartments. Smaller animals, such as gerbils and goldfish, while also increasing in popularity, are no particular threat to the cat since these are not as highly developed. Also, many humans consider gerbils to be overachievers in the reproduction department, and most find it difficult to become emotionally attached to a goldfish.

Domestic cats are relatively inflexible genetically and thus do not vary greatly in size and weight. While there are fewer than forty breeds of domestic cats in the United States, there are at least ten times that many breeds of dogs. Though cats are of less economic importance than horses, sheep, cows, and other animals that man has domesticated, they serve as faithful ratters and mousers and, more importantly, as companions with qualities unequaled in other species. Cats are very good listeners and can be counted on not to divulge secrets. They have excellent eyes. They see well in dim light and apparently can distinguish between colors. Many cats enjoy watching television, especially when animals with which they are familiar are shown. However, cats have been known to attack and sometimes kill the television set in attempting to protect their territory from what they perceive to be intruders.

When hunting in the dark, the cat uses its whiskers as feelers to help avoid obstructions. It has thirty teeth, including eyeteeth that are used primarily for seizing prey. Each forefoot has five toes; each hind foot has four toes. Each toe has a sharp, hooked claw that can be drawn in or extended at will. The cat has keen senses. A pat of its paw acquaints it with the nature of strange objects. It hears beyond the range of the human ear and has a well-developed sense of smell. Cats are among the most intelligent of animals. They are keen observers and have a good memory. They are quick to learn connections between related events such as the sound of the opening of a refrigerator door, or the noise of a can opener, and the presence of food. They are natural imitators and learn a great deal from observing and copying. Their average life length is fourteen years; however, some live for more then twenty-five years.

Most cats, when treated decently, are trusting and friendly. They are grateful for kindness and can be warm and cuddly. They also are independent, strong-willed, and often contrary. They can be docile, contented, and relaxed as well as jealous, quarrelsome, and aloof. The domestic cat is related to many fierce wild animals such as the cheetah, leopard, lion, lynx, panther, puma, and tiger. In the wild state, cats are unlike dogs which typically hunt in packs and are dependent on the cooperation of a pack to ensure survival. Instead, cats are loners; they hunt alone, spend much of their time alone, and seem neither physically nor emotionally dependent on any other animal, including man. Having evolved as solo predators, cats have no need for humans for actual survival and hence no need to accept a subservient position with a human just to gain food or shelter. Instead, they take advantage of the food and shelter we offer and use our houses as their dens, but retain the ability to fend for themselves. The process of domestication has not altered their ability as hunters, and most cats remain proficient and active predators when given the opportunity or necessity.

For those who are fond of all living creatures and do not like to see anything killed, there is a down side to cats. One study showed that peoples' darling cats bring home, on the average, 15.6 dead animals each year. These kills include small mammals, birds, and other small unidentified creatures. This 15.6 kills per cat is thought to represent only half the actual kills since many kills are eaten on the spot or, for other reasons, not brought home. So, a more realistic average number of kills is twice 15.6, or 31.2 kills per cat. There are at least fifty million cats kept as pets in homes in the United States, and at least another fifty million homeless cats. These numbers together indicate that cats kill a minimum of three billion one hundred and twenty million small mammals, birds, and other small creatures each year. Many would consider this bad news. This is particularly so if you happen to be a small mammal, bird, or other small creature. From another perspective, in some areas, the cat's predatory nature succeeds in maintaining a balance of nature. The cat may be the primary or only surviving natural predator of these small animals and, as such, succeeds in keeping their population from expanding to an unacceptable level.

Our cat, Cleopatra, is a Tortie Point Himalayan. This is a fairly new breed of cats, having its start only fifty or sixty years ago. She is a cross-breed, with her mother being a Siamese and her father a Persian. The Tortie Point refers to her coloring which is a cream-white body mottled with seal-brown. Parts of her legs, face, ears, and tail are a dark brown. One front paw is white and the other pale brown. Her nose seems to be about nine different shades of cream-white, brown, and rust. I think her eyes are supposed to be blue, but they are not; they are green. Her hair is too long to call her a short-hair cat and too short to call her a long-hair. She inherited the intelligent and provocative natures of her parents. She is a beautiful combination of her lovely and lazy Persian father and her lively and clever Siamese mother. Yesterday was Cleopatra's seventeenth birthday.

7

This morning I was sitting in the living room with Cleopatra curled up in my lap. I was thinking about the seventeen years we had been together. Cleopatra is a most intelligent animal—I know she is because she keeps telling me she is—and the years have included many meaningful shared experiences. We both have changed a great deal over the years. I think I have mellowed a bit and that she has become more set in her ways; she thinks exactly the reverse. By my way of thinking, she has never been a particularly easy one to live with; however, I cannot accuse her of being dull. By her way of thinking, I just described myself. As I sifted through events of the past years, I remembered one of the early escapades that is typical of life with a Tortie Point Himalayan. I put my thoughts into words and reminded Cleopatra of the time sixteen years ago when we had the cat-in-the-tree crisis.

Cleopatra listens well when she is curled up but she doesn't talk much from that position. She likes to stare me in the eyes when she is talking to me. So, this morning, she listened carefully to what I said but did not make a sound in response. When I stopped talking, she lay in my lap for a while, seemingly thinking long thoughts, and then uncurled, jumped to her stool under the window, gave a toothy yawn, and commented on the long-ago incident. "You seem," she said, "from the way you have described the event, to see it only from your narrow perspective. Let us not forget who is the center of the universe here. Let us talk about it from MY perspective."

I told her I thought she sounded just like the vain, conceited creature I knew her to be and she should be ashamed of herself. Her response was, "I will have you know I am not the least bit vain and conceited, although Heaven knows I have every right to be!" After this illustrious beginning, she proceeded with her version of the cat-in-the-tree crisis. And, I will admit, I was impressed with her insights and with the truths she could so readily apply to others though seemingly not to herself.

"I was just a little kitten, remember, when you had your wife and daughter catnap me from the mansion where I lived happily with my mother and brothers and sisters. After that, you held me against my will and forced me to live in your humble abode. Even then, I was a wise and beautiful creature; not as wise and beautiful as I am now of course, but wise and beautiful just the same. The only thing you had around your place that I really liked was trees. I had never before been outdoors and trees were new to me. I enjoyed climbing the small trees and wiggling out on a limb where you had to stretch to reach me. Remember how I sometimes would hang by one paw and let you pull me down? I enjoyed that almost as much as you did."

"And then one day," she continued, "I was walking across the yard and I bumped into this huge tree. I thought it was a board fence or something so I decided to climb to the top from where I could call for you and have you lift me down. I climbed and climbed but did not reach the top. So, what could I do? I could not just hang there. And I did not know how to turn around and come down. The only thing I could do was just keep on climbing. I finally reached a limb where I could stretch out and rest and then—I can remember it as though it were yester-day—I looked down. The whole world lay spread out below me. I could see all over that part of town. I could see the rooftops, the squares formed by the streets, the fences that divided the houses, and the trash truck stopping to load up on trash. I could see the top of the doghouse next door, the creek behind the next row of houses, and the lake that formed behind the earthen dam. It was a fascinating view but, already, I was wondering how you were going to reach up and lift me down. I did not know what to do. I did not have a rear-view mirror to see to back down. And cats do not go down trees head first. I thought about jumping down but, when I looked at where I would land, I got dizzy and had to hold on tight to keep from falling.

"All of you kept yelling at me; if you had listened instead of yelled, you would have understood that I could not climb down. Two men came from down the street and started throwing rocks and a golf ball inside a sock at me. They gave up on this and tried shooting me down with a bow and arrow. I did not want to get hurt worse than I already was, so I climbed three limbs higher. This seemed to get those on the ground even more upset. And then you turned that fire hose on me and almost blasted me to my doom. What a rotten thing to do!" Cleopatra glared at me and let out an involuntary snarl as she said this.

"And then," she continued, "as wet as I was, I did the only thing I could do. I climbed higher to get away from the idiot with the fire hose. I balanced on another limb and looked down to see what was happening. And then I realized that, now, I could REALLY see the whole world! People looked like little ants crawling around down there. The cars on the highway looked like beetles bumbling aimlessly along. The only immediate problem was that, up that high, the wind blew and moved the top of the tree around. I think I was beginning to get seasick. I spread out between the trunk and a limb where I knew I would not fall, and my queazy stomach finally settled down. I took a good look at all of the commotion on the ground. Tiny people were looking up, gesturing, and shouting. There were ladders and ropes all over. I knew I could never get down and that I was doomed to starve to death. I wondered how it would feel to die of thirst. I knew that, when I got too weak to hang on to the limb, I would fall and be smashed to a pulp. I wondered if I would still feel anything when I got smashed. It was a terrible, terrible happening!"

Cleopatra closed her eyes and shuddered as she recalled the experience. And then she opened her eyes until they seemed as large as saucers and blurted out, "Actually, I loved every minute of it! Never again in my life have I had such fun! Never again have I seen so much excitement and received so much attention. Ah, what a wonderful, wonderful experience!"

She stretched to what seemed to be her full nine-foot length, hung her head over the side of her stool, and continued. "I was glad to get down though. It was exhilarating to find myself alive and safe after giving myself up for dead. And I was kind of feeling sorry for all of you for having to work so hard to get me down. I was thinking I might want to be more careful in the future and not cause so much concern. When people cheered when I reached the ground, I was thinking that, with all this support, I certainly would be able to develop more constructive behavior patterns. And I remember that, while you were glad to see me down, you certainly were hot under the collar. You shook me something fierce and called me all kinds of bad names like fleabag, buzzard bait, and bubble brain. I started feeling so guilty I could hardly bear it. I am sure I would have broken down and cried if it had not been for my innate poise and dignity."

"I think you gave me milk to drink," Cleopatra said, choosing her words carefully. "I wanted water instead but thought it would make you even madder if I complained. You should have known I wanted water. I ate some squished fish and slivered liver but was too excited and upset to eat much. I think I also took a long nap, one of my two-minute specials. When I woke up, you laid a fuss on me again. You did NOT say I had DONE something unfortunate, foolish, or bad; instead, you labeled my whole self as being bad. You said I was a BAD cat and that I should hang my head in shame for causing so much trouble. You said some other things, but I do not remember what they were.

"Somewhere along there I tuned you out and began thinking about how the entire episode was really all your fault. YOU were the one who always encouraged me to climb! YOU were the one who allowed a poor, helpless, little kitten to wander around in that back yard, without any guidance, assistance, or guardrails! It was YOU who took me from my mother before she had a chance to teach me things! YOU were the one who failed to put up caution signs to warn of danger! I was an exemplary kitten who did everything to perfection. Could I help it if I was forced to live with a cruel, careless melonhead? So, since I was perfectly innocent, I put the whole thing out of my mind. And then I remember giving that hoptoad the best spin I have ever put on one.

"I am kind of fuzzy about what happened next. I know I was getting bored with eating and sleeping and hoptoad spinning. I needed something exciting to do. And I wanted to show you that you could not push me around and get away with it. Because of the guilt trip you laid on me, I was still denying that going up the tree was dangerous for me and the cause of a great deal of concern and trouble to you. My denial kept me from being fully aware and my lack of awareness rendered me unable to make very good choices. And that tree just stood there, not fifty feet away, beckoning to me. If you had just picked me up, or rolled a ball of string, or pointed out a flybutter or hopgrasser for me to chase, or slammed the screen door on my tail, I would have been all right. But, no, you did nothing of the kind. You just stood there and practically invited me to get into trouble again. So, I climbed back up the tree."

Cleopatra paused for a minute and stared into space as though searching for a clearer vision of her lost kittenhood. "It was more fun the second time," she said. "I knew how to balance on the limbs, and I knew you would get me down. I knew you would really lose your cool, but I figured you could not insult me any more than you had already. When you did get me down again and asked me why I climbed it a second time, I told you something that was not altogether true. I told you I climbed the tree because that was just something cats do. Well, cats DO climb trees, but they seldom HAVE to climb trees. Mostly, they do it only when and if they want to do it. The truth is I climbed by accident the first time; I really did not know what I was doing and I had no choice, at least not much of one. My life experiences were so limited that I was caught off guard. But I climbed the second time mostly because I chose to do so. I had convinced myself, with your help of course, that I was an innocent victim of circumstances and of your poor judgment and bad attitude. So, since this was all your fault, there was no reason why I should not go ahead and have a fun time. After all, cats DO climb trees."

I stopped her there and asked, "How can you be so sure we ever have choices? Do you have any proof?"

"That is not something I wish to argue about," she answered. "No, it cannot be conclusively proven, but we can go by the weight of the evidence. Remember when you were trying to decide between sitting in your chair thinking and going out on the porch and reading the newspaper? Well, suppose you had known for certain which of the two you were 'fated' to do. I know you well enough to know you deliberately would have done the opposite. So, if you can choose capriciously, there is no reason to believe you cannot choose deliberately. The mistake you make is judging that others always have the same choices you have."

"Remember the story about Amenamhettie, the little Egyptian kitten who was one of my ancestors?" she continued without waiting for my response. "Well, that kitten made a reasoned decision to tame down the Egyptians. It thought over the alternatives, picked the one that seemed the best answer to its predicament, and went for broke. But that was not so hard for it to do. It did not have guilt and denial getting in the way of its awareness. Just think how different all of history would have been if you had been there. You would have fussed that kitten up for being on the wrong side of the river, for not warning its mother about crocodiles, for getting in somebody's garden, and for speaking to strangers. You would have had it feeling so little and bad it would have crawled into a crack somewhere and stayed there until it died."

I stopped her there and asked a question that had been on my mind for some time. "Well, what difference does it really make whether you make reasoned decisions or unreasonable ones? The world is so big and we are so insignificant, what difference does any of this really make?"

Cleopatra paused for a moment before answering. "It makes a difference," she murmured. "Remember yesterday when you tossed a stone into the pond? Well, the ripples in the water created by that stone go on and on forever. Because you tossed that stone, the world never again will be quite the same. Also, the kindness you did—or failed to do—today impacted on others, who in turn impacted on others in an ever-widening circle until the whole world is touched. Everything you do—or fail to do—changes the world forever. Most of the changes you see in the world are the results of small day-to-day actions by simple animals who often think what they do makes no difference. Remember that curve in the road just before you get to the pond? Two hundred years ago, a deer was bounding through the woods headed straight toward the pond when a bumblebee almost flew right into her face. The deer made a quick turn to avoid the bumbler and then continued on her way. Other deer, plus raccoons and other animals, followed in the path she made through the underbrush. The path widened and eventually was traveled by horses and wagons that brought in early settlers. Fifty years ago, the land on both sides of the road was carefully surveyed and mapped. Later the road was paved and houses were built. Now, every day, you drive down that road and around the curve that was created two hundred years ago when a simple deer encountered an humble bumblebee and made the decision to take a sharp left turn.

"But back to my story. As I was saying, without Amenam-hettie's simple gesture centuries ago, cats would never have gotten friendly enough with humans to lead and guide them all these years, and the human race would have died out or returned to its caves long, long ago. So, while that kitten made a decision that changed all of cat and human history, the whole thing would have fallen apart if you had been there instead of here."

"We both made a decision, that Egyptian kitten and I," Cleopatra continued after she cooled down a bit. "Both of us made quick decisions of course. Neither of us spent hours agonizing over what to do. But nothing nor no one MADE us do what we did. What each of us did was our own free choice. But that other kitten surely had more of a choice than I had!

"The truth is that all of us go through life with a weighing scale that we use to weigh and judge everything. However each scale is different. Another's ounce may be your ton, and your pound may not register on my scale at all. You cannot see my life precisely as I see it, and I cannot completely understand your perspective. So, I do not judge how much choice others have. And others cannot know how much choice I have, unless I tell them. And, even then, they do not entirely comprehend. Besides, sometimes even I am not sure of my choices.

"Remember, back then I told you I climbed the tree because that is what cats do? I thought that was true at the time, but as I have said, I now am even wiser and more beautiful than I was then. Now, I recognize that I acted out of choice. How do I know Amenamhettie acted out of choice? Well, I admit I cannot be certain. I simply am acting on my superior wisdom and what she told me... or..., maybe I read it somewhere. Anyway, chalk that one up as certain enough for you to bet your life on but not certain enough for me to bet mine on. What I have learned over the years is that we usually have some degree of choice, but our range of choices and the appropriateness of our choices depend upon how aware we dare to be. And full awareness can be blocked by denial, and denial can result from guilt. And I learned all this in spite of the guilt trips you have tried to lay on me. Now please be quiet! You already have ruined my day and given me a headache by bringing up all those bad memories. You are bad, bad, bad! You should hang your head in shame!"

With this, Cleopatra stood up, yawned, stepped lightly over the arm of my chair, rearranged my lap to fit her contour, curled into a ball with her front paws resting on my leg and her head pressed against my stomach, sighed softly, swished her tail twice, and dropped off into peaceful sleep.

III. Squeaks the Squirrel Saves the Day

I thought my game of golf was dreary, drab, and droll,
Until I saw his triple bogey on the second hole,
I thought my short and simple drive a sorrowful mistake,
Until I saw him slice his shot and land it in the lake.
I rued my lack of skill and cursed my dreadful luck,
Until I saw his perfect putt roll twelve feet past the cup.

8

I was in an unusually grumpy mood when I awoke that morning. Maybe it was the bad news I saw on television last night just before I went to sleep, maybe I had a bad dream, or maybe you don't have to have a reason for being in a bad mood. Anyway, first thing, I went in to wash my face and comb my hair. I spent several minutes staring into the mirror trying to figure where I had seen that face before. For certain, it was somebody I didn't like! I dressed, fixed my first cup of instant decaf, dropped a spoon on the big bone of my bare foot, and spilled part of the boiling coffee on my trousers. The hot coffee soaked through, of course, and boiled my leg. After this ominous beginning, I finished dressing, walked out to the workshop, filled an empty coffee can with sunflower seeds, reached to put the lid back on the feed container, knocked over my can of seeds, got the dustpan and broom, swept up the seeds, put the spilled seeds back into the coffee can and, in the process, spilled half the seeds back on the floor. I backed out, pulled the door shut, forgot to make sure my foot cleared the doorway, hopped around on one foot, and uttered a few well-chosen words.

I took the seeds out and dumped them on the ground for the birds and squirrels. This finished, I walked down the driveway to the street to retrieve the newspaper, discovered too late the giant web the spider had hung across the driveway during the night and, while desperately pulling tangled webs from my face and hair, stubbed on a stone the toe of my already sore foot. I didn't see the newspaper. Either the newspaper woman had missed us again or the neighbor's dog had stolen it again. No! There it was over in the edge of the grass, one whole side wet through from the dew. I picked up the newspaper and jerked off the rubber band that obviously was put there just to annoy me. In the process, I accidently ripped a corner off the front page of the paper and snapped the rubber band against the back of my hand. I stuck the wet, torn newspaper under my arm, rubbed the red spot on my hand, and limped back to the porch to read. On the way, I noticed dark clouds that were half blotting out the sun. The day likely would be another cold, wet, dark, dreary, miserable one.

I threw the newspaper on the table beside my porch chair, sat down, and reached for my coffee that, by then, was barely lukewarm. I missed, knocked the cup over, and sloshed its contents onto the only part of the newspaper that had been completely dry. I went in, got more coffee, sat back down, carefully opened the wet newspaper, and started to read the parts of the front page that were still readable. Over the top of the newspaper, I noticed that the chair across from me again had mildew on the back cushion. I never would have bought the chairs had I known I would have to wash them down with bleach every time it rained. There always is more work to be done than I can ever do. I read the front page of the newspaper. There was nothing but bad news. I looked at the sports page; the home teams had lost again. I looked at the local news section; taxes were going up, and three homes in our end of the county had been burglarized. I heard the rumble of thunder in the distance. Dark clouds were moving in; it was almost too dark to read.

Squeaks the Squirrel, apparently having finished off sufficient sunflower seeds to knock the sharp edge off her appetite, bounced onto the porch, looked at me with a friendly eye, and innocently asked, "What are you doing?"

"I'm reading the damned newspaper," I grumbled. "Or, I was until you interrupted. And I'm halfway through it now and I haven't yet found anything good. It's all bad news!"

Squeaks stared at me quizzically, her tail twitching, and asked "What do you mean by 'read'?"

I tried to tell her about letters forming words, words forming sentences, and sentences telling what the writer was thinking. She seemed to understand.

"You mean you can look at all those little squiggly lines and tell what another animal that lives a zillion miles away is thinking? Wow! Undeliverable, inedible, destonishing! Wow!"

She bounced around the porch, with her tail twitching violently. She paused, stood on her hind legs with her paws folded across her chest, pointed her nose toward the newspaper, and asked, "Where did you get it?"

I told her about the paper woman who delivered it every morning. Except when she accidently missed us, which happened more often than I wanted to think about. Again, Squeaks seemed to understand.

"You mean you get one almost every day? You get to learn what is happening all over the world? What a zillion different animals are thinking and doing? And she brings it right here to you and all you have to do is go out and pick it up? Wow! Undeliverable, inedible, destonishing! Wow!"

Then she yelled at the other squirrels who were still eating sunflower seeds, "Hey, you guys. Look here! He has news from all over! Just came in! All stuck on that big piece of paper. He can find out EVERYTHING while just sitting there in his chair! Isn't that something?"

The other squirrels stopped eating and looked on with keen interest. Squeaks, who could barely contain her excitement, decided to find out what other incredible things I might tell her. She turned to me and asked, "Why do you sit out here to read instead of sitting in your den? What? Because you just like to sit outdoors when it's not freezing? Don't blame you there. Must get gosh-awful cold in your den. That big top on it must keep the sun from shining in. What? You mean it's not cold in there? Stays eighty degrees in the winter and sixty degrees in the summer, you say? Hmm. How do you keep it so warm? What? You mean you don't have to line your den with leaves and you don't have to grow thick fur? Hmm. You mean you don't have to do ANYTHING? You say a little thermos cat does it all and that he does it auto-magically? Bet his paws and ears get singed! But... but... but... wait a minute! I know your cat, the one who calls herself Cleo Patrick, Queen of Denial. We play tag sometimes when she's not asleep. Didn't know she was a thermos cat."

I explained that we were talking about two entirely different things. Again, she seemed to understand.

Squeaks stood there for a minute making sure she had all her facts straight. In a more serious tone, she said, "I'm glad you keep that thermos cat shut up in the house where it can't hurt anybody with its magic. And you say your thermos cat also keeps your den cool in the summer? Oooh! She really IS magic! Imagine that! In there making ice when it's two hundred degrees out here. Wow! Undeliverable, inedible, destonishing! Wow!"

She turned again to the other squirrels. She now had their full attention. She yelled, "Hey, guys, listen up! He also has a pet cat. Not the one he calls Cleo Patrick, but another one that he never lets out of the house. Stays in the hallway, on the wall. Says it's a thermos cat! It does magic! It does stuff that keeps snow and ice out of his den in the winter and keeps it cool in the summer!"

For the squirrels, this was almost too wonderful to believe. They all joined paws and began dancing around in a wide circle, looking at me with envious eyes, and singing, "Wow! Undeliverable, inedible, destonishing! Wow! My goodness! My gracious! My heavens! My gosh! Lucky, lucky, lucky thing!"

I looked up at the sky and saw that the clouds were thinning and that the sun was rising from behind the trees. A soft, warm breeze stirred the morning air. It was going to be a beautiful day. I went back to my newspaper and was surprised to discover unbelievable, incredible, astonishingly good news scattered here and there.

IV. Rosie's Tale of the Wise and Foolish Owl

You neither hear their pleas nor heed their woes
When you are listening only with your ear.
For answers to the questions they propose
Are seldom what they need or wish to hear.

9

Raccoons are supposed to sleep by day and prowl by night. But, from spring until late fall, the three of them I know best often show up in our back yard by two or three o'clock in the afternoon. One spring afternoon, I was getting the vegetable garden ready for its first planting when they arrived. I was busy and paid little attention to them. They usually check out the birdseed that I put on the ground for the doves, drink from the bird bath, and maybe drape over the limb of a tree and watch for us to put out kitchen scraps, which we usually do later in the day. The three include Rosie, the oldest, whom I have known for a number of years. She sometimes has a nasty temper. Bit me once when I accidently got too close to her little ones. All in all, though, she is a nice lady. Intelligent, wise, a good conversationalist.

Jimmie, another of the three, is, I regret to say, something of a thief and a liar. A NICE thief and liar, but a thief and liar just the same. Jimmie always has been one of my favorites. I used to sit on the floor of the walkway to the carport and shell peanuts. Jimmie would sit beside me and eat them as fast as I could pop them out. He was the only raccoon I have ever seen who loves peanuts but absolutely refuses to shell them. He always claims to have a toothache, be allergic to something in the shells, not know how to shell them, or be afraid to pop them open because there might be a big dog inside. And all the time he is making excuses, I am sitting there shelling peanuts for him. Even with all of his mischief, however, he has done only one thing that really ticked me off. This was when he came in one summer day to show off the three new babies. That was when I discovered he would lie about almost anything and that he had been a "she" all along. But the name stuck and she is still Jimmie, the loveable thief and liar.

The third raccoon is "Honest." That's her name, Honest! According to Rosie, Honest is the most honest, plain speaking, open, trustworthy, upright, virtuous animal in the neighborhood. Also, according to Rosie, she is the biggest troublemaker in this and the surrounding six counties.

<h2 style="text-align:center">10</h2>

As I said, I was working in the garden that spring afternoon and not paying any particular attention to the three raccoons. I was putting down seeds for lettuce and spinach when I first heard Honest screaming. I dropped my tools and went over to see what was wrong. Honest was sprawled out on the bare ground holding one paw over a bloody ear and another over a scratch on her neck. She seemed to be close to hysterics. She cried, "Don't let her get away! She tried to kill me! Help! Police! Fireman! Postman! Marines! Air Force! Murder! Mayhem! I've been assaulted! I'm wounded! I'm hurt! Civil rights violated here!"

Jimmie stood back at the edge of the woods brushing her own ruffled fur back into place and wiping a few small spots of blood off one paw. "Don't look at me," she wailed. "I didn't do anything. I wasn't even here. I was home asleep. Didn't even know about it until somebody came by and told me. And, besides, I have a sore paw. Couldn't possibly hit anybody. See! I can hardly lift it. I saw him hit her. Big aardvark with beady eyes. Ugly thing. Went that way. We're just lucky he didn't get me too. Besides, it was her fault. Anybody will tell you she started it. She hit me first. Hit me thirty-four times and was going to hit me again. Was just protecting myself. And, anyway, I probably won't do it again. Not today, anyway. Well, duty calls elsewhere, and I have to run!" And she was gone.

Honest stood up on shaky legs, brushed herself off, gingerly rubbed her wounded ear, moaned softly, and said, "I don't think I have many mortal wounds, no thanks to her. I think I will go down to the pond and wash off all the blood and dirt. I will hurt some, but nothing I can't manage. What do you think set her off like that? She had me pretty much pounded into the dirt before I even knew she was in a tizzy. Hope I don't run into her again today. Well, see you tomorrow if I am not too stiff and sore." And she hobbled off.

Rosie rushed out from behind the tree where she had been watching and called out to Honest, "Wait up! Got something for you here." She handed Honest a watch and necklace. "I think these are yours," Rosie said. "Jimmie took them from you when you were down. I sneaked them back when she was preoccupied with talking to the... uh... talking to him."

She pointed in my direction, so I assumed I was "him." Honest took the items, thanked Rosie, and went on her way.

I still was befuddled by the whole scene. I asked Rosie, "What is going on here? Did you see it? What happened?"

"Well, let me get comfortable here and I'll tell you," she said. She climbed onto the bird bath, lay in the water with her legs hanging over the sides, and told me the following.

11

"It was about three years ago on a spring afternoon just like this one. That was when I first heard the real honest truth about the Easter bunny. Not sure who told me. Maybe my third cousin on my mother's side. I remember him because he had such big ears. And speaking of big ears, have you seen the ears on that yellow dog? Now, that dog.... What? Oh! You say that's not what we're talking about here? What then? Oh, yeah, big fight between Jimmie and Honest. Well, it was the usual kind of thing. Happens all the time. Different animals. Different details. But, same thing, really. As you probably know, while Jimmie is a shrewd little thing, she also has a vain streak running through her. She just spent half the morning brushing up her hair. Came over here to show it off. Ran into Honest. Asked her how she liked her new hairdo. Honest asked, 'Do you really want to know the truth or, are you just fishing for a compliment? Do you want the honest, unvarnished, cross-my-heart-and-hope-to-die, absolute, may-lightning-strike-me-dead, candid, sincere, forthright truth?'

"And Jimmie said, 'Sure. Of course. Absolutely. Certainly. Definitely. Positively. Unconditionally. Unequivocally. The truth, the whole truth, and nothing but the truth. That's what I asked for; that's what I want!'

"So, Honest, who, as you know, is the most wonderfully honest creature and biggest pain-in-the-neck in this whole part of the universe, did an absolutely horrid, beastly, despicable thing! She told the truth."

Rosie paused for a moment to let this sink in, and then continued, "What Honest actually said to Jimmie was that her hair looked like an upside-down hornet's nest that had been abandoned and gone to seed. I thought that was an excellent description. Good choice of words. Described her hair exactly. Couldn't have said it better myself, even if I thought about it all night. Was going to congratulate Honest on the clarity, precision, and lucidity of her choice of words. But I didn't get a chance because that is when Jimmie lit into her. I don't blame her. I would have done it too. What Honest said was a gross, blatant, flagrant, obscene insult!"

This was too much for me. I held up my hands and shouted, "Wait a gosh-awful minute here! You said Honest told the absolute, unvarnished truth and that what she did was obscene? How can the TRUTH be obscene?"

Rosie settled down a little deeper into the water in the birdbath. Her bulk caused small streams of water to pour over the sides. She lifted one paw to swat at a horsefly, settled back down, and then replied. "Obviously, you don't know much about animal nature or about basic communications. But, this makes sense, I suppose, considering that your species is not particularly noted for its perceptiveness. Do you want me to try to educate you a little? Then, please listen carefully.

"When someone asks you a question, it may or may not be something they really want to know. They may ask the question because they want to know SOMETHING, but they are not sure exactly what it is they want to know. Very few actually know the right questions for getting their concerns addressed. The main thing missing in this life is the right questions. An animal will be feeling down in the dumps, like life is dull and nothing is going right. So what does he ask? Something like, 'Do you think it is hotter today than it was this time last year?' Or, 'What kind of medicine do you take when you don't feel much of anything all over?' Or, 'Why do you think my mate acts the way she does sometimes?' Don't bother to answer questions like that! Best respond with something like, 'So, you are wondering why such and such is so and so.' That, at least, lets them know you care enough to listen, and it may even get them to thinking a bit about what it is they really are trying to say.

"Instead of trying to answer simple-minded questions—most all simple questions are simple minded—try sort of repeating back to them what they have just said—maybe using slightly different words. If they are listening, they will realize that their question really didn't make much sense, or that it was not really what they wanted to know. That way, they may come up with a better question. If so, you should treat it just like you did the first question. Don't ever flat out answer a question—unless, maybe, they just want to know your name, or which way is up, or some specific information thing like that. Even then, you may just be wasting your time. They probably don't really care about your name, and 'up' for them may be 'down' for you. If they ever really ask the RIGHT question, it will be a great shock to them. They probably will say, 'WOW!' And you will not need to answer, because they will already know the answer. Answers come easy; good questions come hard. Answers usually come first; then we have to work hard to find the right question to go with the answer.

"Sometimes, questions are asked just to get your attention away from the real issue. Like, this big robber runs into you in the back alley, sticks a gun in your ribs, and says, 'Your money or your life.' And you don't have any money. What do you do? Happened to me once. Know what I did? I asked, 'Should I vote Publican or Demoncrat in the next election?' He got so rattled trying to think of the answer that I took his wallet and his gun and just walked away while he stood there talking about why the Demoncrats were pushing the flea tax and the Publicans were going to take away our sociable security. My walking away was a smart thing to do. So was taking his gun. But taking his wallet is another thing you need to understand: never push your luck too far."

"But why am I telling you this?" Rosie asked. "Do I know the answers to life's questions? Do I have the intelligence, physical and emotional security, knowledge, initiative, and wisdom to understand that which is incomprehensible to most?

Perhaps I DO know a few answers. But I can't be sure YOU have the right questions. So, I simply will tell you stories. You can ignore the stories or use them as you wish.

"I am going to tell you a little story I just heard. So listen up while I tell you about the wise and foolish owl. Then I am going to get up from here, dry off, walk off, and get started on my night's work."

I sat on the ground beside the bird bath, leaned back against the tree, and listened while she began.

"Aristotle was his name and being a Barred Owl was his game," Rosie said. "His few friends called him Ari the Owl."

12

All owls, by the way, except for the barn owl, make up the family *Strigidae*. In nonscientific terms, an owl is a cat with wings. It is an efficient killer of small rodents and other small animals. It is a swift, silent hunter. Yet, on occasions, it can be noisy, rending the night air with raucous courting screams and hoots. The owl is thought by some to be very intelligent. But, in truth, it only looks that way. Its erect posture and large, round eyes give it a regal and wise appearance that is deceiving. Actually, geese, crows, and ravens are far more intelligent. Another misconception about the owl is that it stays awake at night because it is afraid of the dark. This is not true. It stays awake to hunt.

The owl has a wing structure, ears, and eyes that are particularly fitted for night hunting. The forward edges of feathers on the front of its wings are serrated so as to disrupt the flow of air as it flies. This eliminates the vortex noise that otherwise would be created by the flow of air over a smooth surface.

Don't ever tell somebody a secret when an owl is around! The owl is able to locate even faint sounds with remarkable accuracy. Its ears are linked to special cells in the midbrain that are sensitive to differences in the time and intensity of sounds reaching each ear. This, along with its typically intimate familiarity with its hunting territory, permits it to hunt successfully even on the darkest of nights.

The owl has excellent eyesight. This is fortunate since the relatively small size of its nose and the location of its ears does not encourage the wearing of eyeglasses. While the owl cannot see in total darkness, its eyes are particularly well equipped to use whatever light is available. The size and construction of its eyes permit it to collect and concentrate as much light as possible. The owl also can see in daylight, but not as well as at night. This is because, during the day, its eyes have to shut out much of the bright light in order to prevent injury to its sensitive inner eye.

The fossil remains of an owl were uncovered beside the Ten Mile Creek in Wyoming. These bones had lain undisturbed for about sixty million years. The fossilized remains indicated that today's owls have changed little from their early beginnings.

The size of the population of owls depends on the size of its food supply. Changes in farming practices and habitat changes resulting from human encroachment have, in many areas, reduced the number of owls. Also, the widespread use of insecticides has poisoned rodents which, in turn, have poisoned the owls that eat the rodents. Thus, in many areas, the owl occupies a precarious position in its relationship to humans.

The barred owl, or *Strix varia*, lives in the woodlands of eastern North America. It grows to be nearly two feet long. Those who think owls don't give a hoot about anything are mistaken. The barred owl, perhaps, deserves the title of "hoot owl" better than any other. It gives a series of eight or more loud hoots that sound like "ah-whoo, whoo, whoo, whoo; whoo, whoo, whoo, whoo-ah."

13

The tale that Rosie told continued like this.

"Ari the Owl, who was very wise (and very foolish) either ignored or forgot the law that said owls are supposed to be out only at night. It was broad daylight and he was wide awake and perched on a limb of the hickory tree in his side yard. He was watching a million ants divide and relocate a few crumbs of bread when he heard the big news via his neighbor's grapevine. One of the wheels had fallen off the King's chariot! The result of this tragic accident was that the King no longer could take his morning ride about the kingdom. This was terrible news, for any change in the royal schedule usually meant a change in the way the kingdom was governed. And any change in the government was, as usually is the case, a change for the worse.

"As Ari the Owl listened to the frantic announcer describing how the resources of the kingdom were being mobilized to resolve the crisis, he thought about the ants at his feet, the hummingbird in the petunias, and the warm sun at his back. He thought about mountains that, perhaps, held the sky in place, and about the waving limbs of the trees that, perhaps, made the wind blow. He also thought a bit about the poor royal chariot abandoned at the side of the highway with one end of its front axle bare because the wheel was lying in the ditch on the other side of the roadway. And, since he was, like all owls, very wise (and very foolish), he said, half to himself, 'I know the answer!'

"Over the next several weeks, the citizens of the kingdom pushed all other activities into the background so as to direct their energies toward a solution to the problems created by the disabled royal carriage. A royal Citizens' Committee of One Hundred was appointed to consider various options. A blue-ribbon panel of the country's leading scientists worked around the clock on computer simulations of various approaches. Fortunes were gained and lost as first one idea and then another gained ascendancy and then fell into disrepute. Politicians proclaimed the virtues and disadvantages of various approaches. Ministers, priests, and rabbis searched their holy scriptures and prayed long prayers in an attempt to gain heavenly intervention. Ari the Owl attempted to tell a few acquaintances that he knew the answer, but they quickly shuffled him into the background and proceeded with their support of their own favorite schemes.

"By the end of the first month, four ideas were receiving widespread backing. One was to dig a canal from the ocean, some eight hundred miles away, to provide water to fill a network of local canals. This not only would permit a royal barge to carry the King for his morning rounds about the kingdom, but also would provide vast recreational opportunities, a waterway for a public transportation alternative, and potential for a local fishing industry. This plan had the unqualified support of the Drudge Dredge Company, which was owned by business associates of one of the King's mistresses, and the Dreamboat Steamboat Company, which was operated by business associates of the King's other mistress. The second proposal was to transplant ten thousand giant redwoods from California to the kingdom. These would be strategically located throughout the kingdom so as to support a network of tracks for a nuclear powered monorail which would permit the King access to all parts of the kingdom. The redwood forest was owned by associates of the Queen's hairdresser, and the monorail-in-the-redwoods idea was said to have the Queen's full support.

"The third proposal, forcefully pushed by the King's nephew, was to use the disabled carriage incident as an opportunity to tear down the entire kingdom and rebuild it in a grander style in the meadow on the other side of the river. This meadow was, of course, owned by the King's nephew. The fourth, and perhaps most practical of the ideas, was to expand the royal golf course to one thousand eight hundred holes spread throughout the kingdom. By using gasohol-powered golf carts, the King and his court could travel throughout the kingdom without ever leaving what had become the kingdom's primary political and business arena.

"Ari the Owl, who was very wise (and very foolish) tried contacting the kingdom news media to tell them none of these grand plans would work and that he had the true answer. However, all were too busy researching and reporting on the four leading proposals to bother with a mere individual.

"The Royal Citizens' Committee, made up of one hundred of the Kingdom's leading citizens and graft takers, implemented a massive advertising campaign to solicit ideas from the general public. Ari the Owl took a day off from whatever owls do and went to the Citizens' Committee offices, which were located in a new skyscraper built just for that purpose, to try to tell the Committee that he knew the answer. After two weeks of listening to speeches by Committee members concerning how much they appreciated individuals like Ari the Owl who were willing to come forward with new ideas, he finally was directed to the Office of Proposed Solutions, which was located in a dark, damp corner of the skyscraper's sub-basement. Here, he was instructed to go to Room B2-50713 at the other end of the sub-sub-basement, ask for Form Z-10029937 with Attachments E-301 and X-402, complete these in triplicate, and mail them to the Office of Stuff and Things where they would, as a kingdom security measure, be shredded immediately so as to keep any good ideas from getting into the hands of any enemies of the kingdom. Ari the Owl, being very wise (and very foolish), did not bother to do any of this. Instead, he sat and blinked his eyes and thought long thoughts.

"And then Ari the Owl decided on his next course of action. He went straight to the Kingdom University to the offices of a consortium of research organizations that had been awarded a fifty million dollar research grant to conduct a five-year study of the problem of the fallen-off wheel. Ari the Owl spent the next two months going through the academic screening process required to gain permission to address the researchers. Unfortunately, one requirement for admittance was that the candidate must have earned one hundred and five hours of graduate academic credits; Ari the Owl, who was very wise (and very foolish), had earned one hundred and eight hours and, thus, did not qualify.

"Over the next several months, the King had arguments with both of his mistresses, a big fight with the Queen, and a disagreement with his cousins who owned the Gulping Gasohol and Golf Cart Company. All four prominent plans for solving the problem created by the broken carriage were left in disrepute. A new proposal was the talk of the kingdom. Closed-circuit video cameras, mounted on a fleet of blimps operated by remote-control via a relay station to be constructed on the moon, would permit the King to 'visit' all parts of his kingdom without ever getting out of bed. This plan was being pushed hard by the Cottontail Communications Corporation which was controlled by the brothers of the King's new mistress who loved to lie in bed and watch television. Fortunately, Ari the Owl was a renowned expert on the relationships between the phases of the moon and the hooting of owls. Since this type of expertise was somehow critical to the success of the new communications plan, Ari the Owl was, at last, able to secure an appointment with the King and the King's court. Ari the Owl, who was very wise (and very foolish), was given twenty seconds to make his presentation, supposedly to give advice regarding the kinds of signals from the moon that were most likely to cause the kingdom's owls to give a hoot.

"But, nobody had bothered to read and censor Ari the Owl's short presentation, so no one knew for sure what he would say. At the appointed time, Ari the Owl, who was very wise (and very foolish) was ushered into the King's august presence. He approached the King and said in a quiet and trembly voice, 'I know the answer to the kingdom's problem. The answer is, "Put the wheel back on the chariot!"'

"These statements first were followed by shocked silence from the elite gathering. Then someone gave a nervous laugh. The Royal Greeters blew their trumpets to announce the next visitors. And Ari the owl was quietly led away.

"At dawn the next morning, Ari the Owl, who was very wise (and very foolish), was quietly hanged on the kingdom gallows. No mention was ever again made of the incident of the wheel and the chariot. By the end of the day, the wheel was quietly put back on the chariot. The next day, the King quietly rode about the kingdom in the royal chariot just as he had done before the wheel fell off. And life in the kingdom went on much as it had before. Only a few wise ones remembered the incident and knew Ari the Owl had given the correct answer to the wrong question."

V. The Goosenganders

As the LIGHT blazed brightly on their sight,
Four pilgrims judged its heavenly plight.
One swore a firefly's flickering flight;
Another claimed a candle's light.
The third vowed stars aglow at night;
The fourth saw angel halos bright.
I wish I may, I wish I might
Know for sure which one was right!

14

It was Wednesday morning, and I was coming home from my weekly grocery shopping. I was driving mostly from force of habit, my thoughts still back at the grocery store. I had witnessed a simple little incident there that had absolutely nothing to do with me personally, but I was having a difficult time getting it off my mind. Back there in the grocery store, I had stopped my cart in the canned goods department and was checking my grocery list to see what I needed to pick up next. There was an older couple in front of me. He picked up a can of something or other, beans I think, and said to the woman, "Hey, these are on sale. Three cans for a dollar. Let's take them."

She said, "No. That's not the brand I use." She picked up a can from a different shelf, looked at it closely, and said, "This is the brand I use."

"Why do you use that brand instead of this one?" he asked.

"Because this one has better ingredients in it," she answered.

"How do you know?" he asked.

"Because the ingredients cost more," she answered. "See here. This can costs fifty-nine cents."

"But," he said, "that can is a lot larger than this one."

"Well, maybe it's a little larger," she answered doubtfully.

"Why," he said, "can't you see? That one is a lot bigger. Look there on the side at the number of ounces in it. See.

Twenty-eight ounces. These other ones are only fourteen and one-half ounces. Hmm. You know, ounce for ounce, that brand is actually cheaper than this one that's on sale."

"Oh, really?" she said, putting her can back on the shelf. "In that case, put in three of those that are on sale."

"No," he said, "I don't think we ought to get these."

"Why not?" she asked.

"Well," he said, "things are always cheaper in big cans, and I think maybe the other one has better ingredients."

"No," she said, "small cans are cheaper. See. We can get three cans of those for less than we'd pay for two cans of these. Besides, I think the recipe I'm going to use calls for three cans."

"Three cans of what size?" he asked. "Three big cans or three little cans?"

"I think so," she said. "In fact, I'm almost certain."

"Well," he said. "In that case, I think you are right. We probably ought to get three of the big cans."

"Well, all right," she said, as she put three of the larger cans in their cart. "But I still think the smaller cans would be better."

"I think it's a toss-up," he said, as he took the cans out of their cart and put them back on the shelf. "Why don't we just do what you wanted to do in the first place and take one big can and one little can?"

I don't know which cans they eventually chose. They were still discussing when I finished that aisle and moved on to the next one. As I was driving home, I was trying to figure out the logic of their arguments and I was wondering why some people have such difficulty communicating with each other. I had been thinking lately that one reason people often have difficulty agreeing on even the smallest details might be that there is some major difference in their basic assumptions about reality. I had been thinking I was going to start being more observant of the people I'm around to see if I could detect some fundamental difference in point of view that might explain many or most of their minor disagreements. Actually, I suspected that the couple in the grocery store were fundamentally alike and that their conversation made perfect sense to both of them. But I also suspected—and rather hoped—that I was different from them in some fundamental way.

I turned off the highway onto the road that leads past Lake Splash, which is sort of a neighborhood pond. Up in front of me, I spotted two of our resident goosenganders waddling along the edge of the road. I stopped the car, rolled down a window, and yelled at them, "Hey, you guys, what have I told you about walking in the street? Now let's watch it, OK!"

Four goosenganders, in all, live in and around the pond. The first time I met one of them I asked it if it were a goose or a gander. Its pert response was: "Yes! Of course! Certainly! Absolutely! Unequivocally! Are there any other options? Did you come up with that question all by yourself?" Since then, I have learned their names and know the boys from the girls. But the term stuck in my memory, and I remain quite comfortable referring to them as goosenganders.

Fun City, the largest and handsomest of the four, honked, "Roads? Cars? Who cares? I'm looking for goodies. What kind of nibbles did you bring? A medium pizza will serve quite nicely this time of day! Especially if you will throw on some extra mozzarella and go heavy on the anchovies. And, this time, please ease up on the onions and peppers!" He paused for a moment, took a quick look at his calendar watch, and continued, "Ah, grocery-shopping day, and you have bags and bags of groceries in there somewhere! And you got most of them just for me? Oh, thank you! Thank you! Thank you!"

I remembered the first time I met Fun City. I judged immediately, based partly on his deep, deep voice and partly on his arrogance, that he was a male. After getting to know him better, I asked him, and he said I was at least five hundred percent correct. I might have assumed the goosengander walking along the road with him was his mate, Glory, but with Fun City it's not safe to make such simple assumptions. At the time, I did not know Glory well enough to recognize her when I saw her. So, since she said nothing to me and I responded in kind, I politely refrained from making guesses about who she was. As for Fun City, I simply ignored him. While I did have a loaf of bread, a package of rolls, and other goosengander favorites in the trunk of the car, I also had several frozen items which needed to be rushed home before they thawed. Besides, I rarely buy pizza at the grocery store, hadn't had Fun City in mind when I bought groceries, and was a bit put off by his brazen ways. So, I simply rolled up the window and drove off. I could hear him fussing and fuming as I pulled away. From the rearview mirror, I could see him and the other goosengander continue their awkward strut along the edge of the road.

15

For those of you who are scientific minded, goosenganders make up the subfamily *Anserinae* in the *Anatidae* family. They are web-footed birds closely related to the quackenducker and swan. They are twenty to forty inches long and have wide wings. These wings enable them to fly to great heights; sober airline pilots have noted passing them at altitudes as high as nine thousand feet. In addition to being excellent flyers and swimmers, goosenganders can walk quite well on land. They often have long lives, sometimes living to be sixty-five years old, at which time they presumably begin to take advantage of their senior citizens' discounts. Most scientists think North American goosenganders are migratory birds that fly as far north as the arctic circle and as far south as Mexico. Other knowledgeable observers have noted that many never go as far as the other end of the pond.

There are thirteen kinds of wild goosenganders in the United States and Canada. All are quite intelligent, highly gregarious and, normally, monogamous. They typically form strong pair bonds that, except for some occasional messing around, last through the entire adult life of the pair. Many of them nest in shallow holes in the ground which they line with grass, feathers, down and, sometimes, work gloves that someone has accidently left in the back yard. Interestingly, goosenganders tend to keep bankers' hours: while they usually are late going to work, they make up for it by quitting early.

Our goosenganders are of a type called "white-cheeks," a name based on the prominent white patch on each side of their head. The white-cheeks usually eat grains, insects, small water creatures, popcorn, peanut butter and jelly sandwiches, and, of course, pizzas.

Some species, such as the Great Canadian Goosengander, have become virtually extinct as a result of hunting and changes in habitat wrought by encroaching humans. Other species have fared better, primarily because of the relative inaccessibility of their nesting areas. Some goosenganders survive quite well in lakes and ponds in heavily populated areas where they are treated as somewhat reluctant pets. At one time, there were six adult goosenganders in our pond. One was killed by a speeding automobile and the other, according to rumor, was shot by an illegal hunter on the day before Thanksgiving and eaten as part of a holiday feast. Young goosenganders are particularly vulnerable to numerous dangers. So far, no newly-hatched gosling has survived in our pond for more than a few days.

Goosenganders communicate through honks, squeaks, hisses, and "body language." When one is ready to take off for a flight, for example, he or she moves his or her head rapidly from side to side. Goosenganders are large birds and require considerable taxi area to build up enough speed to become airborne. So, their head signals signify, "Get out of my way, stupid. Do you want to be run over by a bus?" A loud hiss means something like, "Get away from my nest!" or "Lay some nibbles on me or I will eat your arm off!"

16

The four goosenganders in our neighborhood pond were of particular interest to me. As I said above, I had been thinking I was going to start being more observant of the ones I am around often to see if I could detect some fundamental difference in points of view that might explain many or most of their minor disagreements. I passed the pond frequently and saw the goosenganders often. Maybe I should stop by and get better acquainted with them. Maybe I could find out if there were any major differences in their behaviors and, if so, what the basis was for the differences.

A few days later, for the first time, I had an opportunity to hold a conversation with one of the goosenganders that was more than just everyday chit chat. It was a warm fall day, a beautiful day to be outdoors. I was walking along the shore of Lake Splash when I met the goosengander whom I have come to know as "Glory." She is a female and the mate of Fun City. She has a shrill voice, sings soprano, and is deeply religious. This was one of the few times I had ever seen a goosengander alone. They usually are in pairs. I asked her why she was alone. Her response was something about down time, personal space, individuality, tired of the same old gaggle bag, and other things that I did not quite understand. What I did understand, from her fussing and grumbling, was that she was in a defensive and grumpy mood. So, mostly just to try to get her in a better mood, I asked, "Why don't you just go drown yourself?"

She replied with dignity, "Don't be silly! Life is much too important to squander in such a frivolous manner. Surely you jest."

We moved from there to a more serious discussion of what life is all about. I suppose you could call it a discussion. Actually, I mostly just listened. Once a goosengander really starts talking, it is difficult for anyone else to get in a word.

"Contrary to what you erroneously might have assumed," continued Glory, "life is not something to be taken lightly. Rather, as the great poet Longfeather said:

'Life is real! Life is earnest!
Drowned or road killed's not its goal.
Goosenganders ever turnest
Toward eternity for the soul.

Fun and games to mask our sorrow
Should not be our destined way,
But to live so, each tomorrow,
We're more pious than today.

In the world's wide sea of twattle,
In the swim and quack of life,
Be not a sinful waggle gaggle;
Find salvation in the strife.

Trust no fathead, frump, or pheasant!
Let the dead grass line your bed!
Uh! Barf up frogs that don't taste pleasant!
Um! Don't think stuff that bonks your head!'"

I think Glory got a bit mixed up on the last few lines, but I suspected that she would never admit it.

She continued her explanation. "The one single thing that is REALLY important in this life is that one believe in and serve the GREAT GOOSE IN THE SKY." She held one foot across her chest and bowed her head reverently as she said this. "There is no ultimate worth in how many nibbles one might accumulate, how pristine one might leave the pond, how well thought of one is, or how many goslings one leaves upon the sands of time. The primary, yea, the sole purpose of life is that it offers each of us a choice as to whether or not we will grovel at the Webbed Feet of the GREAT GOOSE. Those who choose to serve will reap eternal life in the GREAT POND where they will learn to take great joy in doing without all the things they care about the most in this life. There will be no need for nibbles, no need to make goslings, no need to soar, and no need to swim in the cool of a quiet spring morning through a lake's gentle waters in the wake of our much-loved mate with the breezes softly sifting through our feathers. In that GREAT POND, even the tone-deaf will learn to love harp music, and we will wear halos in hot weather and in cold. These are some of the things that are hard to understand, for the gods do not think as we do. But we can be sure that, if we keep the faith, we will die a glorious death and live a joyful forever in that GREAT POND with the GREAT GOOSE tending to all of what She knows to be our needs. Glory! Hallelujah!"

"So," Glory continued, "while we may do many things in this world that seem to relate just to staying alive, the real purpose of life is to make the right decisions and, incidently, to show others that they must make the right decisions so that they, too, fulfill the purpose of their lives. For, alas, to make the wrong decisions, to choose to ignore the GREAT GOOSE and live a life devoted only to selfish nibbling, honking, and preening, will result in being banished for all eternity from the GREAT POND. Yes, banished instead to suffer forever in the ghastly BURNING DESERT of unbelievers where there is no water, where the sun blazes hot, where there is no shelter, where the dry sands blow, where the sharp thorns of the cactus stick in one's throat, and where...."

She continued longer with this discourse, but I became increasingly confused with the logic of her argument and maybe a bit sleepy from the warm morning sun shining in my eyes and the big breakfast I had eaten earlier. Anyway, that was enough of her philosophy for one day, so I took my leave. Glory seemed not to notice my departure but was left standing on a stump with her head thrown back honking shrilly and gesticulating wildly with her wings. We would discuss this subject further some other day when she was less emotional.

17

Several months passed before I had much time for goosenganders or before they had much time for me. I was passing the pond on the way home from the hardware store when I spotted two of them between the road and the edge of the pond. One was waddling in a tight circle around the other who had his or her head tucked under a wing and was, seemingly, asleep. With about every third step, the circling goosengander stretched his or her neck into the air and honked, "Boring day! Boredom city!"

I stopped the car, got out, and went down and sat inside the circle next to the sleeping goosengander. I saw then that the circling complainer was Fun City. He rushed toward me, could not stop in time, collided, and bowled me over. As I lay on my back in the damp grass, he stood over me with raised wings and bad breath and honked in my face, "Nibbles! Nibbles! Nibbles! What kind of nibbles do we have here? What? No nibbles? Rats! Well, got any extra tickets to the jazz festival? No? No tickets! Darned! Money for beer and pretzels at the Swinging Singles? No? No money! Dang! Borrow your car for a little skiing or scuba diving trip perhaps? No? No wheels! Drat! What about some sky diving or a little hot air balloon trip? No? No trip! Damned! Hmm. Well! Oh! I know! It's bungie jumping! Bungie jumping! Bungie jumping! Right? What? No? Hell's bells! No fun!"

Then, with a sigh of resignation, he backed off my stomach, lowered his wings and head, and moaned, "Well, at least we can go for a ride on your motorcycle." His enthusiasm seemed to return as he continued, "I love motorcycles! Speed! The roar of the engine when you scratch off! The smell of burning rubber! The scream of tires on tight curves! Wind in your face! Snack bugs on your windshield! Wait a minute! What did you say? You don't own a motorcycle? Ding! Damned! Darn! Boring day! Boredom city!"

I knew it was a useless question, but I asked it anyway. "Don't you ever think of anything but having a fun time? What are you going to do when you are too old or fat or sick to do things like that?"

The response was immediate, "Old? Me? Fat? Me? Sick? Me? Got to run now! Great things to do down at the other end of the pond!" He flapped his wings mightily and dashed down the slope to the water.

I thought a bit about Fun City. And I thought again about the couple in the grocery store trying to decide which beans, or whatever, they should buy. It occurred to me that, while there seemed to be significant differences between the way Fun City and the couple acted out their assumed roles, there also was a commonality, a commonality that might be more significant than the differences. I wondered if the lives of both might lack some meaning, some vision, some guiding light, some deep interest or concern outside themselves. And I wondered if this might result in their focus being on what seems to me to be frivolous, trivial aspects of life.

Fun City's tirade over the motorcycle had awakened the other goosengander. It was his mate, Glory. She patiently plodded after him, glancing back only to tell me, "He's not saved, you know. That's why he uses those bad words. But the day will come when he must stand before his MAKER. The GREAT GOOSE hears all and holds all accountable. Glory! Hallelujah!"

18

As Fun City and Glory disappeared into the shadows of the trees at the far end of the pond, the other pair of goosenganders pushed their way out of a patch of reeds and waddled over to where I was sitting. The female began picking up the cigarette butts Fun City had carelessly thrown on the grass. The other looked me over with silent, searching eyes. I had never spoken to them but, from what Fun City had told me, I assumed them to be Eden and her quiet mate, Socs.

"I don't know what we are going to do with him," said Eden as she looked in the direction of the recently departed Fun City. "He's a disgrace to the goosengander race, but I really worry about him. He is an atheist, you know. He doesn't believe in anything but having fun. He thinks a dead goose is a dead goose and that he might as well live it up while he is still alive. But I think he really believes he will live forever, always young, always handsome, always energetic, healthy, strong, virile, and ready to do anything to keep from thinking and feeling. He says he believes everything that exists—the earth, the sky, all the animals—is the result of a creative accident, that there is no meaning to life, that we all do what we do because it feels good to us, and that one is stupid to worry about tomorrow. For him, the thing to do is eat, drink, and make merry, for tomorrow, you diet!"

"He has no concerns for the environment, the national debt, or what kind of world we leave to our children," continued Eden. "He seems unconcerned that there are thousands of starving goslings all over the world. He seems not to care that our infrastructure is crumbling, that there is crime in our cities, and that there is unemployment across the land. Of no concern to him are our collapsing family structures, our failed education system, and the oppression and armed aggression in many parts of the world. If you mention to him that the ozone layer is being destroyed, that global warming threatens, and that lands and seas are becoming cesspools of contamination, he will stare with a vacant eye and ask what that has to do with the price of pizza. Instead of concerns about overpopulation, he keeps egging his mate on. His only worry about pollution is that he might trip over it and break a leg. His only concern about global warming is that his snow cone will melt. While I know I ought not to say it, the real truth is that that goosengander is so dumb that, if he died tomorrow, the average IQ in the animal kingdom would go up at least five points!"

I thought the conversation was getting a bit too subjective and, perhaps, a bit vindictive so I tried to change the subject. I asked, "Well, why do you think he is like that?"

Eden stretched her wings and flapped them a few times, took a deep breath, and responded, "Fun City was the last hatched of a very large brood and everybody always gave him lots of attention. He has always had about everything he wanted. When his parents were young, they had a very hard time finding enough food to stay alive and they wanted to make sure life was better for their goslings. They wanted their goslings to have everything they had missed out on. So I think Fun City has never had enough troubles to develop much character. Uh, that doesn't sound quite right because he IS a CHARACTER! But, anyway, I think you know what I mean. He's still just a big, happy-go-lucky, fun-loving, over-grown, uh... handsome gosling. And while I... I... envy him, he does makes me angry. He's not very nice: while he's friendly with those with whom he can have fun, he just snubs everybody else. And if there's one thing I can't stand, it's a snub! If everybody just looked out for himself the way he does this world would be an even bigger mess than it is now. He doesn't do his part; he takes and takes but never gives, and that's not fair. I know that is not the way life should be lived."

This seemed to be a good opportunity to change the subject to something other than the fun-loving, handsome snub, so I asked, "Then, how do you think life should be lived? What do you think life is all about?"

"Well," she replied, "life is about making this a better world. The GREAT GOOSE intended that we have good lives and SHE has given us everything we need to make this a perfect world. The trouble is that some, like Glory, try to get the GREAT GOOSE to do things that they are perfectly able to do for themselves. And others, well, most just don't seem to care at all and some..." she pointed to Socs as she continued, "some say they care, but I don't think they care enough. They don't realize the urgency. The earth is being so messed up that the damage is becoming irreparable. It may already be too late to save ourselves. And, for sure, if everybody doesn't start right now to make a concerted effort to repair the damage, it is certain that the end is near."

Socs, or Socrates if you wish to be more formal, seemed not to notice the conversation. Perhaps he had heard it all before. He had slipped my digital wristwatch off my wrist, held it up to his ear, and wondered why it didn't tick. Then he patted one webbed foot on the grass as he counted off sixty seconds. He compared this with the numbers on the watch and murmured that he thought maybe the watch was a bit slow.

Eden motioned in his direction and continued, "He, for example, could do lots of good things if he wanted to. While he doesn't mess up anything, he doesn't fix anything either. Well, not unless it's one of his toys. Like his telescope that he keeps trying to adjust so he can prove some of his dumb theories like... well, he actually thinks the world is round like a ball and that it is always spinning around. But he can't explain why we don't fall off or why we are not upside down part of the time. And... and any idiot can look right there at the ground," she pointed with one wing as she continued, "and tell that it definitely is NOT spinning! For absolute sure, it is just sitting there doing nothing of the sort!

"But, anyway, he always wants to STUDY things instead of FIX things! He thinks what we KNOW is more important than what we HAVE. Now I will admit that he is kind and gentle. And he wouldn't hurt a flea. He is a vegetarian, you know. He won't even do frogs! And he says it's not because he is interested in maintaining an ecological balance but because he thinks frogs are nice fellows and that they think some very interesting thoughts. Such nonsense! It's not as though they were red meat or something that's bad for the arteries. Everybody knows the GREAT GOOSE made frogs just for goosegander hors d'oeuvres! If we all were like him, we wouldn't be able to move because we would be neck deep in frogs. But, then, I guess if we were all like that Fun City, there would not be a single frog in forty counties. So, maybe Socs balances things out some even when he doesn't mean to.

"In some ways, he's as harmless and useless as she is." As Eden said this, she pointed in the general direction of where Glory was swimming in a tight circle in the middle of the pond. "While she wants to get those frogs SANCTIFIED before she eats them, he just catches them, finds out what they are thinking, and lets them go. Then he goes off and eats grass and stuff. He doesn't know a thing about balance and moderation. Ha! I'll bet he has all kinds of vitamin and mineral deficiencies! He just LOOKS real healthy! I'll bet some day all his feathers will fall out and his skin will turn all green like the grass and other gunk he lives on!"

"And Glory," Eden continued, "is so kind and gentle that she gives me... uh... well, goose pimples. So, it's hard to say anything unkind about her. But the truth is, while she believes with all her heart in the GREAT GOOSE, she doesn't think much of the world the GREAT GOOSE has created for us. She wants to ESCAPE this world rather then LIVE in it. I think that may be because of her first-hatched son. Do you know that clear spot over past those bushes? Well, that's where her first-hatched was killed by a hawk. And you know how mothers are about their first hatched! They always have a special place in their hearts. And, well, I think she mostly thinks about how she wants to move on to the GREAT POND IN THE SKY where she is sure she will spend eternity with her beloved son. And, while I think she is mostly right about that, she spends so much time looking toward the GREAT POND that she is more or less miserable in this life. She thinks her mate is almost sure to end up in the BURNING DESERT, and that makes her very sad, too. I think of the GREAT GOOSE as a loving GOOSE who would never think of sending one of us to the BURNING DESERT. I'm not even sure there is such a place."

Eden paused for a moment and then continued, "But when I really think about him (I was pretty sure she was talking now about Fun City), I'm not certain he will ever be happy in the GREAT POND. I can't imagine his sitting around all day on a cloud strumming on a harp! And I think they had better get some armed guards for all those female angels because he's going to do who he's going to do, and that's a fact. And have you ever seen him when he's had a couple of beers? Well..."

I stopped her there because I thought her enthusiasm might be overpowering her judgement. I redirected the dialogue by asking, "So you, too, believe in the GREAT GOOSE?"

"Well, of course!" she responded. "But much of what she (Glory) believes about the GREAT GOOSE is just plain superstition. She takes myths literally and, so, misses out on the real truths that the myths represent. For example, she thinks Goosengander Noah really did build a huge airplane out of logs, stuff it full of pairs of animals, and fly off to escape forty days and nights of drought. She also thinks Goosengander Jonah actually got chomped down by a giant camel while he was walking across the desert and, later, got barfed up on wet land. Well, a myth is just a myth! These myths tell the real truth about how the earth will turn to desert if we don't tend to it properly. They tell us that what is important is our making the earth a better place in which to live!"

I interrupted again to ask, "Well, IS the world getting to be a better place?"

Eden thought for a minute, and then responded sadly, "Not that I can tell. It seems to be getting worse. Animals just aren't trying hard enough. They are too selfish; they rarely think of the common good."

"Why is that?" I asked.

"Well," she replied, "I think animals were better to each other when they were so superstitious they thought the GREAT GOOSE would zap them if they didn't do right. Now, most of them have done so many bad things WITHOUT getting zapped that they have decided the GREAT GOOSE either is not all that concerned or is not looking. 'So,' they think, 'if no one is looking, I'll just do what's fun for me right now.' We've just got to do a better job of educating and making it clearer to all that we are in this world together and that looking out for each other will make life better for all. If we all cooperated, we could make this world a perfect place. There would be no suffering, sorrow, hunger, danger, pain, or fear. Instead, there would be peace, abundance, cooperation, kindness, honesty, and love."

The sun, by now, was high in the sky. I thought I had the general idea of Eden's view of life. So I said my goodbyes and took my leave.

19

It was the day after my visit with Eden. The raw, cold, windy days of early spring seemed to have passed, at least temporarily. This was the perfect time to take my hammock out of the workshop attic and swing it between two trees in the side yard. Putting the hammock out again gave me a good feeling. After my long winter of contented discontent, this felt like a new beginning. The afternoon was at least half over, and I was sitting sideways on the newly-reinstalled hammock listening to the birds sing. Out by the feeders, there were bluebirds, blue jays, cardinals, chickadees, doves, goldfinches, hummingbirds, juncos, nuthatches, titmice, woodpeckers, and wrens. They seemed not to be doing much other than singing and bouncing around, so I wondered if it might be time to put out more seeds. I looked at my watch to check the time. I realized, with somewhat of a shock, that I did not have a watch! Hmm. How could that be? Then I remembered. Yesterday, when I was down by the pond, Socs had borrowed it. He had not returned it. I forgot about feeding the birds, went into the house for my car keys, and drove down to the pond to try to retrieve my watch.

I parked just off the pavement, got out of the car, and walked to the edge of the pond. I sheltered my eyes from the sun that had half disappeared behind the trees and looked out over the pond for some signs of life. The only movement was the glitter of the sun's last rays as they bounced off the slight ripples of the pond surface. The air was warm and still. All was quiet except for the distant cawing of a crow and the low drone of a beetle in its flight. I cupped my hands to my mouth and shouted over the waters, "Hey, you guys! Is anybody home?" There was no reply. The pond seemed deserted. I walked back toward the car. I would try again another time.

But then I heard a rustle behind me and looked back to see a goosenganders rushing up the bank toward me. Its wings were dragging as if it were almost exhausted. "Stop! Don't go! Wait up! I've got your watch!" Socs sagged to the grass in front of me and lifted a wing that held a watch loosely stuck between his feathers. I gently removed it, put it back on my wrist, and waited for him to catch his breath.

He recovered quickly, stood up, flapped his wings a few times, honked a few times to clear his throat, and explained, "Sorry I kept your watch, but you were so busy talking with Eden the other day that I didn't think it polite to interrupt. Just now, we were down behind the bank where you couldn't see us. I had the watch in my beak so as to make sure I didn't drop it while I was climbing the bank. I slipped on the bank and had a hard time climbing up. But here I am and there is your watch. Thank you for lending it to me."

He paused, cleared his throat again, and continued. "Now, about the watch," he said, "there is what I suppose you would call the good news and the bad news."

"What is that supposed to mean?" I asked.

"What I suppose you would call the good news is that it really IS waterproof, just like it says on the case. You have my personal assurance that it is water tight."

"So," I asked, "what is the bad news?"

He seemed not to hear the question. He said, "Do you know why it doesn't tick? It has a battery inside! It runs on electricity! And that is why it doesn't tick! Inside, there is a small electric motor and all kinds of wheels and gears and things that make the motor turn the disk that has numbers on it so you can tell what time it is. That quartz thing is important too. Did you ever notice the word 'quartz' printed on the case? The quartz is a small crystal that makes the watch keep accurate time. Uh. Did I say accurate time?

"Well, here is what I suppose you would call the bad news. I have made some careful observations over the past twenty-four hours. I adjusted a pendulum so that it exactly matches the timing of your watch, and I compared the motion of the pendulum with computations of changes that I noted in the relative positions of Ursa Major—I think you call it the Big Dipper—and the constellations of Cassiopeia, Cepheus, and Camelopardus. I double checked this against the light rays bouncing off the nebulae Orion, the confluence of Jupiter's third and eleventh moons, and the change in the distance between Saturn and Venus. I made the necessary adjustments to compensate for the nutation of the earth's axis caused by the moon's gravitational pull, the perturbation of Venus from the North Star and Pegasus, the temperature, wind direction and speed, the relative humidity, the shifting of the ozone layer, and the local elevation. I am reasonably confident of my calculations, and I can tell you your watch is running slow. I think you will be shocked to know that if you use that watch, you will lose almost a full minute over the next five million years. I thought it might be a weak battery or a loose connection, but I checked those out and I am reasonably certain that you have an imperfect quartz crystal. And I will be honest and tell you that I don't know how fix it."

I was a bit surprised at all this, but I was determined not to let it show. I acted on the principle that the best defense is a strong offense and asked, "When you said you had what you SUPPOSED I WOULD CONSIDER good news and bad news, what did you mean by SUPPOSE?"

He looked up at me with a surprised look on his face and replied, "So, you noticed that. Very observant of you. I mean VERY! Well, what I meant was that it's not particularly good news or bad news to me, but I thought it might be to you."

"You mean you don't care whether or not water gets into my watch or whether or not my watch keeps correct time?" I asked, showing more feeling than I intended.

"Well, no, not really," he replied. "If it gets a little water inside, there will just be a little less on the OUTSIDE. There will still be the same amount of water in the world, so what's the difference? And, if you ever got really thirsty, you could just swallow your watch. Might even keep you from dying from thirst some day. And as for losing time, what's the big deal? If it didn't keep time at all, look at all the time you would save! You would have all the time in the world to do everything you ever wanted to do. And remember that time is relative to speed. So, if you want the watch to run faster, YOU run faster. If you run fast enough, it will keep perfect time. Well, that is, relative to your present speed which, if my observations are correct, is basically zero."

I was beginning to feel some irritation. I hate smart-elicky ganders. I stared at his neck and wondered how it would look tied into a knot.

He settled down into the grass, looked up with a quizzical expression on his face, and murmured, "You don't know how good it is to talk to somebody like you who seems to understand what I'm talking about. Thank you for being a good listener. Most animals think I'm some sort of nut, you know. But you seem like a very perceptive and caring person."

Maybe I would not tie his neck into a knot just yet.

"Mind if I wear my eyeglasses?" he asked. Without waiting for a reply, he pulled them from under his wing and perched them on his beak. "I really can't see much without them, you know. But I don't wear them when I'm around others because the sight of a goosengander wearing eyeglasses seems to upset some. I made these out of bottles that people threw into the pond. Same as I did my telescope and microscope lenses. Glass is wonderful stuff. You can see through it or see yourself in it, depending on how much courage you have. But I am afraid most see through it because they want both to escape from themselves and to keep a barrier between themselves and what's on the other side of the window. And when they do dare look into a mirror, they usually see what they wish they were instead of accepting and being delighted with what they really are. Do you understand what I am talking about? That's good! I was pretty sure you did."

"Did I ever tell you about the tenor?" Socs continued without a pause. "I didn't think I did. He is a frog, you know. Most frogs sing bass, but he is a tenor. First frog I ever met. That is, after I was old enough to know what one was. Found him under a log down by the dam. Was almost noon. He was asleep, I think. Only had one eye open. Wrong eye. I came up on the other side of him. Didn't see me. Almost noon, but I already have said that. And I was hungry. Caught him up. Looked pretty good to me. Started to put a gulp on him, but hesitated. Wasn't sure which end was supposed to go down first. Wasn't sure if I was supposed to peel him first. Maybe I was supposed to whack him a few times first. So much to learn!

"He asked me what I was planning to do. I said I thought I was supposed to eat him. He said he wished I wouldn't. I asked why not. He said he just didn't think he would enjoy it. He said it seemed like more fun for me than for him and he didn't think that was quite fair somehow. I said that's what the other goosenganders did with frogs. He said that was true, but if I did the same thing everybody else did, I would never learn anything new. I asked how he would like to learn what it is like to be eaten. He asked how I would like to learn what it is like to be taken by the EVIL ONE. I told the frog I wasn't sure what he meant by the EVIL ONE. He explained to me that the EVIL ONE is that huge black dog that's short on tail and long on tooth. I said I thought being taken by the EVIL ONE would be a TERMINAL experience and that I thought there were lots of other kinds of experiences that would be more appropriate for that period of my life."

Socs came back to the present for a moment and said, "Terminal experience! Wasn't that a neat phrase for such a young lad? The frog assured me that he agreed with me and that he, too, wasn't ready for a terminal experience. So I put the frog down. He made good sense to me. Smart fellow. Interesting fellow. Turned out that he sang in an opera company. Presented every Saturday night. And, sometimes, in the middle of the week. He's still performing, you know. Since that first experience with a frog, I catch them, ask them if they are ready for a terminal experience and, if they say not, I have them tell me why not. Learned a lot that way. Experiences. Experiencing others. That's what it's about, you know."

The sun had disappeared behind the trees and the pond lay in soft shadows. A few mosquitoes were beginning to circle me and check out my bare ankles. The day was ending, but I was reluctant to leave. "I have to go," I told him. "Can we talk again soon?"

While seeming to ignore the question, he answered it in his own way. "When we get together again, I want you to tell me some things that I have been wondering about. Do you know what proponents of the Big Bang theory are saying about the possibility that some stars may be older than the universe? What is the relationship between random molecular reshuffling and the development of DNA? Do you know about Fermat's last theorem, what Gautama would think if he came back to earth and saw how Buddhism has developed, and why, when you drop a piece of toast, it always lands buttered side down? I thought you did." And then, without another word, Socs waddled slowly down to the pond and swam into the gathering darkness.

20

It was Easter Sunday, and my schedule was a bit different from usual. I arose while it was still dark and drove down to the fast foodery for coffee and a grease biscuit. On the way back home, I passed the pond just as the first orange rays of light began to illumine the soft mist that rose from the shimmering surface of the water. It was a magic dawn, with the dogwoods in bloom, the first green appearing on the poplars and oaks, and the sweet smell of spring in the air. I stopped the car, rolled down the window, and waited in the stillness of the morning. All was serene and soft and cool. All was at rest, so it seemed. The world lay sleeping in the silence and safety of the dawn of a sacred day.

And, then, a faint voice seemed to float on the silence. I sensed rather than heard a sweet, tender voice trembling tentatively in the cool, still morning air. I listened carefully for the direction of the sensation and walked slowly along the dew-strewn shore toward what now seemed to be the music of angels. I saw nothing at first. And then, as I came out of the far side of a small copse of shrubbery, I saw Glory standing in a clearing by the shore of the pond. This was the very spot where her first-hatched had been killed by a hawk. I was surprised to see her, for I had never before seen a goosengander up this early. But I was even more surprised, and moved, by the beauty of her clear, soft soprano voice as it wafted gently through the morning air. With her graceful head pointed skyward and her wings folded as if in prayer, she sang her version of an old and sacred hymn.

"GOOSE OF AGES, please help me.
May I find my way to Thee.
Let the waters of the flood,
From Thy regal wings which flowed,
Be for me a certain cure
For my sins. Please make me pure!

Should my sorrow be complete
And my wings forever beat,
These could not, by one degree,
Make me safe or make me free.
So, to Thee, no gift I bring,
But simply to Thy mercy cling.

Now I sing this humble song,
Ere my feeble breath is gone.
For when I fly to skies unknown,
I'll behold Thee on Thy throne.
GOOSE OF AGES, please help me.
May I find my way to Thee."

I waited quietly until she was silent and then, without disturbing her time of worship, walked slowly back to the car. On the floor of the car was a piece of bright red ribbon that had, some months before, been left there when a gift was unwrapped. I took the ribbon, walked back to the place where Glory stood, and gently tied it about her graceful neck. Not a word was said. We simply looked at each other and, with a nod of our heads, acknowledged our awareness. I walked back to the car and drove home.

21

When I passed by the pond again a few days later, the surface of the water sparkled from the rays of the noonday sun.

I shaded my eyes with my hand and explored the pond and shoreline. At first I saw nothing, but then something seemed to be moving over on the grass at the edge of the pond. It was a pair of goosenganders. One was lying on the ground in an awkward position somewhat like an airliner after a crash landing. He was lying on his chest with his tail in the air and his beak flat on the ground. His wings were spread and lay limply on the grass. His eyes were closed, and he moaned softly. Glory was poised at his side with her wings folded and her head stretched toward the sky. Her high-pitched honks and squeaks filled the air. I interrupted her reveries and asked what was wrong. She leaned over the sprawling form of Fun City and replied, "He really has it bad. I'm praying for him but I apparently don't have enough faith because he's not getting any better."

"Is he hurt badly?" I asked with some anxiety.

"Oh! He's not going to die, if that's what you mean. He just has a super bad case of the blahs."

I took a closer look at Fun City and, from his looks, gathered that Glory's diagnosis was correct. He obviously was sufferer from a bad case of depression. He half opened one eye, looked up at me, and said in a pitiful voice, "If you are going to do anything for me, do it quickly 'cause I'm going fast!"

"What, exactly, is wrong?" I addressed the question directly to him.

With a wistful moan, he said, "I'm not even going to ask if you have any nibbles. Nothing is going right for me. I'm afraid I have the triple blats and blahs."

I sat in the grass beside him and lightly stroked his head and neck. He continued his low moan. "Maybe it would help to talk about it," I suggested.

He looked up with sad eyes and said, "I don't think anything will help. When your time comes, it's time to go. And there's nothing you can do about it."

He looked over at Glory, who still was hovering nearby, and murmured, "Uh, would, uh, you, uh, mind, maybe, uh, giving me a little privacy here?"

Glory, appearing only mildly offended, said, "Of course I wouldn't mind." She stepped easily into the waters of the pond and swam at an angle toward some trees that shaded the far shore.

As she swam, Fun City called after her, "Uh! Thank you, uh, for trying to help!" She responded with a toss of her wing as she swam on.

Fun City glanced at me shyly, took a cautious look around for eavesdroppers, and continued. "This morning, I found a... a... a grey feather in my tail. I'm... I'm getting old! And... and..." He again looked cautiously around to make sure no one else could hear him and continued in a whisper that I could barely hear. "And... and... well, I'm LOSING it, if you know what I mean!"

I responded that I really was not sure what he meant. So he continued, "Well, I'm losing IT! You know, LOSING IT! I used to enjoy, er, well GANDERING AROUND. But, now, I don't particularly feel like it. Not every day, or every hour, like it used to be. I'M LOSING IT!" He sobbed softly for a minute or two and then got his emotions under control enough to honk his nose and start again. "Like I have told others, in this life, one might as well eat, drink, and make Mary, for tomorrow you die! But life has been so short and there were so many fun things to do. And now it's about over. And I don't want to die! I'm too young to die! What am I going to do?"

I really did not know how to respond. I thought and thought and finally, from sheer desperation, asked, "What do suppose the other goosenganders think?"

He considered this for a minute and then answered, "They're no help. At least I don't think so. She," he pointed one wing in Glory's direction, "is a fine goosengander. She is so caring. She would do most anything to help anybody, except on Sunday. But... but, in some ways, she is such a... such a... well, a GOOSE! But she really believes what she preaches. She found a nest of field mice down by the dam and spent the better part of a month trying to get them baptized. Five were drowned in the process, but I hear the remaining three are doing fine. She's very controlling. I wish she would stop telling me how to live my life. I would almost let her baptize me just to make her happy. But I keep remembering those five mice; she really gets carried away sometimes. She has a firm belief in angels and devils and all kinds of crazy stuff. And there's not an ounce of proof that any of it is true. Her kind of superstition is just something animals have made up because it makes them feel good." And then he added wistfully, "And I almost wish I were dumb enough to believe it too. Maybe it would make me happy."

He was quiet for a while and then began, again, to sob softly. I continued to stroke his head and neck and to smooth down some of his ruffled feathers. I asked, "Do the other two goosenganders think the same way?"

"Well, no!" He pointed toward the pair of goosenganders in the middle of the pond as he replied. "Eden is a save-the-whale type. She thinks we should spend our lives building an Eden, whatever that is, right here on earth. She has all this junk that she's collected and she spends a great deal of time trying to find animals who are very poor so she can give the junk to them and make them happy. I understand she has a very hard time finding enough poor animals who will take stuff, so it is piling up on her. But she is optimistic; she probably will figure out some way to recycle the junk and make it into something I can eat. She does lots of good things, of course, and some of her ideas are not so bad. She even convinced me that I should pick up my stuff and not leave such a mess everywhere I go. Well, she convinced me, but I guess I don't actually DO it. But at least, now, I feel bad when I don't do it. And she has other good ideas like, for example, she has shown me that dumping my old engine oil into the pond gets the water all greasy. So I've stopped doing that. Now I'm careful to dump it into that storm sewer up by the road.

"She really works hard at the things she believes in. She is involved in more causes than a squirrel has acorns. I understand she now is heading a drive to get animals to counteract global warming by leaving their refrigerator doors open. And I can't say she is wrong. She has only been at it a few weeks and, already, it seems a bit cooler to me. She is convinced that we can make the world better and better until it will be so good we can hardly stand it. But I think she is fighting a losing battle. You only have to look around to see that the world really is getting worse and worse. She says we just haven't yet tried hard enough and, I don't know, maybe she is right. But if she doesn't stop fretting so much over everything, she is going to find grey feathers in HER tail!"

I could not help noticing that Fun City was reviving a bit as he talked. This was encouraging, so we continued. "What about him?" I asked, pointing toward the other of the two goosenganders who now had drifted close to the shore where we sat. "What does Socs think?"

"I don't know," Fun City responded. "He doesn't talk much. He reads all the time and seems to be very curious about everything. He is always studying something. I should think it would make his eyes hurt. But he is a nice enough goosengander to be around. He never tries to tell you how to live your life, and he is a good listener. The others think he's nuts. I think he may be a little nuts, but I agree with him about some things the others think are crazy. Like, he thinks the earth is round. And I think he is correct. After all, the pond is sort of round, pizzas are round, the sun looks kind of round, and the moon is round part of the time. So, why shouldn't the earth be round, too. I'm pretty sure it started off square but, then, the corners sort of got broken off and left it as round as a coconut cream pie. So, while he may not be playing with a full deck, at least he has all of his aces and kings. He seems to be interested in what others are doing and what they think about things. He seems always to be trying to learn stuff. But what good will all that learning do when he drops dead? The other day, I saw a frog that got run over by a truck. He was as flat as a pizza. What good did all he ever learned do him then? You can't take it with you. His brain was squashed as thin as a sushi nibble. And, uh, did I say pizza? Uh, did I mention sushi? Did you bring up the subject of coconut cream pie? Uh, ah, do, uh, do you, ah, by any chance have some crackers or, maybe, an apple?"

Fun City definitely was going to live! He munched a couple of stale cookies I found in my jacket pocket and, being somewhat refreshed, continued. "Some of them don't seem to think I'm very bright either. And maybe I'm not. They think I look at life from a short-term rather than a long-term perspective. And they are correct about that. Long term, we are all going to die, the sun will explode, and the universe will collapse. Long term, our existence not only is temporary, it is pointless. Nothing really matters! So, why waste time looking at the long term? And I know for certain some other things about the short term that they are really mixed up on. Life IS short term, so that is all you have to worry about.

"Do you want to know what this short-term life is really all about? Well, I can tell you. The answer is very simple and very short. It is spelled S-E-X. Sex is what it's all about. It is recreating your own kind so you don't become extinct. Like dinosaurs! If they had spent less time slouching around in swamps and more time having sex, there would have been more of them, and they would not have got themselves extincted out. You can't call a species successful if it has been extincted out! So, the only thing any animal has to do is reproduce itself. If it does this, it is a success. If it doesn't, that is the end of the species. Do you know about bollygronkers, zingdoobers, and wakklesockets? Of course you don't! And why not? Because they did not reproduce faster than they got killed off! For all the zillions of years of evolution, success has been measured by ability to survive. It's all right to get put down or eaten up IF, and that's an 'if' with a capital 'I' and capital 'F', IF you have reproduced sufficient of your own kind to keep the species alive. So, what is life all about? SEX! What is a successful life? One in which you reproduce lots of your own kind before you get put down! Am I a success? You can bet your pin feathers I am! VERY successful!"

Fun City paused again to catch his breath and inhale the last of the stale cookies and, then, he continued. "Now, these other goosenganders, they really are a bunch of softies, nice softies, of course, but softies just the same. I've got to be an example for them, got to show them how to be a success and how to have fun. If I've got to die, I've got to die, but I will be brave about it. I won't cry. I will go down winging and swinging. I will be brave to the very end, I mean to the VERY end!" He was standing tall now. He looked like his old, well, no, his YOUNG self. "Yes!" he continued, "To the very END! To the [gulp] very... end...?"

The last few words were spoken so softly I barely heard them. But the crisis was over. Fun City was almost, but not quite, as good as new. At least he would cavort and carouse for a few more years. As he waddled away in a strong, straight line toward the pond, I saw something I had not noticed earlier. On his right leg was a clumsily-tied bright red ribbon, a gift from Glory of one of her favorite things.

22

I hate those days when the sun doesn't show. We had had rain for four days, and it looked as though it would rain forever. I decided to go out anyway, just to get out of the house. I drove to the pond, opened my umbrella, and walked through the wet grass and steady rain to the edge of the water. Two goosenganders, Glory and Socs, swam over and climbed onto the bank. Glory spread her wings and stretched her neck into the air as if to try to get as wet as possible. She said, "Wonderful day! Cold, rainy, damp, dark, wet, wonderful day! A simply marvelous day! Great to be alive on a day like this." She looked at my umbrella and said, "Had an uncle who had one of those things. Used it on bright, sunny days to keep the weather from getting to his head. Said if you didn't keep the bright, sunny weather off, you would get the fever. Must have known what he was talking about because he never had the fever. If everybody did environmentally correct things, we wouldn't have bad weather like that. All the days would be beautiful like today. Well, got to swim!" She splashed back into the pond and swam into the wind and rain.

Socs shook the water from his wings and said, "I was hoping you would come again soon so we could talk some. Can you tell me the latest on the Palomar Observatory? Have they found anything new? I understand there is some controversy over the Dead Sea Scrolls. Know how much of them they have translated? Did you get a new watch yet? Want me to check it out for you? What do you want to talk about? You can't just sit here in the wet grass, can you? You don't like to get rained on. Right? Why don't we go up there under those trees where you will be more comfortable."

Socs and I relocated under some nearby trees where the rain came down in droplets rather than in torrents. It was a bit more tolerable for me there. I sat on a reasonably dry rock and held my umbrella down close. Absolute comfort is not necessary when the company is good. Socs sat at my feet, and we talked.

Socs does not respond well to small talk, so I got right to the point. "What I really would like to know," I said, "is about your basic philosophy. I would like to know what you think is really important and why you think it is important."

"I don't much like to talk about that," Socs responded.

"Why not?" I asked.

"Well, mostly because I don't seem to be able to say it so anyone understands what I mean. Perhaps that is because some of it is pretty fuzzy to me. When others tell me things, they seem to know all the answers. And I really do NOT know all the answers. I have just barely started trying to find ANSWERS. I am still trying to figure out the QUESTIONS!"

I wasn't sure I understood exactly what he meant, but I was pretty sure we were not going to get very far unless we shifted gears and started in a new direction. So, I said, "The other three goosenganders seem to have quite strong opinions about things. So why don't you tell me what you think about their ideas?"

Socs murmured, "I suppose I could try to do that."

"Why don't you start with him," I suggested, pointing in the direction of where Fun City lay in the pouring rain on the other rim of the pond.

"Interesting specimen," Socs responded. "I think you already have found out all about him. Really is not much to say. But I can reaffirm what you already know. The most difficult thinking he ever does seems to be thinking about how best to avoid thinking. Well, that is not quite right. He DOES think about certain things. He is a gourmet cook, so he obviously thinks a great deal about food. And he likes to fly up on that big oak tree limb that reaches over the water—bet you have never seen a goosengander on the limb of a tree—and swan dive into the pond. Bet you didn't know a goosengander could do a swan dive. Actually, a swan can't do a swan dive. Fun City can though. Exceptional lad. Had to do lots of thinking to figure out how to do that.

"And have you ever seen him wind surf? Doesn't use a board and a sail like most do. Just spreads his webbed feet, gets up on them, holds his wings to the wind, and off he goes. He thinks those kinds of things are really serious stuff. So there is a matter of perspective here. When I think about thinking, I think about SERIOUS thinking. But what is SERIOUS? Isn't it largely a matter of perspective? I don't think gourmet food, swan diving, and wind surfing have much to do with the real meaning of life. But he thinks they have a great deal to do with it. And he thinks the things I mess around with are TOTALLY unimportant. So, who is going to say which of us is right? I can't. I can see only from my own perspective, and he can see only from his. Did you say it must be difficult for us to communicate with each other? Thought you did."

Actually, I had not said a word.

He continued, "We never speak to each other. Well, hardly ever. No point in it. Rather talk to frogs. Interesting little fellows, frogs. There was this family of eight frogs that I used to know quite well. Met them over on the other side of the dam. They lived in a little puddle there, that is, until a long dry spell caused them to have to move. Did you say I was off the subject? Thought you did. What was the subject? You are right! We were talking about what I think about Fun City's ideas. Well, the truth is I don't think much about them at all. Haven't thought about them for a long, long time. Might never have thought about them again if you hadn't asked. But now that you have put me to it, let's see, what DO I think? Well, here's what I think.

"First, I don't agree with him when he says everything he does is predestined, that he always does exactly what he HAS to do. That he has no choices. Or, for that matter, that none of us ever has choices about anything. I think I agree with his mate that all intelligent animals have choices. Not many choices, perhaps, and we can't tell for sure what choices another animal has or does not have. No point in anything if we don't have SOME choice. Not everything, though, has choices. Grass and rocks and water don't seem to have choices. Don't know about earth worms, honey bees, and slugs. Don't seem to have much, if any, choice. Run mostly on instinct. You know about instinct, of course. All of us have some, probably couldn't breathe if we didn't. But some creatures are born with their internal computers already stuffed full of data. They never learn anything. They just run on the data they already have. I think that's what instinct is, just data we have that we didn't have to learn. Don't quite understand weeds and grass. Can't say they run on instinct because they don't have a brain. Don't know how they run. They can't talk. Wish they could so they could tell me how they run. Don't know what I would eat, though. Hard to share ideas with something and then chomp it down.

"To the extent that you can learn, you have choices. Because, the very fact that your brain is developed enough to experience things and learn from them also means that your brain is complex enough to discriminate. Discriminate is a big word that means you can choose one thing over another. Being ABLE to choose and CHOOSING to choose, though, are altogether different things.

"Intelligence is another good word here. Intelligence is the ability to discriminate. Everything else being equal—and that, by the way, never happens—the more intelligent animals are, the more choices are open to them. Up to them whether or not they take advantage of their opportunities. Glad you understand all this. Maybe you can explain it to me sometimes. Some creatures that have intelligence choose not to make much use of it. They choose not to be very aware. Being AWARE! Now that's a good term! Could be that the only real choice we have is how AWARE of reality we will be. Being aware can be most painful. And it can be very hard work. Dangerous, too, because it can lead you into all kinds of strange places you didn't even know existed. Being fully aware could be TOO painful or TOO dangerous for some. Might cause them to flip out and just go into a tizzy.

"From my perspective, he (Fun City) seems not to be particularly aware. I can't be sure, of course, but he seems to me never to have been aware enough to experience the wonder and awe of being aware. He seems to be earth bound, even if he does fly well. He seems never to have really seen the stars. He seems never to have really heard the angels sing. He thinks he has it all, but I wonder if he senses that he may be missing the real essence of life. He may be choosing not to choose. He may be choosing not to be aware. But, to the extent that he is able to make choices, he is living the way he chooses to live. We all do what we really want to do, and he is doing what he really wants to do. And that's all! Don't know anything else about him. Well, except the delicious cabbage roll he makes sometimes—when he can get a cabbage, of course. But, like you said, you are not interested in that."

I still had not said a word.

"So," said Socs, "you think I ought to try to straighten him out. Think I ought to convince him he is all wrong and that he should do differently. Why should I do that? I couldn't do it! And, even if I could, I wouldn't. He would be living MY life, not his. And one can never really live unless it is his own life.

I'm not sure how an animal changes. And I'm not sure he should change. Sometimes change seems to be triggered by some traumatic event that lets one know in no uncertain terms that he can't go on the way he's been going. But, such change seems about as likely to be a change for the worse as a change for the better. More positive change seems to occur when one has a solid physical and emotional base. Such a base provides the security one needs to dare to take a close look at himself. Maybe one has to learn to like himself before he can do very much about changing himself."

"I'm not sure what, if anything, my responsibility is toward Fun City," Socs continued. "If I am honest with myself, I will admit that I really am not very interested in him. I just try to get along with him without getting him all riled up. I've told him his cooking was delicious. That seems to please him, and I don't see how saying that can do him any harm. I didn't say anything about his swan diving until he right out asked me what I thought about it. I told him that was hard for me to say since swan diving was not something I had a great deal of knowledge of or interest in. That seemed to upset him some, but I didn't know what else to say. He wanted to teach me how to dive, but I told him I thought I was too old for that. He said I wasn't much older that he was. I said I didn't know he was that old, and that he certainly looked younger. He seemed to like that."

Socs paused here and seemed to be in deep thought. Finally, he seemed to get his thoughts straight and continued. "I think I have not quite said something important about my relationship with him (Fun City)," he said. "I want to be helpful wherever I can. To the extent that he seeks help from me and is receptive to any help I might be able to provide, I want to be there for him. And I would like the same from him. I think I can accept that the way he lives his life is, from his perspective, right for him. But, also, I think my value system and the way I live my life are right for me. I think the best thing I can do for him is to be true to myself. I will be as close to him as I can given that he is he and I am I. But I can't change who I basically am in order to be a close friend and helpmate to him. I will accept him the way he is and I will try to let him be. And I hope he can do the same for me."

"Now his mate (Glory), is a different thing altogether," Socs continued. "I don't seem to have much of what you call 'feelings' but, if I did, I would feel sorry for her. But feeling sorry for her does not show much respect, and there are some things about her that I respect. So maybe I'm not using the right word here. What's the right word? Maybe 'sympathize' or 'empathize' would be better. Anyway, I hurt when I see her hurt. Part of me wishes I could do something to keep her from hurting, but I am not sure whether this is to reduce HER pain, or to reduce MY pain. And, another part of me sees something positive in her hurting and just wants to let it be. Do you have mixed feelings like that? Thought you did.

"So, like I said, I don't have much feelings about anything. Different that way. But I guess if I really knew I would not do more harm than good, I would do almost anything to be helpful to her. Don't know what I can do though. I've spent lots of time thinking on it and I just don't know how to be helpful, other than to do what I already do. And that's just to let her know I like her and that I respect her pain and her struggle with life. Don't think that helps her any though. She just thinks I'm some kind of nut. Don't have any arguments with her about that. May be the only thing we agree on. She struggles mightily with herself. She wants so badly to be loving, caring, helpful and positive about life. But these are hard for her because she's so full of negative feelings. She takes great pride in her humility and seems to be trapped by her feeling of superiority. She can't stand the thought of the possibility that she may be less than perfect. If she isn't the GREAT GOOSE's perfect disciple, then she thinks she is nothing, and all her beliefs and hopes come crashing down around her ears. Can't talk to her. She isn't open to anything new. If any significant awareness was ever a choice for her, she seems to have rejected it."

"And you are wondering why I don't try to get her to understand that much of what she believes simply is not true," said Socs. "You are asking why I don't try to show her some new truths? That would be cruel, that's why! It would be like taking a cripple's crutch away and making her walk on a broken leg! She would hurt too much if she dared let even a flicker of new light into her closed mind. Logic doesn't work where strong emotions are involved. And I think her self-esteem may be too low for her to deal with things any better than she does now. That's all I know about her. Want to talk about anything else?"

"Well, what about your mate (Eden)," I asked. "She seems to be quite different from the others."

"Yes, she is," he replied. "And, if you are wondering, I agree with her about a great number of things. She thinks we are in the midst of a global environmental crisis and that life on the earth as we know it is doomed if we don't do something dramatically different and do it now. And I more or less agree with her. Where we differ is she finds this global environmental crisis to be DREADFUL as well as interesting; I find it to be INTERESTING as well as dreadful. She thinks much could and should be done to reduce pain and suffering in the world. I suppose I also agree with her about that. But I don't necessarily agree with her about HOW this should be done. I fear some of her efforts in that direction are ill conceived and short sighted and that she often, in the long run, causes more pain and suffering than she cures.

"She is a lot younger than I, you know. She was only sixteen when we first met. And, I think I was about, maybe, two thousand years old. I think she sometimes wishes I were younger and more interested in the things that interest her. And there are some other things about her you probably don't know. She will not mind if I tell you. There are good reasons why she focuses on making this a better world. It keeps her from hurting so much that she would not be able to stand it. She hurts for her children and for all the children of the world. She cares about them all and wants to make things less painful for them. She doesn't understand why a loving Creator would create a world where there is so much pain. So, while she believes there is a GREAT GOOSE, she doesn't LIKE the GREAT GOOSE or TRUST HER very much. That leaves her feeling responsible for trying to fix some of the things she thinks the GREAT GOOSE refuses or neglects to fix."

Socs paused for a moment, closed his eyes, shuddered, opened his eyes, and began again in a voice so low I could barely hear. "It was late on a dark and stormy day like this, except it was in the winter when the cold winds blow. We left our nest for a short time and went to look for food. Our six goslings were almost grown then. We left them in the nest.

75

Looking for food took longer than we expected, and it was dark when we got back to the nest. Our goslings were gone! We don't know if they were killed—there were no signs of a struggle—or if they just decided they were grown up and it was time for them to go. She never had a chance to say goodbye! We never saw them again and never knew what happened to them. So every year since then, on dark and stormy nights when the cold winds blow, I hear her walking along the shore of the pond calling, 'Here! Here! I am here!.'

"I go to her and ask her why she is walking through the dark and stormy night, walking while the cold winds blow, and calling, 'Here! Here! I am here!'?

"She answers, 'I'm calling to let them know I'm here to help. I am calling for my little ones. They may need something. They may be hurt.'

"She won't come back in. I can hear her as she walks all through the night calling, 'Here! Here! I am here!' When the night finally ends, she comes back to the nest. She falls into a fitful sleep and sleeps all day."

Socs paused again before continuing. He obviously cared deeply for Eden; her hurt was also his hurt. And then he went on, "All in the world are her children. She wants to find the ones who are lost and hungry and hurting and offer them a safe harbor in the storm. The focus of her life is to stop the hurting by trying to make the world a paradise where everything can live together in harmony. A place where her children will not need anything. A place where her children will not hurt."

"She really can't do that, of course," he continued. "The world wasn't MEANT to be a place of perfect peace. But she can try, and she does try. I cannot fault her. From her perspective, she does a great deal of good. The world WOULD be a kinder, gentler place if all were like her. But, and I don't mean this to be sarcastic, it would be even MORE kind and gentle if there were no living things in it. But, with no living things, what would it be worth?"

He stared out over the pond for some time and then stood up. He hung his head and said in a sad voice, "I wish I could help her not to hurt so much. She's... she's... well, I like her a lot. I... I don't know anything I can do to help her except let her know how I feel about her. I... I don't think I want to talk any more today." He walked slowly to the edge of the pond and swam out to join Eden.

23

It was one of those hot, muggy days of early summer when staying in the house with the air conditioner on seemed to make good sense. But I had been inside most of the week and had cabin fever. Heat or no heat, I had to get out for a while. I decided to walk to the pond. Since the pond is almost three-quarters of a mile from the house and the road is hilly, I thought I was being pretty ambitious. I was. I was red faced and sweaty when I arrived. Two goosenganders were lying in the sun seeming not to mind the blazing heat. One was humming a hymn as she lay with head down and eyes closed. This must be Glory, I thought, dreaming of eternal peace in the GREAT POND. Her sleep was disturbed by my heavy footsteps and heavier breathing. She stood, yawned, stretched her neck, and gave her wings a few flaps. And then I noticed the red ribbon was back around her neck.

She noticed that I noticed, so we sat down together and she explained. "I gave my ribbon to him when he was so down, you know." She pointed in the direction of the sleeping Fun City as she talked. "He needed to be cheered up. But I probably should not have done it. He lost it the same night in a poker game. He is a sinner, you know, and he plays poker with Big Drake the Quackenducker and that crowd. I had to buy it back. Paid eight sun-dried polliwogs. Was worth it though. I'm going to keep it this time."

The mention of sun-dried polliwogs shook Fun City awake. He stood up, walked over, looked in my pockets for food, honked his disappointment, splashed into the pond, and swam away.

"So you are angry with him," I said.

"Angry? Of course not!" she replied emphatically. "Followers of the GREAT GOOSE never get angry! They live modest, simple lives and are kind and gentle to everybody even when they have been mistreated like I have been by that no good, rotten... uh, um... by that mischievous lad. The GREAT GOOSE has given him all kinds of opportunities to repent, and I have always tried to be a good example to him. But he finds the joys of this sinful world to be greater than the eternal joy of the GREAT POND. But who am I to judge? All I can do is pray for him and continue to show him the WAY. The GREAT GOOSE, who sees all, knows all, and loves all, will be his judge and tormentor when the day comes when we all shall face eternity."

"So you think he is the way he is because he just chooses to be bad. Is that it?" I asked.

"Well of course," she replied. "Everybody has choices about everything they do. Nobody MAKES you do wrong."

"So you think, if you were in his shoes, you would make different choices from the ones he makes?" I asked.

"We don't wear shoes!" she replied grumpily.

"Sorry about that," I apologized. "What I meant was do you think the difference in your environment as you were growing up might make a difference in what you believe?"

"Of course not," she replied. "We grew up about the same. His mother believed in the GREAT GOOSE same as mine did. We've both been exposed to the WORD since we were goslings. The environment was very good for me. And what is good for a goose is good for a gander! The truth is he just CHOOSES not to believe because that would take his fun away. If you want to BELIEVE something, you just BELIEVE it. It doesn't take any thinking. It just takes FAITH!"

I thought I knew all I was going to find out about how she felt about Fun City, so I asked, "What about the other two goosenganders? Do they have faith?"

Her spirits seemed to soar as she thought about the other two. She fairly shrieked, "Those two are the very worst kind! The ABSOLUTE worst! I mean BAD NEWS! Don't get me wrong though! Good friends of mine. Fine pair! Wonderful pair! Kind, law-abiding, helpful, pillars of the community, great neighbors. Love them both! Nice! Sweet! Wonderful! But, the WORST KIND!

"If you are honest and admit you're not a believer, others know where you stand and they know not to let you interfere with their faith. But those two CLAIM to believe when they really don't. Like, for example, Eden says she doesn't think much of what the GREAT GOOSE says in the GOOD BOOK is literally true. Now you know if you can't believe every last word of something, you can't believe any of it. She says myths and stories that tell the truth are different from stories that are literally true. But, if the stories aren't literally true, they are just something somebody made up, like stories he (Fun City) makes up when he comes staggering in at one o'clock in the morning! And, if everybody can make up their own stories, how could we ever know what really is the truth?"

"And Eden thinks this earth is so great!" continued Glory. "Doesn't believe the earth's just a place for us to abide until we can go to the GREAT POND IN THE SKY where there is neither suffering nor sorrow. She keeps wanting to fix this place up, when the GOOD BOOK plainly says the GREAT GOOSE is going to destroy it along with all those who don't believe. And she doesn't think the GREAT GOOSE DOES anything! She thinks WE have to do everything and that the GREAT GOOSE just gives us moral support. She doesn't pray for THINGS because, she says, the GREAT GOOSE won't answer. Maybe SHE won't answer her because she's not a believer. But SHE sure answers me! If I need something, like frogs for lunch, I pray for it. And if the GREAT GOOSE thinks I should have frogs, I get frogs. I pray for the sick animals, too. And they get well! That is, unless the GREAT GOOSE calls them on. I think the GREAT GOOSE is punishing her for her unbelief. I think that is why the GREAT GOOSE took all her little ones back a few years ago. I think the reason I lost a lot of my little ones is because he (Fun City) is such a no-good, rotten sinner. And I will always despise... uh, um, recognize that the GREAT GOOSE will hold him accountable."

She paused for a moment to catch her breath and continued. "And that mate of hers, what a loser! He THINKS all the time! Nothing worse than those who THINK! They believe they're so smart. They think they know more than the GOOD BOOK or anything. They're just going to think themselves right into the BURNING DESERT! Socs says he believes in the GREAT GOOSE... in the abstract, whatever that means. He says the GREAT GOOSE is just one way of defining or describing the ULTIMATE BEING, whatever that is. He says everybody tends to create their own GREAT GOOSE in their own image. Says he asked a big garden spider about her view of the ultimate being, and the spider said she didn't know much theology. All she knew was that the GREAT KEEPER OF THE WEB has eight legs. I'm pretty sure that is heresy and will get you zapped by the GREAT GOOSE! I wouldn't be surprised to see him get it any time.

"He looks at stars and things and says this earth is just a small bit of the universe. He thinks so big that he can't accept the simple truth that those stars and things are just stuff painted on the inside of the sky, and that the sky is just a big lid that covers the earth. And he thinks one animal is just as good as another. Won't eat frogs! And the GOOD BOOK plainly says the GREAT GOOSE created all those animals for us goosenganders to abuse... uh, ah, USE.

"And he doesn't believe the GREAT GOOSE created everything in six days. Says she DID it but used a thing he calls evolution. Says we probably are descended from Perodactyles or something like that—some awful kind of creature. Thinks some other animals are superior to us in some ways. Thinks some of your kind have better brains than we do. What foolishness! Why,... uh, ah, no offense intended here... but, uh, ah, you can't even fly and can't half swim! Nice enough, of course. At least, some of you. But better brains? Here I am telling YOU all kinds of things you don't know. Can you imagine your telling ME anything I don't already know? Anyway, like I said, those two are the ABSOLUTELY WORST KIND. The scourge of the earth, a bane to all true believers, crabgrass in the lawn of life, the cloud behind every silver lining, sticks in the wheel spokes of the bicycle of life. They're... uh, ah, they're a fine couple, of course. Kind, considerate, helpful. Wonderful couple! Wonderful! Love 'um!"

She stopped there and seemed, for a moment, to think deep thoughts. She continued in a softer, more thoughtful voice. "I know quite a bit about what some of the others think about me. They are partly right, but mostly wrong. They laugh at my occasional imperfections and remark that the GREAT GOOSE is not doing such a good job with me. But I really try! And I pray for them. I'm not sure I can say the same for them. They think my faith is in vain because everything about my life doesn't work out perfectly. But things in their lives don't work out perfectly either! Do they judge that to mean THEIR beliefs are all wrong? Do they have any idea what my life would be like

WITHOUT my faith? No, they don't. I say of them, 'judge not that you be not judged!'"

She stopped again and seemed to struggle to get her breath. She shook her head vigorously from side to side, flopped her wings a few times, stretched her neck, and waddled toward the pond. She looked back over her shoulder and called, "Glad to tell you things you want to know. Ask me things any time. Better be soon, though. The end is near. Each day may be our last. The signs all point to the imminent approach of doom. Always glad to be helpful. That's what believers do, you know. Always helpful! Glory! Hallelujah!"

24

I caught Cleopatra the Cat when she was wide awake. Now that is a rare accomplishment. She was walking back and forth across the living room floor obviously in a dither over what she should do next. When she isn't sleeping or eating, she gets bored easily. This was one of those boring times. I lay down on the carpet, propped up my chin with my hands and elbows, and asked, "Want to talk?"

She stopped her pacing and responded with, "That depends on what you wish to talk about."

I said, "Want to tell you about the goosenganders and see what you think about them."

She settled down on the floor in front of me and said, "I have a busy day planned. I have little time to spare. But, since you are really needy, I will take time for you. But please. PLEASE! This time try to talk efficiently and to the point."

I countered with, "You certainly don't have to put yourself out any. If you don't want to talk, just say so."

She lay with one eye on me and the other on the mantle clock, and replied, "I thought you said you wanted to talk about goosenganders."

The little snit is a darling cat! I told her, briefly, about my encounters with the goosenganders, a bit about each of them, their personalities and basic philosophies. And then I asked, "Do you understand what I'm trying to say?"

"It seems to me," she answered, "the important thing here is whether or not YOU understand what you are trying to say. What is going on with you is that you know all these things about the goosenganders, but you do not quite know how to put them together. You have the bits and pieces but not the big picture. And you want me to fix it for you. Right? Well, speak up. Time is money here, you know. I do not have all day."

"Well, you are basically correct," I offered. "Do you think I've just run across an exceptionally weird bunch? Or are all animals more or less like them?"

"They seem like an ordinary bunch to me," she said. "They are pretty much representative of all thinking animals. We are not talking hopgrassers, flybutters, or roachcockers here. We are talking flybirds and mammalarians and, maybe, reptilians; those that are intellectually more closely related to the specie *Felidae* or, for simple minds, cats."

"Now, back to these four goosenganders," she continued. "Each of them is a clear example of one of the four primary categories of what we might call 'life focuses.' But, before we talk about these four categories and how the goosenganders are representative of them, you need to know about one other category or, maybe, noncategory.... But, for you to understand about this noncategory, I will have to provide you with some elementary education. If I do not, I will lose you completely.

"There was this psychologist named Maslow Von Pussycat. He came up with a useful idea that he expressed as the Hierarchy of Needs. According to this hierarchy, one's physiological needs—to you, that means the need for food, water, oxygen, and golf every Monday—have to be met before one can be motivated to attend to higher level needs. Once the physiological needs are met, one is able to attend to his safety needs. Once the safety needs are met, one can address one's need to belong and be loved. Once one has a sense of belonging and being loved, one can address one's need for self esteem. There is another step called self-actualization, but it would be of no concern to you; only cats have it all together enough to be concerned with that one.

"Now, all of your goosenganders are operating on a pretty high level so, obviously, their physiological and safety needs are being met. But a poor animal that is half starved and scared half to death is not thinking about belonging, or being loved, or self esteem. He just wants food and the dogs off his back. On Maslow Von Pussycat's Hierarchy of Needs, this poor, starving, scared animal is operating on a lower level than are your four goosenganders. This poor animal does not fit into any of the four life focus categories. Rather, he represents a fifth category or, the way I like to think about it, a noncategory. I am telling you about this noncategory because I know you will run across lots of creatures who are in deep, deep trouble. In your thinking, you will try to force-fit them into one of the four primary categories of life focuses, but they just will not fit. So now you know why. But, now, let us stop for a moment and check you out. Does your odd way of thinking permit you to process any of what I have just said? Are you in there somewhere? Do you understand?"

"Don't be so catty," I growled. "Of course I understand. I now know everything I want to know and much I don't want to know about your noncategory. Now let's get around to what I originally asked about, the four goosenganders. You say they are representative of four main categories of life focuses? Well, tell me what you mean by that. Hey! You! Come on! Wake up!" I had to shake her awake. If she is not busy with something, she goes off in a hurry.

"You did not have to scream at me. I was awake all the time," she complained. "The four goosenganders are perfect examples of the four life focuses. One focuses on the gods, but does not care much for what the gods have created; another focuses on what has been created, but does not care much for the gods who did the creating; another cares for NEITHER the gods NOR what has been created and thus typically assumes that life has no inherent meaning; and number four focuses on BOTH the gods AND what has been created. If one-word descriptions will be helpful to you in remembering the four life focuses, you might try 'god,' 'earth,' 'fun,' and 'wisdom.' While most animals' values overlap into several of these categories, one value always is paramount."

25

Here Cleopatra stood up, moved over about two inches, lay back down, stretched out into a more comfortable position, and continued. "The one you call Glory," she said, "is an example of the 'god' group. She thinks the primary purpose of intelligent life is to appease the gods. This focus comes in different forms, of course. Among your kind, the Greeks and Romans had multiple gods; the Jews, Muslims, and Christians have their single god; and the Buddhists have their nirvana, or ultimate reality. Other animals have their own versions. Do not make the mistake of thinking all who attend churches, temples, mosques, and other 'worship' structures are the 'god' category. Only some of them, probably the minority, are. Most go there for social, business, or other reasons.

"The primary thing about animals in this 'god' category is that they think all animals are inherently evil. As you can imagine, this does not contribute greatly to their having high self esteem. In fact, it casts a gloom over them that many of them work quite hard at trying to cover up. They always say they are very happy when, in reality, they are involved in a life-or-death struggle with all this evil. They remind me of quackenduckers swimming in the pond: they are calm and serene on the surface but paddling like the devil underneath. And, as if just being around all this evil is not bad enough, some of them believe their god will punish them severely if they do not repent of the evil with which they were born. Some of them think even infants get punished by their god if they die before they get old enough to repent their way out of their sinful natures. Others think you do not get punished unless you have reached the age of countability. Some say that is when you are old enough to count to ten; others say it is twelve.

"Many in this category focus on escaping this earth where everything is born evil, and going on to something better. And they think the way to make sure they escape this evil world is to appease their god, or gods, usually by making some kind of sacrifice. In most cases, the sacrifice can be made by somebody other than the one receiving the benefit. Sometimes the one actually making the sacrifice does it voluntarily; in other cases, he does not have any choice. In most cases, the primary thing the one receiving the benefit has to do is make himself believe the sacrifice actually works. As long as he really believes this, he is assured of pie in the sky by and by; if he stops believing, he is a goner. This puts him in the position of having to believe something that he may not have had a chance to really think out. And he may be afraid to give it a great deal of thought because, if he does think it through and decides he does not believe it, he is, as I said, a goner. So, since his whole future existence, before and after the death of his body, depends on his believing, he is not particularly open to arguments about his beliefs.

"This 'god' group are motivated primarily by fear, fear that their god will punish them severely if they misbehave or if they come up short on believing whatever it is they are supposed to believe. But, if you think that is really bad, think for a minute! Would you rather they NOT believe what they believe and just be bad? If it were not for their fear, some of them might do all kinds of bad things!

"And are not all of us motivated a certain amount by fear? Fear of failure, fear of not being what we wish to be, fear of not being loved, fear of wasting our lives, fear of illness and pain, and fear of our own stupidity? Those in this category are so afraid of their god that they dare not blame HER for any of the bad things in the world. Instead, they lay most of the blame on some evil or misguided spirit. But some of the blame they accept as their own; however, they claim the only reason they did anything bad is because the evil or misguided spirit made them do it.

"Ones in this category also are motivated to help others but, often, the motivation is not so much caring for others as it is trying to obey their God by getting others to believe as they believe. If they can persuade others to believe, they usually get some kind of brownie points or extra credits.

"What I find most interesting about the 'god' group is that they claim their god, or gods, loves them and that they love their god, or gods. In reality, many of them think their god is stern, vengeful, and cold. And, a word of caution here, be careful of those in this category. While they may be warm, smiling, and confident on the outside, many also may be frightened, stern, and cold on the inside. Getting to what is on the inside, however, is difficult, because they must wear a facade to make sure nothing gets in the way of their believing whatever it is they are supposed to believe.

"In some segments of the 'god' category, while the adherents to their particular beliefs will not admit to it outright, they do not expend much effort on trying to love their god; instead, they worship and adore the one who made their sacrifice for them. It is hard for them to understand their god, but comparatively easy to understand the sacrificed one who, typically, is another animal much like themselves. This probably is a good thing because it sometimes tends to soften them, particularly when they think the one who made the sacrifice did it voluntarily. They probably feel there was some love involved, and this sets a good example for loving themselves which, in turn, sometimes makes it possible for them to love others.

"Another interesting thing about the 'god' group is their views on the sanctity of life. On the one hand, some of them are violently opposed to abortion. If you do one of those abortion things, or even think hard about it, some of them will take you out, put a noose around your neck, hang you from a limb of the nearest tree and, when you are good and dead, cut you down, stomp you to a pulp, and then fuss at you something fierce. On the other hand, many of them support the death penalty on the basis of its being an eye for an eye and a tooth for a tooth.

"You may be thinking I am being unduly harsh with the 'god' category. But, remember, we are talking about thinking animals here. If you want sweetness and light, stick with buttercups and pansies! Keep in mind that, except for cats, the whole animal kingdom is in pretty much of a mess. And, as I think I have mentioned, there certainly is a good side to those in this 'god' category. They usually do not steal television sets or beat their wives. They try to stay out of trouble because they cannot afford to get their god angry with them. So most of them end up being quite decent animals. They make, comparatively speaking, good neighbors and good citizens. They dress up in nice, clean clothes and go to their meeting houses on Sundays or whenever. And some of the more dogmatic ones beat their children to a pulp if they do not go along and sit nice and straight. But do not EVER tell one of them your god is better than their god! THAT will get you forty years in the electric chair!"

Here Cleopatra stopped her discourse and pricked up her ears. She obviously had heard something that disturbed her. She jumped on her stool by the window and peered intently down the driveway into the gathering darkness. I was curious to know what had gotten her attention so I suggested we go out on the porch and see if there was anything unusual about. Cleopatra agreed, made sure I went out first in case there was danger, climbed on top of the barbecue grill, and began swishing her tail back and forth with considerable vigor. I stood still, looked, and listened. And then there it was. First, I heard clanking sounds and what seemed to be chains dragging on the gravel of the driveway. Then the fuzzy outline of some strange apparition slowly emerged from the evening shadows. The sound of low moans and rattling chains grew louder as the wraith-like form grew nearer. Cleopatra responded with a low growl from deep in her throat. She seemed to expand to half again her regular size as the hair on her back stood on end. The form moved up close to the porch and collapsed at the edge of the lawn. The noise of chains stopped but the moans grew louder. I went over to take a closer look and realized the fallen form was none other than Jimmie the Raccoon.

Jimmie's fur was ruffled and dirty, her eyes appeared to be bloodshot, and on her right rear leg was clamped what appeared to be a bear trap. Poor Jimmie held up her undoubtedly mangled leg so I could get a closer look at the trap and the chains attached to it. I reached out to her but she stopped me before I could touch either the chains or her entrapped right rear leg. "Please don't touch me," she said. "I'm in too much pain right now. Besides, it's too late. I'm a goner for sure. Goodbye cruel world. I'm going now to live with the GREAT RACCOON in the GREAT HOLE in the GREAT OAK IN THE SKY where they serve fried chicken for breakfast, baked chicken for lunch, and chicken and dumplings for dinner."

I stopped her there and asked her what in the world had happened and what she thought we should do to help. Her response was, "Please don't force me to think right now while I'm fast passing from this earthly realm. I am starved to death, as I suppose you can see. Got caught in this cruel bear trap and have not had a bite to eat for six weeks or five years. Finally, after a long and valiant effort, I managed to chew through the chain and get free. Had just enough strength left to drag my cruelly-injured body here to your place. I knew what a kind and generous creature you are, and I knew this was the one place where I could get help in my misery and starvation. Oh! I think I am going now. I see visions of food; hot, steaming food; warm, scrumptious food; and cool, delicious, nourishing food. Goodbye, cruel world, goodbye."

I rushed into the house, pulled out half a chicken that was left over from our dinner, and rushed it out to my poor, starving friend. I fed her small pieces of the chicken and gave her a bowl of warm milk with which to wash them down. Then I started again to remove the cruel jaws of the bear trap from her poor right rear leg. Again, she stopped me.

"Rather you didn't touch that," she said. "Cost me fifty dollars. I'll snap it off when I get home. Still have a few more houses to visit before it gets too dark for them to see what bad shape I'm in. Thanks muchly, mightily, and kindly for your munificence, magnanimity, and generosity in providing me with this opulent banquet. I will be eternal grateful and will be back tomorrow at this same time to see if you wish to outdo yourself with another grand repast."

With this, Jimmie packed the remains of the chicken into the bag she always wears around her neck, used one front paw to wipe the grease from her whiskers, and used the other front paw to gathered up her chains. She disappeared into the darkness. All was quiet except for the thump, thump, thump of Cleopatra's tail as she snapped it against the barbecue grill cover.

I didn't think she was going to say anything, but she did. She murmured in a voice so low I could barely hear, "I hope the gods are kind to fools."

She turned to me and growled, "Did you not notice that, when she first came in, she was limping on her LEFT leg?"

26

Several days passed before Cleopatra again was in the mood to talk about the goosenganders. From her place on the glass-topped table on the porch, she reviewed the last part of her previous discourse and then continued where she had left off. "I was talking about how each of the four goosenganders fits one of the 'life focus' categories," she said. "I think I suggested short names for each category: 'god,' 'earth,' 'fun,' and 'wisdom.' Last time, we talked about the one you call Glory who represents the 'god' focus."

"The goosengander you call Eden represents the second category, the 'earth' focus," she said. "The ones in that crowd make up an altogether different gaggle of geese. Unlike those in the 'god' category, who think all animals are born evil, the 'earth' group think all animals are basically good and would, in their natural state, be kind and gentle with each other all of the time. They think, for example, the only reason cats kill and eat mice is because cats were deprived of something or other when they were kittens. They think perhaps the cats' mothers were too strict or, at the other extreme, never could learn to let them go and just kept on babying them even after they grew up. I believe they think cats would, if they had been reared in a supportive, appropriate environment, eat lettuce and, perhaps, potatoes, boiled or baked, with the skins on.

"Those in the 'earth' category usually are a sober, steady bunch. They often are into tofu, compost heaps, natural foods, no chemicals, no preservatives, planting trees, solar heat, geodesic domes, spring water, grow-your-own vegetables, take-your-own-bags to the grocery store, no red meat, simple dress, herbal medicine, and natural childbirth. Some of the more extreme like to live in communes where the entire group can keep everything simple and back to nature. Many of them grew up around members of the 'god' group and may have once been members of that category themselves. But, when they smartened up and realized that their god was not going to zap them when they did something wrong, they also realized SHE was not going to give them any brownie points for doing things right. And if their god does not punish or reward, what DOES SHE do? For many of them, it is easy to believe SHE does nothing at all. Maybe their god just set this old ball spinning and then went away and took a catnap! Anyway, lots of those in the 'earth' group are left with nothing much to work with except the earth and what is on it. If the gods are asleep, the only thing to do is fix things yourself.

"I think the unfortunate thing about the 'earth' group is that so many of them end up realizing they have spent their lives working hard for an ideal that they are further from than when they started. This is not necessarily their fault. But the simple truth is that others mess things up faster than the 'earth' group can fix them. As a result, the earth's physical environment seems, in many ways, to have stayed about the same for millions of years and, in others, to have gotten worse and worse. Neither does there seem to be any appreciable change for the better in the intelligent animals who live on the earth. While some animals learn a number of new facts, their basic natures seem unchanged. The best thing I can say about the 'earth' group is that they rarely do anybody or anything any real harm. Well now, wait a minute! Let me think about that statement you just made! Yes! Good thing I stopped you there! That statement is not altogether correct. Many of them are rabid pacifists. For example, they come out strongly against the death penalty. In fact, they are so violently opposed to violence that they think those who disagree with them should be taken out and shot.

"You probably are thinking nobody could possibly be other than supportive of animals who are trying to make this world a better place in which to live. But you are wrong; the 'earth' category actually has some powerful enemies. Opposition to making the world a better place comes mostly from two sources. First, the 'fun' crowd, with their typical short-term view of things, often get upset when the 'earth' group want to do something that interferes with their fun and games. They sometimes, however, are supportive, particularly when they see some of their recreational areas being destroyed by commercial interests. Other strong opponents of the 'earth' group are those of the 'noncategory' type who are in a desperate struggle to survive physically. Would you care what happened to the earth if you were starving, homeless, and cold? Of course not!

"Those in the 'god' category are quite supportive of the endeavors of the 'earth' group as long as the endeavors do not detract too much from their own full-time job of pacifying their god. They are supportive primarily because most of them admit that this IS their creator's world whether they personally like the world or not. Oddly enough, while those in the 'god' category claim to be anxious to leave this old world and go on to a better one, they seem strangely reluctant to get the show on the road. And often they will cooperate in trying to keep the earth from falling apart until they get finished with their own lives and, maybe, their children get finished with theirs. Those in the 'wisdom' category usually are quite supportive of the 'earth' group. They just seem to be considerably more casual about making this a better world. They think the world is working out basically as it was intended and that, if they start messing around with it, they well may end up doing more harm than good.

"I personally think the logic of the 'earth' group sometimes goes off the deep end," continued Cleopatra. "For example, remember the pretzel worm case? There were, as far as anybody knew, only two pair of pretzel worms left in the whole wide world. And they were a major food source for whackle birds, glizzard lizards, and squishy fishes. So what did this 'earth' group do? They protected those two pair of pretzel worms against all comers. They ran off all their enemies so the worms could go forth and multiply. Now, tell me again what you did most of the day yesterday? Right! You spent the day squshing, squishing, smashing, swatting, stomping, smurfing, and otherwise trying to obliterate all those pretzel worms that are eating up the trees and falling off all over everything. And you know, of course, about whackle birds, glizzard lizards, and squishy fishes! They now are extinct! The last ones starved to death while the 'earth' group were protecting the pretzel worms, which were the extinct creature's primary food supply! And then there is... uh... purrrrrrr."

Cleopatra yawned deeply, spread herself a bit more firmly on the glass table top, and was asleep. I would wait thirty minutes or so and see if we could continue the conversation. This was a good time for a break. Earlier in the afternoon, I had thawed a frozen chicken to cook on the grill as part of the dinner I was preparing for my wife and me. I fired up the gas burners, went in the house and got the chicken, came back out on the porch, placed the chicken pieces on the grill, and sat in my porch chair to read the newspaper. In almost exactly thirty minutes, Cleopatra awoke. She lay on the table at the edge of the porch with one eye half opened and half-heartedly watched the birds pecking at the bird seeds on the ground. She showed slightly more interest in the jays and cardinals who flew under the walkway roof as a shortcut from the edge of the woods to the seeds. They whizzed through only a few feet above Cleopatra's nose.

I kept one eye on the newspaper and the other on the cooking chicken. I had gotten up and was turning the chicken pieces with tongs when I saw a raccoon cross the yard and head our way. Cleopatra opened her other eye and turned her head a few inches to get a better view. The raccoon stopped on the porch steps, sniffed the smokey, aroma-laden air, and turned a pleading glance in my direction. In a whinny falsetto, she said, "Please kind sir, my name is Pathetic and I am so hungry. I have not had a bite to eat in six or eight months. I am so weak from hunger that I could not have walked up the hill to get here if it had not been downhill. I have a sister named Jimmie with whom you might be acquainted. She speaks highly of you and says you are a paragon of virtue. She said you sometimes manage to find a scrap of bread or half a chicken for poor unfortunate ones like me. And I am soooo hungry."

I went to the workshop and got her half a coffee can of dog food. She quickly ate it and asked for more. She told me the reason she was so hungry was that she selected her diet with full attention to avoiding the destruction of any endangered species and with maintaining an ecological balance. I scooped up another can of what I assured her was healthy, preservative-free dog food packaged in a biodegradable bag. She, again, ate the dog food and, again, asked for more. I had accidently dropped one small piece of chicken through the wires on the grill, and it was badly charred. I gave it to Pathetic and told her that was the last she was getting. She ate quickly, thanked me excessively, and left. As she was leaving, I noticed that a tiny, greasy scrap of the chicken had stuck to her face between her nose and her eye.

Two minutes later I again saw a raccoon approaching. She marched up to the porch and said in a familiar voice, "This is Jimmie checking in as usual to take care of any scraps of bread or half a chicken that you might be trying to get rid of."

I went to the workshop, got her usual can of dog food, came back out, and put the food on the ground for her. She ate a few bites of it, seemingly without great enthusiasm, and then stuffed the balance into the small bag she usually wears around her neck. I told her about the visit we had just had from her sister, Pathetic. Jimmie's response was, "Didn't know I had a sister. Must have been one of my cousins on my father's side of the family. They are ALL pathetic. Anyway, glad you were able to help her out. Uh, if she comes back tomorrow night, will you help her out again? What if she comes back again tonight? What if she comes back again in about five minutes? She will get hungry again in a hurry, you know, after not having anything to eat for six or eight months."

Something here did not seem quite right, but I was not sure what it was. I had not told Jimmie that Pathetic claimed not to have had food for six or eight months. But, maybe she heard it somewhere else. There was something else, maybe something about Jimmie's appearance, that seemed to trigger something in my memory. I scratched my head and tried to figure out what was going on here. I took a closer look at her. I was not sure at first but, then, as Jimmie turned to leave, I was certain; on her face, between her nose and her eye, was stuck a small, greasy scrap of chicken.

Cleopatra looked up at me with a scornful eye and said, "Sometimes we realize people in the world are not as smart as we thought they were and wish they were. I remember when I had just received my Ph.D. degree. I realized that I now was one of the "smart" ones. And then I had this sinking feeling and I said, 'God, help us all!'"

27

Again, several days passed before I was able to find Cleopatra in the mood to continue our talk. She lay stretched out on the carpet at my feet with her rag mouse between her paws. She flipped the mouse across the room, decided to ignore it for the moment, and stared at me as she usually does when she has something to say.

"Now," she said, "before you let yourself get distracted, what we are talking about here are the four categories of life focuses. We have talked about two of them: the 'god' group who think the primary purpose of living is to appease, or please, their god, and the 'earth' group, who are dedicated to making the world a better place in which to live. Now we are to the third category, the 'fun' life focus. Usually, the motto of those in this category is 'eat, drink, and get married, for tomorrow you die.'

"These are interesting animals as you learned from your association with the one you call Fun City. The distinguishing feature of those in this category is that they believe there is no inherent purpose or meaning to life but, since there are no pleasant alternatives to living out their lives, they might just as well select something to occupy their time. They usually select some activity and devote themselves to it as a means of gaining some satisfaction out of life. Many in this 'fun' category are more sober and steady than your Fun City. Instead of some of the more obvious pleasures, many of them are more into things like stamp collecting, walking the length of the Appalachian Trail, studying the breeding habits of the Mediterranean Fruit Fly, or climbing Mount Everest. Some are like the 'bean can couple' in the grocery store; they keep themselves preoccupied with activities that appear to me to be more frivolous than fun.

"Many tend, because of their particular mind sets, to make good researchers and scientists. Much of our knowledge of the physical and biological world is the result of their efforts. They are not as likely as some of the other groups to be swayed by sentiment. They usually call a spade a spade. They tend to keep us going in a reasonably straight line where other types would have us going off in nine different directions at the same time.

"Most in this 'fun' category believe very strongly in their unbelief. The idea that religion is only for children, old women, and half-wits is something they preach about religiously. There is no point in trying to reason with them because they are very proud of their disbelief; they have a strong emotional attachment to it. It gives them an identity, sets them apart, and makes them feel superior. They are adamant that they will not believe in anything they cannot feel, taste, smell, hear, or see. So, they have a super-strong faith that all the universe is the result of random events, that there is no evidence of a creator, much less one who cares about its creation, and that there is no meaning to life other than what we accredit to it out of our own needs. These are the basic tenets of their creed and they devoutly believe in them in spite of the fact that they are not supported by anything they can feel, taste, smell, hear, or see.

"Some of my best friends fit this 'fun' category. They usually are pleasant to be around, at least for short periods of time. Unless they are in a funk, and that happens to them fairly often. There is hope for some of them because they usually are not superstitious and they know something about logic. Notice I said they know SOMETHING about logic. I did not say they know a LOT about it! For example, they do not seem to understand that nothing is absolutely certain! If you want certainty, just sit where you are, do not bat an eye, do not move an inch, do not breathe. Just sit there, turn green in the face, and die from lack of oxygen. Why do that, you ask! Well, because there is no absolute certainty that you should do otherwise! Rarely, if ever, are we one hundred percent certain of anything. If forty-nine percent of the data in our internal computer says go south and fifty-one percent says go north, we go north and consider ourselves fortunate to be able to be so sure we are doing the logical thing. We operate successfully by going by the weight of the evidence. Like in a court of civil law. The evidence is virtually NEVER all in one direction. There ALWAYS are several possible truths. We have to pick the ONE truth that is best supported when we review the available evidence.

"And there are things in this world that we cannot feel, taste, smell, hear, or see that still are very real and very important in making decisions. And there are some major life factors that are not supported by what we can feel, taste, smell, hear, and see. If the logic supported by our five senses was the ONLY kind of logic, your mother would have eaten you alive when you were first born. You probably would have some allies or accomplices, but you would have no friends. You would not enjoy the beauty of the flowers or the sunset, you would never dream long dreams, you would never be touched to tears by the mewing of a newborn kitten, you would never climb mountains simply to see what is on the other side, you would never gaze in awe at the starry heavens, you would not be moved by a song, and you would never know the wonder of loving and being loved."

Here, Cleopatra grew quiet, her eyes slowly closed, and her easy, regular breathing indicated that she was asleep. I found this a good time to stand up, stretch a bit, get a cold glass of lemonade from the refrigerator, settle down again, and wait for Cleopatra to finish another nap.

Her nap, however, was interrupted by what seemed to be a knock at the back door. I put down my glass of lemonade and paused for a few seconds to make sure I heard correctly. I had. The knocking was becoming louder and more persistent. I yelled, "Patience there! I'm coming!" and headed for the door with an aroused Cleopatra padding softly along behind. We have a doorbell at the back door. Whoever was at the door apparently was either too short to reach the push button, too nearsighted to see it, too ignorant to know what it was for, or too thick headed to care. Actually, he was all four of these. It was an opossum, a stranger to me. He spoke up immediately, "Were you expecting someone named Patience?" he asked. "Well I'm not him. I'm a fully-authorized, licensed, and bonded solicitor of food donations for BEGGARS. If you don't know, that stands for Benevolent Enlightened Gatherers of Groceries for Animals Requiring Sustenance. My name is Occupant the Opossum and I have all kinds of identification to prove I am completely legitimate."

To prove his point, Occupant reached in his pocket, pulled out a stack of mail that he claimed was his, and showed me the name on the envelopes. Sure enough, all of the mail was addressed to "Occupant." He also showed me his business card which, unfortunately, was too dirty and grease stained to read, and his official badge which looked suspiciously like the lid from a can of cat food.

I tend to be a trusting soul, so I said, "I will see what I can find, for you do appear to be honest, upright, and beyond suspicion."

"I do?" Occupant asked. "What do you know about that! Actually, I don't believe in any of that stuff. Truth is, my motto is 'eat, drink, and pick berries, for tomorrow you make pie.'"

I decided not to comment. I looked in the pantry, found a half loaf of somewhat stale bread, and handed it to Occupant. He took it, examined it carefully, and said, "This fine gift is muchly depreciated but could you, perhaps, as an extraordinary show of generosity and magnanimity, throw in a handful of peanuts or something like that?"

Actually I did have a jar about half full of roasted nuts. They had been around for a long time and I probably would never eat them. I brought them out and placed them on top of the half loaf of bread that Occupant held in his arms. He thanked me again, asked if I wanted a "recipe" for outcome tax purposes, reached for his pencil and receipt book, dropped the bread and jar of peanuts, bent over to pick them up, dropped his tin badge, reached to pick it up and dropped.... Anyway, I told him I did not need a receipt, helped him get himself together, turned him facing in the direction in which I assumed he wished to go, and gave him a slight nudge. He was off toward the edge of the woods.

I heard a soft noise behind me and turned to see Cleopatra sitting on the floor, holding her front paws over her eyes, and moaning.

"What's with you?" I asked.

"Nothing at all," she answered. "It is just that there are some things in this world that I cannot bear to watch, and what you just did is one of them."

I left her to her moaning and walked as quietly as I could to the edge of the woods to see what had happened to Occupant. I eased up to the large poplar tree and, using it for cover, peered around to where I seemed to be hearing voices. What I saw was Jimmie the Raccoon taking the bread and jar of nuts from her accomplice, Occupant, or whatever his real name might be. Clearly, Jimmie was the brains of the operation. She stuffed the bread in the bag she always wears around her neck. Whatever could she be doing with all the food I had seen her collect at different times and stuff into that bag? She opened the jar, poured out a paw full of stale peanuts, and handed them to the opossum (who obviously was working for peanuts). She pushed the jar into her bag, helped the opossum to his feet, pointed toward our neighbor's house, and said, "Over there next."

I promised myself I would never again allow myself to be outsmarted by the clever Jimmie the Raccoon. Whether or not I would keep the promise is another story for another time.

28

Cleopatra was awakened from her nap on the living room carpet by the noise of wind in the trees, rain on the skylights, and the crash of thunder. She did her usual stretches, jumped onto her stool by the window, pressed her nose to the glass, and watched the rain fall and the lightening flash. She purred softly, "This reminds me of your Socrates. He and those in the 'wisdom' category of life focuses will not settle for something as simple as wind, rain, or thunder. They have to put them all together into something as complex as a storm. No wonder so few understand them. And no wonder there are so few of them. From what you have told me about your Socrates, I do not think I would like to be around him much. He sounds more than a bit weird to me. Are you sure you want me to try to explain to you what goes on with him?"

While I agreed with Cleopatra that Socs might be considered a bit weird, I pointed out that I had enjoyed his company and found his points of view to be most intriguing. This seemed to rub her fur the wrong way.

She growled, "Maybe you should just move the old boy in here and make a house goose out of him. That way you could enjoy his company all the time."

Cleopatra reluctantly permitted me to scratch her ears as I spoke in a conciliatory voice. "Remember, I'm asking you to tell me about Socs but I've never asked HIM to tell me about YOU."

This apparently satisfied her and she continued. "As I was attempting to explain before you interrupted, your Socrates and others in the 'wisdom' category have some big ideas that go so much against what most of us think and feel that it is difficult to find words to describe them. But I will try. I think you said you have not talked with him very much. And that is just as well. The more you talk with him, the more you are going to get confused. But remember, while he probably knows what he is talking about, I not only know what he is talking about, but I also know how to tell it in words that there is some chance you will understand."

"The primary characteristic of those in the 'wisdom' category," continued Cleopatra, "is that they are extraordinarily interested in solving the mysteries of the universe. They want to know how the universe came to be, how it works and, more importantly, why it was created. They want to know how the living things in the universe live and work and have their being and, more importantly, what purpose the living things are intended to serve. And they celebrate life and their connection with all of creation—usually in a quiet, sober way—because they think life is basically good. They attempt to solve the mysteries of the universe by beginning with their own observations and experiences; examining the accumulated myths, knowledge, and wisdom of the ages; and drawing tentative conclusions on the basis of logic and the weight of the available evidence.

"According to those in the 'wisdom' category, when they look about them in an attempt to understand the universe, the core and essence of what they see is not so much forests, oceans, and mountains. It is animal life. More specifically, it is INTEL-LIGENT animal life. From this, they conclude that intelligence is the core and essence of the universe. Are they able to prove this? No, they cannot. But think about it! While forests, oceans, and mountains are bigger and more visible, they do not dominate the intelligent animals. The intelligent animals dominate them. They can cut down the forest, dig up the mountains, and fill in the oceans. So, their conclusion! Not conclusively proven but, according to them, supported by the weight of the evidence. The universe was created to produce, sustain, and enhance intelligence.

"Since, in all their observations and experiences, those in the 'wisdom' category have never known anything to come into being without a source, they believe intelligence could have come only from an original source of intelligence. They refer to this original source of intelligence as the Creator. They believe this Creator, the original source of all intelligence, also is the creative force that shaped the universe and sent it spinning into time and space.

"Those in the 'wisdom' category focus their lives on gaining insights into the nature of this Creator. They do this because, they claim, to the extent to which they can comprehend the Creator, they can comprehend the INTENT of creation. However, according to them, there is a dilemma here. There is no way they can know anything about the Creator and the Creator's intent except by studying what the Creator has created. Thus, they attempt to discover the intent of creation by gaining a greater understanding of that which has been created, an understanding, in particular, of intelligent creatures.

"Those in the 'wisdom' category claim that, when they take a close look at intelligent creatures, they see creatures that are driven by insatiable inner forces to become more than they already are. They see creatures that, once their physiological needs are met, have strong, ardent, earnest, sometimes desperate needs to love themselves and be respected by others. And those in the 'wisdom' category claim that when they observe intelligent creatures who have high self esteem—that is, creatures whose physiological needs AND needs for belonging and to love and be loved are being met—they again see driven creatures. These creatures are driven by an insatiable curiosity that comes into full power when their lower-level needs are realized. Did you ever hear of curiosity killing the cat? Well, that was a false rumor.

Actually, curiosity is what keeps the cat so very, very alive. And curiosity is what keeps animals like your Socrates constantly on the move to discover new things about the physical universe. He is interested in and curious about the creatures who live in the world, and he values connections with each living thing.

"Those in the 'wisdom' category believe these persistent urges to belong, love and be loved, and grow in knowledge and wisdom are indications of the Creator's intent. They think the intelligence, purpose, and caring reflected in this intent can come only from an original source of intelligence, purpose, and caring. They think it logical to believe this Creator, as the ultimate intelligence, purpose, and caring, is perfect in wisdom, perfect in designing and creating, and perfect in love. Thus, they claim, this intelligent, purposeful, caring Creator does not make mistakes. Since SHE is the ultimate intelligence, SHE dots all the 'i's and crosses all the 't's. SHE leaves nothing undone or half done. Since SHE is purposeful, SHE does nothing without a purpose. Everything is planned, structured, formed, organized, arranged, designed, and patterned just the way SHE knows it should be. Since SHE is caring, SHE created a world where all things are interrelated, where connections can be established, and where love can be experienced.

"Since this creator is intelligent, does everything perfectly and for a reason, and is caring, it follows logically, according to those in the 'wisdom' category, that the world and all the things in it must be working perfectly, for a reason, and in a manner reflective of tough love. Now, this is where things get difficult for most of us. It is hard for us to think of things as being perfect. They seem FAR from perfect to most of us. Think of the crime, violence, hate, poverty, and the desecration of this planet! Is the world perfect, or is it a complete mess? How can such conflicting viewpoints be reconciled? Those in the 'wisdom' category would say the 'complete mess' is mostly the result of choices that humans make in the process of growing, something the Creator could prevent only by taking away free will. And they would say the primary thing the Creator wanted to happen in the universe IS happening, in spite of the way we have messed up the earth. They would say even this messed up world is perfect for serving its basic purpose which is to produce, sustain, and enhance intelligence."

"Notice, here," continued Cleopatra, "that those in the 'wisdom' category have NOT concluded that the creator's PRIMARY intent was to produce happiness, contentment, serenity, pleasure, gaiety, bliss, rapture, tranquility, peace, safety, security, satisfaction, or certainty. And why not? Well, these are means toward ends rather than ends in themselves. And, in some ways, the desire for and striving for these things are more important than the possession of them. Which would be more likely to learn new things, an animal that is completely satisfied, happy, and contented, or one that is somewhat dissatisfied, unhappy, and discontented? So, you say it is the latter! Well, there may be a few exceptions, but you are mostly correct. Most intelligent animals will, if they see any chance of satisfying their wants, be driven to tear half the world apart trying. And, fortunately, there is a chance they will learn some worthwhile things in the process. But once they get what they want, what happens next? Right! They will be quite satisfied—for about two weeks. And then they will think of something new they want. This new want will tend to make them dissatisfied, unhappy, and discontented. So, then, they will start working and learning again in an attempt to reach their new goal.

"Many creatures seem to go through endless cycles of severe emotional ups and downs. This, at least in part, is because they attempt to satisfy their basic needs the easy way and by inappropriate means. Remember Maslow Von Pussycat's Hierarchy of Needs? Most intelligent animals are in desperate need of a sense of belonging and loving and being loved. They mistakenly believe they can satisfy these needs and, thus, gain high self esteem, by buying a new car, belonging to the right club, owning a beach cottage, being a super racquetball player, having the right hairdo, or earning their second million dollars.

"Actually, having these things may cause other animals to ACT more friendly and approving and may cause the owner, for a while, to think he likes himself better. But what happens if these things are lost? No more friends and no more liking themselves, that is what happens! Material possessions, power, and prestige can only give pseudo-self esteem; they cannot give the REAL THING. And, until one has the REAL THING, one is going to be vulnerable, suspicious, and anxious.

"Those in the 'wisdom' category are less likely than others to value material possessions. Oh, they want to be reasonably comfortable and secure, but they do not strive for material possessions to boost their self esteem. They not only VALUE knowledge and wisdom but also ACT from a base of knowledge and wisdom. They understand enough about life to accept the negatives as well as the positives and to see that the wholeness of life necessitates both. They have the courage to EXPERI-ENCE life moment by moment and the desire to share life experiences in close community with others. They see enough of the entirety of life to regard it as wondrous, awesome, and spectacular. Thus, they live in eager anticipation.

"Those in the 'wisdom' category also are comfortable with tension. They think the Creator deliberately placed intelligent creatures in a state of tension. For some animals, the tension is between their desire for short-term pleasure and their need for long-term satisfaction. For others, it may be the result of having to prioritize seemingly equally-appropriate alternatives. Animals often think they want to get rid of the tension in their lives but, according to those in the 'wisdom' category, if animals are perceptive, they will recognize that such tension most often serves a useful purpose. The tension within an atom is what holds it together. The tension between atoms is what holds molecules together. Tension holds the planets and stars in their places. And a certain level of tension is what makes life mean-ingful. If you ever see an intelligent creature that is free from tension and is truly satisfied, a creature that is completely blissful, happy, and contented, you should dig a hole and bury it because its useful life is over! Just ask your friend, Socrates. Is there tension in his life? Of course! He will tell you that he struggles every day from early until late because there is so much more that he wishes to learn.

"This characteristic of thriving in a state of tension, how-ever, applies only to INTELLIGENT creatures. Do you remem-ber Casey the Canine? Stupidest animal I have ever seen. If you give that dog a soft bone, a ball to bounce, a warm bed, and a pat on the head, he will almost die from sheer bliss. You can ask him what he wants and he will ask you if you are crazy. How could he possibly want anything. He already is well fed, warm, comfortable, entertained, and secure. He could lie right there forever—and he practically does—without ever having an original thought or ever having even the faintest urge to do anything insightful or creative. Why would anyone ever wish to own a dog?"

Cleopatra jumped to the floor, glared at me, and demanded, "Put me down a fresh can of that hashed herring or, maybe, crunched croaker. And then it will be nap time. After that, there is one more thing I wish to tell you about those goosenganders, if I can remember what it is."

I opened a can of cat food, put half of it in Cleopatra's dish and the other half in the refrigerator for her late night snack. She would be ready to talk again in her own time. She ate, retired to her stool in the living room, and soon was fast asleep. I sat in my chair beside her and watched her flank rise and fall with her slow breathing. The thunder and lightning passed and the rain ceased. All that remained of the storm was an occasional distant grumble of thunder. I sat in my chair and listened to the quiet.

I thought I heard a door slam. My wife was in her study working, and I was sure she would not be slamming doors. The noise seemed to have come from outdoors, from the direction of my workshop. I remembered that I had opened a window when I swept the workshop floor that morning. But the eves were wide enough to keep out rain, and the wind had not been strong enough to blow open the door. I turned on the outdoor lights and went out to the workshop. The door was closed and everything seemed, from the outside, to be secure. Only when I opened the door and turned on the workshop lights did I realize I had been burglarized.

The trash can in which I store sunflower seeds was completely empty and only a few scattered seeds remained in the bird food container. The bag of dog food had been ripped open and cleaned out. I looked at the window I had left open and noticed the screen had been cut neatly along one edge. The burglar apparently had entered by the window, carefully smoothed the screen back into place, and made his exit through the door. I cranked the window shut and started to turn out the light and leave. It was then that I noticed the note stuck to the side of the sunflower seed container.

The note read, "Thanks muchly, mightily, and kindly for your munificence, magnanimity, and generosity in providing me with this opulent banquet. I will be eternally grateful and will be back tomorrow at my usual time to see if you wish to outdo yourself with another grand repast." At the bottom was another note. It read, "Footnote: If you will look over on the table, you will find one coffee can full of sunflower seeds and another full of bird seeds. These should see you through the morning. Signed, sealed, and delivered by Jimm...."

The "Jimm..." was marked through and under it was written, "The Masked Moocher." Obviously, Jimmie the Raccoon had struck again. I was puzzled, though, at her leaving two coffee cans of seeds behind. I wondered if she might be not only shrewder but also nicer and wiser than I had thought.

29

A week later, while I was in the yard pulling wild strawberry vines out of the flower beds, Cleopatra did a walk-about to survey the yard to make sure everything was being maintained to her satisfaction. She walked over to where I was working, stepped into the middle of the flowers, and lay down. A bumble bee buzzed down to check out a flower blossom. Cleopatra jumped up, took a swat at the bumble bee, missed, and fell flat on her face. She looked up at me as though hoping I had not been looking. She said, "I bet you saw that. And I bet you are going to call me clumsy, clumsy, clumsy!"

"Oh, no," I said. "Pretty much the same thing has happened to me lots of times."

Cleopatra raised her head and said, "Really? Happened to you? Lots of times? Clumsy, clumsy, clumsy! You ought to be more careful."

I thought for awhile and then said, "Well, Miss Know-It-All, maybe this is a good time for you to finish telling me about Socs and the 'wisdom' type. Remember, you stopped in the middle of it the other day."

Cleopatra yawned and replied, "Yes. Actually I have said everything about his type I wish to say. I know you are going to talk to him again one of these days. I understand from what you have said that he must be the world's best listener. So you can ask him anything I have not covered or you do not understand. But there is one more thing I would like to tell you about the four gooseganders and the four focus-of-life categories they represent. And then I never again want to say or hear anything about them! So hear my last words on the subject.

"You should never ask all four of them the same question. You would just be wasting your time. The four will never be able to agree on even the simplest things. For example, suppose someone comes by where the four of them are swimming and says, 'Good morning!' One will answer, 'Depends on whether or not you have made peace with the GREAT GOOSE!' Another will say, 'How can you say that when the air is all polluted and the sky may fall in?' Another will exclaim, 'Depends on what you brought me for lunch and whether or not you have extra tickets to the ice hockey game!' The other will say, 'That is a great question and a great concept. Let us sit over here for a few days and discuss the physiological and psychological ramifications of it!'

"Since you have understood only about half of what I have said and will quickly forget most of the other half, let me tell you one thing more that you might understand and remember. I think what you really want is what most of your kind want. You want a simple answer to a complex question. So here is something you can put on a bumper sticker. 'The search for the meaning of life IS the meaning of life!'" Cleopatra yawned, dropped her head, and was asleep, right in the middle of my flower bed.

30

I watched the old man as he made his weary way down the path. He obviously was struggling to stay on his feet as though the next fall might be the one from which he would never recover. There were pain and suffering in his face. While his eyes showed a strong will to live, they also reflected the sorrows of a lifetime. The cross he bore upon his shoulder pressed into his flesh; the weight of it seemed, at times, almost more than he could bear. But he walked on, slowly placing one weary foot in front of the other, bearing his burden as best he could, feeling deeply not only awe and wonder but also, perhaps more keenly, life's pain, suffering, sorrow, and fear.

I looked long and thoughtfully at the man. The mirror in which I looked was old, cracked, and distorted, but it reflected the truth well enough for me to see. I looked in fright, sorrow, and awe at the reflected light of the yesterdays of my life. I saw the small, individual incidences that, together, make me what I am.

I heard again the last dying chirp of the robin I, as a child, had thoughtlessly killed. I saw again the baby robins as they died one by one, in spite of my tearful efforts to save them. I saw the still, staring eyes of the baby squirrel I had to destroy because of the severe injuries it had received from a cat. I heard again the blast of the shotgun as one of my neighbors shot and killed Randy, the wonderful raccoon who made the mistake of taking a few ears of corn from the neighbor's garden. I saw again the baby deer with the broken foot standing as best it could and looking up through pain-glazed eyes at its mother who stood by in distress and licked its face. I heard, again, the anguished screams of a friend's tiny daughter as the hospital staff fought to save her from the disfiguring and life-threatening scalds from the pot of water she had pulled off the stove. I watched as the horrified and guilt-stricken parents attempted to make sense of the tragedy. I saw again the ugly wounds on the corpse of the teenaged victim of an automobile accident. I saw the multitudes of frightened animals fleeing for their lives from flaming forests and jungles that were being cleared to provide more food for the ever expanding intrusion of the human animal. I saw abused children, raped women, and enslaved men. I saw multitudes struggling through a life that had little meaning for them. I saw them pushing on against the tide, existing, reproducing, and dying, often without ever having really lived. At times, I thought I saw a Creator who looked with indifference and disdain at that which He had created.

I turned from the images, but I could not rid them from my thoughts. What does it mean, this sorrow I see and feel so deeply? Why do I both embrace it and deny it its rightful place in the story of life? How is it that, much of the time, I am able to look squarely at the sorrows of the ages and still feel a deep sense of peaceful, joyous meaning, a meaning that embraces both the ugly and the beautiful? Why do I still see the world as a sad, lonely, but lovely place, and life as a sad, lonely, but wonderful thing? Can it be that REAL beauty and REAL wonder can be known fully only when these are intertwined with the realities of pain, suffering, sorrow, and fear? At those times when I have chosen to be aware, when I have dared to look at the full reflection of my life, I have seen clearly that I have had my fair portion of joys, victories, and proud accomplishments. But, like pieces in a jigsaw puzzle, these have been intermeshed with anguish, defeat, and failure. Is this what life is meant to be? If so, why? Why can we not enjoy the light without having, also, to suffer the darkness?

This was a good day to go to the pond. There were a few things I would talk about with Socs.

I saw Socs just as I rounded the curve in the road that led past the pond. He was standing beside the road by the bridge that spans the stream watching the road as though half expecting me to appear. I parked the car, got out, and sat in the grass beside him in the small triangle of a meadow formed by the stream, the road, and the woods. We sat for a while with neither of us saying anything. But I felt his presence, and the troubling images I had brought with me seemed to retreat a bit deeper into the shadows of my being.

Socs was the first to speak. "The last time we talked," he murmured, "you asked me some questions I did not answer. That was because I was not sure of your questions. I have thought about them some. I think I know now what you were trying to ask. You were asking me who I really am. And I am, of course, like you, the sum total of my thoughts and emotions. You wanted to know how my thoughts and emotions differ from the thoughts and emotions of others. You wanted to know the primary focus of my being. You wanted to know what I have that I can share with you and how receptive I am to knowing you. You wanted to know what vision I have of the unseeable and what I know of the unknown. Yes! Those are the things you were trying to ask me. I saw in your face, as you drove up today, a calm, reasoned sorrow. I was glad to see you come. On this particular morning, I need someone to share with me, for a moment, some of the visions and dreams that both comfort and haunt me."

Socs was silent for a while. He seemed to be looking into the heavens as if at some distant vision of time and space coming together to form new meaning. With seeming effort, he pulled himself back to the present and continued to talk in his low, soft voice. "Did you see the deer with the broken foot?" he asked.

"She died! The hawks and dogs carried off her remains. Nothing is left that shows her humble birth, her short and simple life, the pain that struck her so unexpectedly and terribly, her fear and suffering and, finally, her lonely passing. We have seen, you and I, down through the ages, ten thousand innocent, helpless, creatures. Creatures that hold hope and promise close to their bosoms. Creatures with curiosity and, sometimes, with generosity and caring. We have seen them crushed and left to die, with horror, fear, and disbelief in their eyes.

"And they are not alone, for we also, you and I, look on with horror, fear, and disbelief. Where was the Creator when the pain struck? What noble purpose was served by their swift passing? What plan was advanced? What lesson taught? You wonder about these things. And so do I."

Socs stood up, walked down to the edge of the stream, stared into the rippling water as though at some dark vision forming from the foam. He returned. He sat with his feathers pressed against my leg and continued where he left off. "I have tried to find the sources of pain and suffering and I would like to share some of my thoughts with you. I think the pain and suffering in this world have two primary sources. First, there is what we might call the 'natural disaster.' This includes phenomena such as tornadoes, volcanoes, earthquakes, and diseases. Second, there are the things we bring on ourselves and each other out of our carelessness, callousness, ignorance, indifference, and greed. No matter how hard we try to think otherwise, the Creator ultimately is responsible for both of these. And what we, you and I, are struggling with today is to find meaning in these seemingly meaningless assaults on our senses of fairness, reason, logic, sympathy, caring, and love.

"Tornadoes, volcanoes, earthquakes, and infectious diseases! I talked with the Creator about these one day—I don't mean LITERALLY, but talked just the same. The answer She gave me was that She did not know how to create an earth that had the characteristics required for intelligent life but was free from, well, volcanoes, for example. She said She did not know how to make a ball with the earth's mass that did not have a molten center. She said if I ever figured out how to do it, She would consider doing it that way next time. She said there were lots of things She simply did not know how to do.

"She mentioned that She did not know how to create a universe that was always nice and safe but still could hold a planet in place at just the right distance from a sun to provide the temperatures required to support intelligent life. She talked to me about how living creatures need lots of water, and how water erodes the surface of the earth. She noted that the surface of the earth had to be somewhat unstable so that upheavals, such as those caused by volcanoes and by pressure on the sea floor could, in time, push up new mountain ranges. She noted that, if it were not for these upheavals and their ability to counteract the effect of erosion from wind and water, all the deep places of the oceans would get filled in, the high places would be leveled and, eventually, the surface of the earth would become completely smooth. If this happened, it would be somewhat difficult for us to live on the earth because the entire surface then would be covered with eight thousand feet of water."

Socs stood up, stretched his neck and wings, moved around to where he could sit facing me, and continued. "I also asked the Creator why we have to have diseases, such as those caused by bacteria and viruses. She said She did not know how to create conditions that will allow the development of germs we consider beneficial but not ones that we consider harmful. She mentioned that germs are essential for many things, such as making the soil suitable for growing things. Without bacteria, we soon would starve. She said what She had done was create a universe in which conditions would exist that would support intelligent life. She said I could not imagine how immense this universe is, or how complex it is, with all its parts working together to maintain just the right balance to make life possible. She said that, EVEN IF SHE HAD WANTED TO, She could not have made this world the nice, safe place we sometimes think we want. I believe her! I think if She could have done those things and, if She had thought they were the right thing to do, She would have done them! If you think I am wrong, you must tell me where I am wrong."

He paused. I did not speak. "So you think what I have said is fairly close to the way it is?" he asked. "Then I will go on to the next thing."

Socs shifted his position a bit, rested his neck on my leg, and continued. "The next thing we will have to consider is that the Creator made a world in which intelligent creatures seem to do all kinds of things that are hurtful to themselves and others. Most of the sorrow in the world is the result of our own misguided choices. Why did the Creator have to do it that way? I have asked Her about that too, and She said intelligence without choice is a contradiction of terms. It is similar to talking about round squares, or a front without a back, or up without down: there just can't be such a thing! As long as we have choices, we can choose to do the destructive thing as well as the constructive thing. I think that is the same as saying we can choose to do what seems good for us in the short term, or we can choose to do what seems good for us in the long term. If She took away our right to make bad choices, we would be reduced to mere robots.

"'But,' you say, 'We don't always have choices!' Well, we do too! I think what you really mean is that we don't always have the choices we would like to have. Sometimes we have to choose between alternatives when we don't like any of them. But that is not the same as having no choice. I agree that there are rare occasions when it SEEMS we have absolutely no choice. For example, if you climb a tall tree and slip off a limb, you have no choice but to fall to the ground. You can't fly, and you can't fall UP. So you fall down. You don't have any choice about that. But you DID have a choice about climbing the tree. And you DO have a choice about how you deal with the falling down. You can either accept the inevitable or you can claw and scream every inch of the way! I also agree that, when we do have a number of choices, we sometimes choose not to exercise our choices. But, isn't that just another way of choosing?

"Some choices are very difficult. Quite often we choose not to be aware of our choices. Some animals are so frightened or beaten down by life that they choose not to be aware of much of anything. This is the same as choosing not to think, choosing not to use our intelligence. It also is choosing not to hurt so much! Intelligence is not an unmitigated blessing. If we choose to use our intelligence, choose to be aware, we put ourselves in the position of being aware of pain as well as pleasure. I think most of the choices we make that are destructive to us, or to others, are ones we make when we choose to put limits on how aware we will be.

"Sometimes our being aware leaves us only with a choice between hurting now and hurting later. And, if we really are not strong enough to bear the hurt, choosing not to be aware may be a wise choice. Often, though, we can bear more than we think we can. When we choose not to be aware, not to use our intelligence, we lull ourselves into a half sleep where we can believe the pain will never happen. And, to the extent we continue choosing not to be aware, we may not ever suffer, although others may suffer because of our choices. But, in most cases, we won't really LIVE either! Someone recently told me that life was so tough for him that he did not know whether to go kill himself or go play golf! And that is a serious decision to make. I'm not sure of the best choice for any particular animal at any particular time. It all depends on how much living they wish to do, which is the same thing as how much HURTING they are willing to do."

Socs paused, looked me straight in the eyes, and said, "Stop me and ask questions if I say something you don't understand or you think is not true." And then he seemed deep in thought for what must have been at least two minutes. I lay back on the grass with my hands under my head and listened.

Socs began again, "Back a few minutes ago, I said something I thought you would question. But you didn't, so I will. I said the Creator told me that, EVEN IF SHE HAD WANTED TO, She could not have made this world a nice, safe place. What did She mean by 'even if she had wanted to?' I asked Her about that and I found Her answer hard to understand. She said, if She had made the world without turmoil and stresses, we would not have the motivation to change, learn, and grow. She said, without turmoil and stresses, we never would have evolved past the stage of worms crawling about in the primeval slime. And She said She never intended for animals to live forever. I wonder what She meant by that! I think what She meant was that life is meaningful ONLY because it is not forever. When we USE life meaningfully, we do it mostly because life is in limited supply. Perhaps the whole meaning of life is wrapped up in how aware we choose to be in what little time we have. Maybe awareness is the thing that gives us the experiences of a thousand years in the short time allotted to us here. Maybe awareness advances us on the road through eternity even while we are still earth bound.

"Let me stop a minute here! Do you really understand what I mean by AWARENESS? I don't mean merely knowing something exists, having a superficial knowledge of something, or understanding the mechanics of something. What I am talking about is reaching out with all our senses and actually becoming a part of what we observe. I mean not only understanding the what, where, when, why, and how of something, but actually, in a real sense, EXPERIENCING it. I mean accepting and dealing with that of which we have evidence. I mean refusing to hide from reality, even when this refusal requires facing difficulty, danger, and heartbreak.

"Let me think of an example that might help me better understand what I am trying to say about awareness. Suppose your mate tells you she doesn't want to live with you any more. If you choose not to be aware, there are several things you might do. You might pretend you didn't hear her, you might suddenly decide you never did like her and that you would do well to be rid of her, you might convince yourself that she is a dishonest person who has deceived you for years, or you might decide you are a worthless character who really doesn't deserve a decent mate. There may be some truth to any or all of these possible responses, of course, but they are superficial ways of looking at the situation.

"If you choose to be truly aware, you will not need to defend yourself in such a manner. You will... well, first of all you already would have known something was weakening the relationship, and you would have addressed it before it became a crisis. If you are truly aware, you will see clearly what caused the two of you to get together in the first place and why you have drifted apart. You will understand your own strengths and weaknesses and how these have impacted on the relationship, and you will understand and accept as reality her perspective. You will see that each of you has made past decisions that, at the time, seemed correct. You will understand how both of you must change if the relationship is to continue. You will see realistically the costs and paybacks of these changes for each of you and will make a reasoned decision concerning how to proceed. And, perhaps more importantly, you will see how this changing relationship relates to both your lives, connects with others who may be involved, and meshes with the sum total of existence. If you choose to be fully aware, you will not be angry or devastated, you will not blame, and you will neither stop caring nor permit your caring to become an obsession."

Our thoughts were interrupted by noises from the edge of the pond. The other three goosenganders had found something to eat and were having a loud conversation about who saw it first and how to divide it fairly. The interruption apparently presented Socs with some new thoughts, so he shifted gears with his conversation. After standing tall to see what the racket was about, he said, "One of them (Glory) thinks the sky will fall in most any day because the Creator has put up with as much of our sinning as She can stand. Apparently everybody has had all the chances to do right they are ever going to have. So, according to her, it is time to pack everything up and move on to the rewards and punishments that go to the game-of-life's winners and losers. The other one (Eden) also thinks the sky will fall in most any day. But she thinks it is because we have trashed our world to the extent that it will just curl up and die. The other one (Fun City) is extreme in his choice not to be aware. He just wants to know what's for lunch. As you know, I don't completely agree with any of them. The one who thinks we are trashing the earth is partly correct. We ARE damaging the earth. But the earth will not curl up and die. WE may curl up and die, but IT won't! Maybe someday, in the far distant future, it will blow, but not because of what we have done to it. This world has... well, all the time in the world. We are the ones who are just camping here overnight."

The background noises now had ceased. Socs walked over toward the road and I thought perhaps he had finished talking and was leaving. But he turned around, returned to where I was sitting, settled down beside me, and continued his discussion. "You were asking me what I think is the real meaning of life, and I don't think I have yet told you. It is difficult for me to find the right words. I believe I can feel it, but I have a difficult time saying it. But I will try. We are not here to be happy. Of all the things in this wide world, happiness has been the most overrated. We are here to grow, to learn, to understand, to accept and merge with reality, to love and be loved, and to bond with each other and with all creation. This world is ideally suited to this purpose.

"The uncertainties of life and the certainty of death prevents our sitting back and relaxing. The harsh realities push us continuously onward in our search for understanding and meaning. The world's vast beauty can be seen only in contrast to its harsh realities. So, while life for each of us may be a terrible, desperate struggle, it has sufficient rewards to motivate us to choose, at least most of the time, to 'go play golf' rather that 'go kill ourselves.' While we were designed and created never to be fully contented, we can find an exciting, joyful, meaningful existence. We can choose to be aware and we can change our expectations to fit the stark realities of life and death. Through doing this, we can find contentment in our discontent!"

"I think I said," continued Socs, "that we are here to grow, to learn, to understand, to accept and merge with reality, to love and be loved, and to bond with each other and with all creation. Why do these things matter? Why are they important? I'm not sure, but I think I know. It may be because these are the only things that are real. These are the only things you can take with you when you leave this body, this earth, and this life. You may ask why you can't take stagnation, ignorance, misunderstanding, divisiveness, indifference, and alienation with you. It's because you can only take things of substance with you. Ignorance and indifference, for example, have no substance. They are the ABSENCE of knowledge and love. Things of substance are eternal. The LACK of something never had an existence. I cannot show you the hat I never had or speak to you from knowledge I never gained. Negatives cannot fill a void; they ARE the void.

"If we assume the Creator created for a purpose, what could that purpose be? If the here and now is all there is, what good is any of it to the Creator? But what could come after this life? In what corner of the universe is eternity located? Is not time relative to speed? If you were to move at the speed of light, time would stand still for you. If you moved a bit faster, time would turn backwards and you would begin to move into the past. Perhaps our concept of time and place is relative to our earth-bound, time-bound environment. Certainly a few million years here or there seem to be of no great concern to the Creator. Perhaps, in reality, the entire universe as we know it is one single atom in a tail feather of a giant goose who lives by a giant pond in a far bigger universe. In this life, our physical being limits our ability to grow, to learn, to understand, to accept and merge with reality, to love and be loved, and to bond with each other and with all creation. But, when our physical being ends or changes at what we refer to as death, perhaps these limits will be lifted. Perhaps we will understand things that are beyond the capabilities of our simple, animal brain. Maybe we have just begun to live and grow. Perhaps this day is only a small part of eternity, and perhaps our awareness today is only a tiny window opening into the possibilities of knowing other aspects of unlimited time and space."

The shadows were lengthening. The fireflies were signaling the end of another tiny segment of eternity. Socs rose slowly to his feet, walked across the road, slipped silently into the still water, and glided purposefully into the gathering darkness. I turned the car around and drove home. This was, perhaps, the most meaningful conversation I had ever had. And I had not spoken a single word.

31

Cleopatra likes to ride in the car—that is, if conditions are just right. She likes the air conditioner on, back seat to herself, slow on the curves, and not over forty-five miles per hour. I decided to go to the pond, and she wanted to ride with me. I scrounged around in the refrigerator and found a bag of stale rolls to feed to the goosenganders. I opened the rear car door, let Cleopatra in, then got in the front seat and fastened my safety harness. Before I could start the engine, Cleopatra jumped into the front seat, slashed open the plastic bag, and killed and ate three of the rolls. I asked her why she had not told me she was hungry. She said she had not been hungry but that, as I should know, animals had to follow their instincts, at least part of the time, or they would lose them. She had attacked the bag of rolls because that was a good way for her to work off her "predatory aggression" without hurting anybody. With this, she jumped back into the rear of the car and began taking an after-snack bath. I unfastened my seat belt, got out, walked around the car, opened the other front door, gathered the several loose rolls off of the floorboard, took out the floor mat and shook off the crumbs, and got back in and buckled up. Finally, I was on my way. Cleopatra had finished her bath and was deep in an after-snack nap.

I heard the noise and confusion before I got close enough to see what was going on. I parked the car, pulled Cleopatra's ear to wake her up, and we walked over to some low shrubs on the bank of the pond. All four goosenganders were milling around, honking, and flapping their wings in obvious agitation. They all were talking at once while gesturing toward the shrubs. We walked closer and took a good look. Curled up under one of the shrubs was a full-grown opossum. He was sobbing and was obviously in great distress. Between the sobs, I could hear what seemed to be, "Oh! I'm hurt! I'm hurt! Save me! Don't let me die! Call 911, quick, somebody! Call 911! Emergency! Code Blue! Emergency! Pain! Agony! Torment! Misery! Help!"

32

Opossums make up the family *Didelphidae* and are the only marsupials native to North America. The largest group is the Virginia opossum, or *Didelphis Virginiana*. When full-grown, the opossum is as large as a house cat, has course grayish-white hair, a pig-like snout, large naked ears, a long hairless scaly tail, about fifty long sharp teeth, and dark beady eyes. It also tends to slobber most of the time. If you like pretty, dainty creatures, you should stick to goldfish, parakeets, or butterflies. Only its mother could love an opossum, and that likely is because of her small brain.

When opossums are first born, they are smaller than honey bees. They suckle for the first several weeks from their position inside their mother's external pouch. After this, they depend on their mother for a month or so longer before going it on their own. Under ordinary conditions, an opossum is slow. When it is in a frantic rush, however, it is VERY slow. Its brain is as quick as a steel trap that has rusted for seventy-five to one hundred years. Yet, the opossum has survived virtually unchanged for millions of years. How has it managed to do this? First, it simply is not smart enough to get into a great deal of trouble. Second, it has the ability to play "possum." To do this, it flops limply on its side, closes its eyes, and hangs out its tongue. When it is in this condition, no decent, law-abiding animal will touch it. Third, fashion models rarely ever pose in opossum coats, so trapping opossums for their fur has never been a lucrative business. Fourth, while opossums do not stink to high heaven, they do have an unpleasant odor. Animals with a keen sense of smell will not touch them. And fifth, opossums are heavy breeders. They have one to two litters each year, with each litter consisting of five to eighteen young. Standard equipment for the mother is only thirteen milk stations; therefore, when there are more than thirteen young in a litter, the last born starve to death.

Opossums in the wild eat frogs, snakes, lizards, other small animals, eggs, berries, and persimmons. In populated areas, they prefer sweet corn and garbage can contents. They are nocturnal animals and feed mostly at night. They communicate with barks, moans and, occasionally, with growls. The clicking of teeth and tongue is a courtship gesture. A hiss is a signal of danger or fear. An opossum's tail is prehensile and is used for grasping things such as material for lining its den, or for suspending itself from a tree branch when it just wants to hang out.

33

Cleopatra is a quick cat when there is an emergency. She marched up to the sobbing opossum and said, "Hush! Hush now, and tell us what is wrong! We cannot help if we do not know what is wrong." She handed the opossum a tissue on which to blow his nose and wipe away his tears.

The sobbing subsided and was replaced with a moaned response. "Well, Ma'am, my name is Oppie and I'm bad hurt. Was walking down the road last night minding my own business. Big car came along, was speeding, didn't have the right of way, bad brakes, mutted guffler, license expired, driver obviously intoxicated, didn't dim his headlights, blinded me, and then ran over me. Hit and run driver. Didn't even slow down. Ran right over me before I could get out of the way."

One of the goosenganders interrupted and said in a matter-of-fact tone, "Broke his tail. Broke it right there in the middle. Clean break, no lacerations, just a good clean break. Just needs resetting and a few splints. Maybe a spot of penicillin for any infection and a sedative to calm his nerves and help him sleep."

The other goosenganders chimed in with comments such as, "Maybe we should call emergency. Maybe we should cut him open and check for eternal injuries! Will his Blue Goose/Blue Shield insurance pay? Did anybody check his pulse to see if he's still alive? Should notify his next of kin. Knew a horse one time that had that; they had to shoot him. You mean he's been under that bush since last night; bet gangrene has set in. If we had a thermometer, we could check his temperament! Bet it was that big man from the funeral parlor trying to drum up business. I think we need lots of hot water here! Know where there's some hedge clippers; maybe should just lop his tail off up close. Did you check his head to see if he has a brain discussion? Ought to have a blood transfusion. Blood? Oh, I think I'm going to faint!"

Cleopatra looked up at me and purred, "Remember when we were talking the other day about different perspectives? Well, I want to show you what I meant." She turned to the milling goosenganders, flexed her claws, and shouted, "Now, all of you hush up for a minute! Here is what we are going to do." The four goosenganders fell silent and gathered around her. She IS a persuasive cat!

Cleopatra continued, "If he were going to die from this, he would already be dead. So there is no big emergency. I am going to give each of you a turn to tell what you think should be done, and then I will make a decision. Understand?" All nodded their heads in agreement. "All right! You first," she said to the goosengander on her extreme left. Oppie crawled partly out from among the shrubs so all could see him better. With each low moan, he looked up to make sure he still was the center of attention.

The first goosengander to speak obviously was Fun City. He had a cookbook in his wings and was thumbing eagerly through the pages. He spoke up, "Well, here's what we have right off. There's opossum casserole, opossum au gratin, opossum en brochette, opossum mignon, opossum pilaf, opossum ragout, opossum rissole, opossum suchi, opossum fritters, and braised, boiled, poached, baked, barbecued, roasted, sauted, stir-fried, and pan-fried opossum. And here's an old southern favorite: possum stew and sweet potatoes. Got to have sweet potatoes! Keeps the meat from sliding down too fast. Who has sweet potatoes? Hey, I know what we'll do. We'll throw a big party! Invite everybody! Social event of the year! Food! Drink! Games! Fireworks! This is big! I mean, BIG! I'll go start a cooking fire while the rest of you figure out which recipe you want! Then we'll plan the party and get invitations out." He started toward the trees to pick up dead limbs, but Cleopatra stopped him.

"Just hold on," she ordered, while gently sliding a paw full of razor-sharp claws along the side of his beak. "You stay right here while the others have their say!"

"Well," Fun City protested, "If they want to cook him some other way, that's all right with me. Or if they just want to eat him raw, that's all right, too. But if you find him awfully greasy, don't blame me for it. And a party is a party. Everybody knows I know how to throw a party. So what else is there to talk about? It's going to be great! I mean, GREAT!"

Cleopatra hissed, "Shut up and SIT!" He shut up and sat. She turned to the goosenganders standing next to Fun City, and asked, "What do you think?"

Glory looked up from the book she held and said in her shrill voice, "I don't know why we are even talking about this. It doesn't matter what we think. We are not supposed to think! It tells us right here in the GOOD BOOK what we should do! Right here, it tells about this scruffy character who was traveling between two cities when he fell among some bad ones. They stole all his stuff, beat up on him, probably broke his tail, although the BOOK doesn't mention that specifically, and went off and left him for dead. Several came by and saw him lying there suffering and, though they ought to have known better, they passed by on the other side and didn't help him at all. Another one came by, saw him, took pity on him, tied up his wounds, and took him with him so he could take care of him. And right here in the GOOD BOOK are the words as plain as day that we should 'go and do likewise.' Obviously, the GREAT GOOSE has sent this poor, miserable creature to us so we can baptize him and then tie up his wounds and take care of him."

Oppie had not said a word when Fun City had been talking about cooking and eating him. Perhaps he did not understand the concept. But he had heard about Glory and the baptism of the eight field mice, five of which were drowned in the process. He began to tremble with fear, and moaned, "Please, why do I have to be baptized? I don't want to be baptized!"

Glory was ready with an answer. " That's so you will get rid of your sinful ways, live a life of righteousness and, when you die, spend eternity with the GREAT GOOSE in the GREAT POND. Not in the main part of the GREAT POND, of course, but I'm pretty sure they have an annex or something for the likes of you."

Oppie's fear seemed to increase and the tears began to flow again. He said, "I thought I did right already, except when I got run over by a car, and I didn't do that on purpose. And I don't know anything about sinning. How do you do that? And I don't want to go to no GREAT POND. If I ever die, I want to be with the GREAT OPOSSUM in the GIANT PERSIMMON TREE IN THE SKY."

Glory seemed to be getting a bit hot under the feathers. She responded, "He's one of those heathens, all right. And the GOOD BOOK says right here that the GREAT GOOSE said to her followers, 'Bind him hand and foot, and cast him into the outer darkness; there, creatures will weep and gnash their teeth. For many are called, but few are chosen."

She closed her book, turned her back, muttered something that sounded like, "Deliver us from evil," and then was quiet.

The next goosengander spoke up in a thoughtful voice. "What we have here is an opportunity to show our friendship with all creatures and make this a better world for all of us. We CAN live together in peace and harmony if we just accept that the GREAT GOOSE loves all her creation and that we should do likewise. What an opportunity to set up a shelter for the homeless! A place where poor lost miserable creatures like this one can stay and be happy while we find them a good place to stay permanently. Maybe a soup kitchen, too! Where hungry ones can eat healthy, organically-grown food. I already have a big pile of it if one of you will just help me bring it down here. The others of you can go out and search high and low for some more homeless ones. When you find them, don't take 'no' for an answer. Some of them just don't understand what is good for them. Bring 'em in even if you have to whack them on the head a few times. This can be the dawn of a new day when we can show that we are the GREAT GOOSE'S eyes, ears, wings, and feet to be used to do HER work in this world!" This, of course, was Eden. She had had her say, so she sat down and waited.

Socs was the last to speak. He seemed not to have been listening to the others but had been feeling of Oppie's fur, checking out his bare ears, and making a few tentative attempts to straighten the broken tail. He spoke as though talking to himself, seemingly not noticing that the others were there. "Interesting thing about getting hurt. Makes you think and feel new things. Wonder what this experience means to him. Hard to tell from what he says. Maybe hasn't had time to sink in yet. I'll ask him about it again next time I see him. Hard for one animal to exactly understand a different specie. Brains are put together different. Different ratios of data from learning versus instinct. Different ways of sensing the environment. Different ways of communicating. Different degrees of awareness of how they think and feel. Some seem not to be aware just because of the way their brain is built. Others seem to be able to CHOOSE whether or not to be aware. Those who are less AWARE don't seem to be quiet as ALIVE. But they don't seem to hurt as much either. Good balance. Good system. Fair to everything, in an odd sort of way."

He then turned to the others, seemed to notice them for the first time, and said, "Whenever you are ready, we will patch this boy up and send him on his way."

Cleopatra held one paw up to her mouth to keep the others from hearing and purred in my ear, "Remember when I said these four, with their totally different basic perspectives, would never be able to agree on even the simplest thing? Well, I rest my case."

And she was right, of course. But not altogether. The four might disagree in principle, but they were capable of uniting in action. Eden held Oppie's head to her breast to comfort him, Glory tried to give him a reassuring pat on the head without touching him too much, and Fun City, in spite of his violent protestation that he would have nothing to do with this, helped pull the broken tail out straight. There was a great deal of moaning, wailing, and offered advice as Socs did the doctoring. The last I saw of Oppie, he was walking gingerly back toward the woods where he lived. His tail was sticking straight out behind held rigidly in place by two straight splints that Socs had smoothed down with his pocketknife.

And holding the splints in place was a bright red ribbon.

VI. The Fight of the Century

If betting on bingo or lotto or loo
Is your way of gaining an edge,
I'll make an appointment tomorrow at two
To sell you the Brooklyn Bridge.

34

It was the day of the big fight. The media billed it the fight of the century. The bets were down and crowds were gathering. Odds were set at a thousand to one in favor of The Killer, who had been champion for almost two years. These odds would have been higher except that few could raise enough money to bet on the champion, and very few were willing to bet even a penny on the challenger.

The Killer was undefeated in fifty-two fights, and the experts were unanimous in predicting another victory. The challenger was considered by the experts to have absolutely no chance, in spite of the supposed possession of a "secret weapon." The secret weapon was thought by most to be just another contrivance, and various stratagems tried by past challengers had not proven effective against the awesome might of The Killer.

The Killer was considered by many to be the most powerful animal of all time. Certainly the record of fifty-two straight victories was unsurpassed. There was talk of making The Killer supreme ruler for life. Others were frightened of The Killer's awesome power and considered it to be a threat to all the animal kingdom. One thing was certain, on this particular day, The Killer reigned supreme; no other animal was or ever had been considered the equal.

35

This story actually had its beginning about fifteen months ago when I was attempting to decide on the best way to invest a few dollars in the stock market. I had read all recent issues of the Wall Street Journal and had done extensive other research on the half-dozen stocks I was considering buying. I had considered the cash flow, debt-to-earnings and price-to-earnings ratios, book value, likelihood of dividend maintenance, competitive position in the industry, industry prospects, historical perspective, and management capability of each of the companies under consideration. Finally, I decided three of the stocks would be good buys but the other three should be avoided like the plague. Before placing my buy orders, I decided to make one more trip to the library to read what the experts were saying about the six stocks. Somewhat to my chagrin, they were virtually unanimous in recommending that anyone owning the three stocks I intended buying should sell them immediately. They also strongly advised purchasing the three stocks I had rejected. What was I to do? I certainly did not consider myself an expert on the stock market or on any other investment options. So, I went with the experts; I avoided the three stocks I originally intended to buy and bought the three I originally intended to avoid.

Now that was about fifteen months ago. Since then, I have carefully followed my three stocks and have seen them steadily decline in value. The stocks now are worth only slightly over half what I originally paid for them. The experts now are divided in their advice about them. Some still recommend them as outstanding buys, particularly at their current low prices. Others, perhaps the majority, now declare that only an idiot would have bought them in the first place and that they should be sold immediately. And what happened to the three stocks I originally intended buying but, because of the advice of the experts, did NOT buy? You guessed it! They have steadily increased in value to the point where they currently are worth about double what I would have paid for them. And what are the experts saying about them now? You guessed it again! Part of them now claim they originally strongly recommended them and say the rise in price shows how astute they are. Some of the others recommend them as a new buy opportunity; after all, look how well they have done! A few of the more honest ones who originally found them unfavorable still claim they are dogs that ought to be sold immediately.

Recently, I noticed we had saved a few more nickels and that it was time to invest again. I had a few ideas for some long-term investments that might, in time, help me recoup some of my loses over the past fifteen months. But I still felt uneasy about my expertise in the area of finance. I decided, again, to check with the experts to see what investments they currently were recommending. My five full day's research of various investment newsletters, financial journals, and advice from local stockbrokers provided me with a great deal of information. Unfortunately, there was little agreement among the advice givers. The only consistency was that virtually all were confident they were right and that all of the other experts were cowering idiots. The recommendations included buying municipal bonds, gold bullion, growth mutual funds, tax free government bonds, options on hog bellies, electric utility stocks, health care stocks, junk bonds, time share condominiums, raw acreage in New Mexico, certificates of deposit, baseball cards, variable annuities, convertible bonds, and stock in Joe's Same-Day-Surgery and Aluminum Siding Company. These were most helpful to me in making my investment decision. My wife and I simply blew the whole bundle on a two-week vacation in the Bahamas.

What I am saying is that my unshakable faith in experts is considerably shaken. Not just about financial investments, but about practically every aspect of life. Over a lifetime, I have found the experts in virtually every area to be wrong about as often as they have been right. I now have decided to be a contrarian. Whenever I have time and opportunity to search out information needed to make an informed decision, I follow my own inclinations rather than go with the experts.

My resolve to follow my own inclinations was put to the test by the upcoming big fight. I had known for at least a week of the Killer's scheduled title defense and I decided that, before I put my money down, I would try to figure out what I personally—without any expert advice—believed about the big fight. So, I did what I often do when I am puzzled about what is going on in the animal kingdom: I asked Cleopatra the Cat. She doesn't claim to be an expert on everything and she says she would be quick to admit it in the unlikely event anything she does or says ever turns out to be wrong.

36

One morning several days before the fight of the century was to take place, I was able to catch Cleopatra when she was neither sleepy nor hungry and, thus, was in one of her good moods. I asked her, "Are you betting on the big fight?"

"I am unsure of your definition of 'betting,'" she responded. "Do you mean gambling, venturing, wagering, speculating, chancing, hazarding, or risking? Do you mean in a formal, legal sense, or are you referring to an informal, mental attitude? Could you speak clearly and precisely, please?"

"Well, never mind," I growled. "I just wanted to know if you agree with what all the experts say about the fight and, if not, why not. But don't put yourself out here just because I happened to be the one who feeds you and cleans your litter box!"

She purred a quick response. "I probably would miss you if you had to be replaced. After all, you have been around here for a long time. But.... What you are asking here is why there should be a fight at all if the outcome already is established. And, if the outcome is not certain, how could so many experts be wrong. I will try to explain this to you. But, first, I will have to back up and give you some fundamentals."

We were on the porch at the time, so I relaxed in my chair and Cleopatra sat on the glass-topped table next to me. She continued her explanation. "First, you have to understand about risk and gain. On any kind of bet or any kind of investment, what you have to gain is proportional to how much you risk. Now, that is not always one hundred percent correct because other factors often are involved. But it is a basic principle from which to start. IF everybody in the world were equally astute and equally knowledgeable and IF everybody had plenty of time, you could pretty well bet on or invest in anything and come out about even over the long haul. This is because everybody would understand the risks involved in the bet or investment and they would set the potential gain or loss to fit exactly the amount of risk involved.

"Let us say, for example, that someone was flipping a coin, a well-balanced coin that was not heavier on one side. You could afford to bet your dollar against someone else's dollar that the coin would turn up 'heads.' If you continued this long enough, and if the coin flipper did not charge you for his work, you would always come out about even. But, if the coin flipper charged you five or fifteen percent of the amount bet every time he flipped the coin, you would, in the long run, always lose money. And the coin flipper, inevitably, would get rich. Incidentally, that is the way all legal betting works; the ones managing the betting always get their cut.

"Another aspect of betting or investing is that you may not have all the time in the world. So, if you start off losing, you may not have enough time to catch up. Also, losing a bet on one flip of a coin does not change the odds for future bets. If you lose fifty times in a row, the odds for the next toss of the coin still are fifty-fifty. However, the longer you make these fifty-fifty bets, the better the odds of exactly breaking even. Thus, the less time you have for your bet or investment to make money for you, the less risk you can afford to take.

"Here is another example. Let us say you were betting on a roach race. Roach Ricky is rated at one chance in thirty of winning the race. Theoretically, this means if Roach Ricky raced thirty times at these same odds, he would win once. Also, theoretically, if the track did not take any of the money, you could bet one dollar on Roach Ricky in thirty different races and end up exactly getting your money back. Though betting on the thirty races would cost you thirty dollars, you would win back exactly thirty dollars when Ricky won his single race. So, in the long run, you always would come out even. So, you are asking me, how can you ever come out ahead when you bet? There are two ways. First, you can be just plain lucky. But do not count on that. Theoretically, in the long run, you will have about as much bad luck as you will good luck. Second, knowing something others do not know could give you an advantage. Let us say you know Roach Ricky and you know he recently broke into the bag of ginseng roots you stored under the sink. He may be raring to go. He may be unbeatable. And you may be the only one who knows this. If so, your inside knowledge might put you in a winning position.

"But, I hear you saying, I do not wish to bet or gamble. I wish to INVEST. We will talk about this. But, remember, we no longer are talking about the big fight and whether or not you should bet on it. We now are talking about how you can keep me in minced mackerel. For this, we will use a different example. Let us say you have about one hundred dollars to invest and you are considering three options. One is a one-hundred dollar government bond that matures in one year and pays five percent interest. Another is putting one-hundred dollars in the bank at three percent interest. The third is a one-hundred dollar bond, paying twenty percent interest, issued by a financially-distressed corporation. Let us consider the advantages and disadvantages of each of these.

"First, the government bond. Now, if you lend your lawn mower to someone, their use of your property is worth something. The use of your money also is worth something. You might refer to this as the 'going rate' or 'fair return.' Let us say that, in this example, everybody who knows about bonds and interest rates thinks the actual use of money for one year, without figuring in any risk, is worth about five percent. In other words, they figure the 'fair return' is five percent. Since, with this government bond, you are virtually certain to get your money back at the end of the year, along with your five percent 'fair return,' this is a sound investment. You can assume that the five dollars in interest you will receive at the end of the year is a fair return for the use of your one hundred dollars. This is pure investing and will keep me in chopped chicken; virtually no gambling is involved. Next, let us consider the option of putting your money in the bank. Here, you get only three dollars instead of five for the use of your one hundred dollars. So, are you being cheated? No. Not really. The bank offers some conveniences that the government bond does not. The bank lets you put money in a little at a time instead of all at once, and it lets you take your money out if you happen to need it before the year is up. But you have to pay for these conveniences. In this case, you paid two dollars for the convenience. If you did not need the convenience, you wasted two dollars.

"Now, the third alternative is a bit more complicated. When you cash in your one hundred dollar corporate bond at the end of the year, you are assuming you will get your one hundred dollars back along with twenty dollars for the use of your money. But that is not exactly correct. Actually, assuming all goes well, you will get back five dollars for the use of your money and fifteen dollars for the gamble you took. Why do I say this? Well, as I said before about the government bond, we are assuming that about five percent is a fair return for the use of your money for one year. We cannot change the rules just because it is a corporate bond. Returns on INVESTMENTS do not vary a great deal. If you insist on a gain higher than what is considered a fair return, you will have to gamble. With this corporate bond, you gambled. You made a bet that the corporation would actually be able to do what they hoped to do, which was to pay back your one hundred dollars, plus five dollars for the fair use of it, plus fifteen dollars for the chance you took. So, if they paid you off, consider yourself to have been lucky— foolish perhaps, but also lucky. And, in this example, the corporation was, in a sense, unlucky. They had to pay out an extra fifteen percent they could have kept if they had known for sure—and could have convinced potential investors—they would be able to pay the money back as promised.

"But what if they could not pay you what they promised? What if they could not pay any interest at all? Or, even worse, what if they could not even pay back all of your one hundred dollars? Were you cheated? No! Not really. You simply gambled and lost. That is the chance you took when you went for the twenty percent gain rather than for a more reasonable five percent gain. However, IF those who know about bonds and interest rates are correct in setting the odds, IF you have unlimited money to invest and gamble with, IF you are going to live forever, and IF you are willing to consider your recent loss as simply an expensive learning experience, you do not have to worry. Just buy more of the same type of distressed corporate bonds and there is a good chance you eventually will get your newly invested money back plus the five percent fair return for the use of your money. But, here, I will offer you a word of advice. You are neither young enough, rich enough, nor bright enough to gamble like that!

"With all betting, when you gain, somebody else loses. When you lose, somebody else gains. No REAL profits are made; one person is just smarter or luckier than the other. Now, here is life rule number one: Never bet on your luck! Luck is just that! It is LUCK. You cannot depend on it! So, just say NO! Life rule number two is: Be careful thinking you are smarter than the other fellow. You may just think you are. If you are correct in thinking you are smarter than the one you are betting against, and this is based on good evidence, you do not need advice from me. But, if you think you are super smart when you really are dumb as a post, there is not much point in my trying to teach you anything. Hmm. Wait a minute! Why AM I trying to teach you something?

"Now, when it comes to real profits, genuine investing is altogether different from gambling. Suppose, for example, you use your one hundred dollars to buy stock in a company that is financially healthy, has good management, and is going to use the money to buy new machinery so that a product can be produced cheaper and sold at a good profit. In such a case, you actually can gain without anybody having to lose. Of course, EVERY company CLAIMS to have adequate financing, good management, good opportunities, and a certainty of making a big profit; therefore, do not take the word of your brother-in-law, your barber, or the stockbroker who is going to make a profit from selling you the stock! The TRUTH about a potential investment is worth something! Do not try to get accurate information for free. If you do not invest time or money to get the truth, you simply are gambling again, and somebody likely is going to make a bundle—and it will not be you! What I am saying is there is a big difference between gambling and investing. In investing, nobody has to lose; in gambling, nobody can gain unless somebody loses.

"Now, back to the big fight you asked me about in the beginning. First, do you believe the official odds of one thousand to one are based on good data and sound judgement? If so, do not bet at all; the only ones sure to make money are the ones who handle the bets. Do you think the odds are NOT based on good data and sound judgement; do you know something about the fight that the so-called experts do not know? What? Tell me about it! So, you really do not know anything except what you have heard, which is the same thing everybody else has heard. Then, do not bet! Put your money in tinned tuna or a new cushion for my bed! You say you can, for sure, put in one thousand dollars and, when the fight is over, collect one thousand and one dollars, less fifty cents that goes to the bookies? You say, fifty cents is a good profit for doing nothing and taking no risk? You are asking me why you should turn down a sure thing? Remember when I said those who are dumb as a post should not bet? End of lesson! Nap time! Go away!"

Actually, I had never really considered placing a bet. There are enough chancy things in my life already without going out of my way looking for trouble. I restricted my pre-fight activities to trying to learn a bit about The Killer's background. I did this, not to gain knowledge that would help me predict the outcome of the fight, but just because I was curious.

37

Now, let us move back to the present and the big fight. As I said, the bets were down and the crowd was mostly in place. The match was to begin at high noon. Tension was building! Small birds (including chickadees, goldfinches, and titmice), along with frogs, voles, moles, and lizards, filled the front rows. Black birds, blue jays, cardinals, woodpeckers, mockingbirds, robins, doves, juncoes, crows, several sleepy hoot owls, and forty-six squirrels lined up behind them. Next were opossums, raccoons, hare bunnies, quackenduckers, goosenganders, and two wild turkeys. Bringing up the rear were deer, one wild pig, and five neighborhood dogs. Zillions of other creatures looked on from prime seats in nearby trees and the top of the compost heap. Cleopatra the Cat observed from her favorite spot on top of the chimney.

And now for some details about the champion and the challenger! First, The Killer!

The Killer was a small, brown, female hare bunny, with a chunk chewed out of one ear as a result of an encounter with a cat when she was an infant. She was quite young when she gained the title, the Killer.

This is how it happened. There was a small, brown, shoe hound who went through our neighborhood very early every morning to see if anyone had left shoes on their porch or in their yard. The shoe hound collected shoes, took them home, and carefully lined them up in a neat row across his owner's front threshold. This usually got the poor beast some attention, often a scuff on the head which he took as a sign of affection. He made his rounds very early so that no one would catch him taking shoes and fuss at him. Thus, he rarely ran into another animal.

But, back a couple of years ago, something unusual happened. A tiny, inexperienced hare bunny, who had gotten her days and nights mixed up, happened to get up even earlier than the shoe hound. A few sleepy birds noticed this and put out the word that the rabbit had beaten the dog UP. In the telling, this got translated into "beat UP the dog." Several animals managed to get close enough to the bashful but honest shoe hound to ask him for the truth. The shoe hound allowed as how, even though he had been getting up earlier and earlier, the hare bunny still had beaten him up every morning for the past two weeks. This lead to a rumor of a vicious hare that destroyed dogs twenty times its size. Because of this undeserved but awesome reputation, the hare bunny acquired the name "Killer," attracted the attention of a resourceful promoter, and was scheduled for her initial boxing match which she won handily. Then, as her number of victories increased to an astounding fifty-two without anything even resembling a serious challenge, her reputation reached its current peak.

And now, the challenger! The challenger was Bimbo the Deer, youngest daughter of Bambi III. This was to be her first match. She had agreed to it only because she did not have the faintest idea what a boxing match was. She thought they had said "box of thatch," and that thatch was something she could eat without having to forage all over. She was not an impressive challenger, however her handler, Murphy the Mole, liked the way she dodged and feinted one day when, as a fawn, she confronted her first butterfly. He had conceived the idea of the secret weapon, but not even Bimbo knew what it was.

38

Actually, The Killer was not a hare bunny at all; she was a rabbit. But I have always referred to her as a hare bunny, and I'm not going to stop now. Hares and rabbits form the family *Leporidae* and, while hares often are called rabbits and rabbits are called hares, this terminology is not technically correct. Part of the confusion derives from the jack rabbit's really being a hare, and the Belgian hare's really being a rabbit. The Killer actually is a cotton tail rabbit of the genus *Sylvilagus*.

The rabbit is smaller than the hare and has shorter legs and ears. Its young are born in underground burrows which it sometimes digs itself. At other times, it uses a burrow abandoned by a badger, groundhog, or woodchuck. The young rabbits are born without hair and with their eyes closed. The rabbit breeds like, well, a rabbit. There are from two to six young in a family and there may be several litters each year. The rabbit can bite; it has a double cutting edge on its upper front teeth.

The cottontail weighs between two and three pounds and is common through most of North America. It likes to stay in heavy thickets or thick grass where it can hide from its enemies which include birds of prey, coyotes, bobcats, wolves, and dogs. The rabbit depends on its speed and excellent hearing to defend itself against enemies. It is not overly bright. It does not live long enough to learn much. A rabbit is fully mature at eighteen months, middle aged at five years, and senile at ten years. The rabbit communicates through its senses of sight, smell, and hearing. It hears signals made by movements such as a body rustling in the grass or another rabbit signaling alarm by stamping on the ground with its hind feet. The rabbit makes low nasal grunts during sexual contact and a high treble scream or squeal to signal distress. It is a strict vegetarian and eats mostly bark, herbs, and grass. Our neighborhood rabbits appear to eat mostly grass, clover, and birdseed. While they often appear in the daytime, particularly in early morning and late afternoon, they come out mostly at night.

39

The sun was high in the sky, and the fight of the century was about to begin. A hush fell over the crowd as the referee and judges were introduced. The crowd looked on in awe as the Killer came in from the woods and made her way, thumpity, thumpity up to the ring. As was her custom, she was the first to step through the ropes. The crowd roared! The Killer nodded an acknowledgement, flexed her front paws, smoothed her whiskers, danced a little jig to loosen up the legs, and sat on the stool in her corner. After fifty-two fights, she showed little emotion.

The challenger slowly approached from behind low bushes where she had been hiding. She stopped in amazement, stomped her front hoof to signal danger, and pushed her ears forward toward the noise, a mixture of cheers and hisses from the gathering crowd. Her trainer, Murphy the Mole, urged her forward and she stepped tentatively and trembling into the ring. The roar from the crowd reached a frenzied pitch. A few old timers nodded to each other acknowledging that they now realized Bimbo the Challenger did, indeed, have a secret weapon. The Killer also recognized that something was dramatically different from any of the fifty-two previous fights. What was this secret weapon? It was simply that the challenger actually had shown up for the fight! This had never before happened. In all the other fifty-two fights, the challenger, after hearing of The Killer's awesome reputation, had been so overwhelmed with fright that he or she had simply refused to show up. In each case, The Killer had, of course, won by forfeit. But this fight was different; the challenger was standing, if not boldly, at least on her own four feet, right there in the ring with The Killer.

While the crowd stood, screaming and shouting, the referee called the two combatants to the center of the ring and gave them their pre-fight instructions. The instructions were simple though somewhat biased toward the champion: no horning in, no tail swishing, no splitting hares, and no hare pulling. This out of the way, the referee asked if there were any questions. Although the challenger was thought to have asked for a sample from the box of thatch, her voice was lost in noise and confusion. The two combatants were told to return to their corners and, at the sound of the bell, to come out fighting.

DONG! The bell rang and the fight was on. Bimbo, the challenger stepped forward and looked all around for the box of thatch. In her search, she almost ran into The Killer. To brace herself against a possible collision, Bimbo raised her front hoof. The startled Killer, still befuddled at the idea of a challenger's actually showing up for a fight, thought the hoof was going to come down on her dainty head. She fainted dead away!

The crowd screamed and pressed forward. Some were thought to have been trampled in the melee. The referee began his count. One, two, three, four, five, six, seven, eight, nine, ten! Then he continued counting until he reached at least one hundred! The Killer was still out! The referee finally raised the challenger's front hoof and declared her the winner! A new champion was born! The new champion, Bimbo the Deer, looked in bewilderment at the roaring crowd, flinched from the unconstrained pounding of her trainer, Murphy the Mole, and murmured something that sounded like "I can't stand all this violence and bloodshed!" Trembling with fear and frantic of being overwhelmed by the pressing crowd, she sprang out of the ring, bowled over a few fans in the ringside seats, plowed a furrow through the milling crowd, and disappeared into the deep woods. She was never again seen in these parts. The Killer, now renamed the "Faint Hearted," recovered sufficiently to return to her burrow, settle down to a typical bunny life and, by the end of the summer, rear two broods of six bunnies each.

VII. The Pessimist and the Optimist

Should Mousy flee the skulking cat
Or stand and face his fearsome foe?
The answer to such trials as that
I must confess I do not know!

40

I was tired and somewhat discouraged. For several weeks, I had worked hard at a job that was not going well. I had become reasonably certain the task was beyond my capabilities but I hated to give up. I've heard so much about how perseverance against all odds is the way to success. How can one avoid feelings of failure from trying and giving up or from persevering when all is lost? How can one know when to quit and when to keep on trying?

The morning breeze was soft and the air was warm. Perhaps this was a good time to put aside my worries and spend an hour or two outdoors lying in my hammock and reading a book. Sometimes just getting away from a concern for a short time has lead to my being able to approach it later from a new perspective. I collected the few things I needed to ensure my comfort and made my way to the side yard.

A hammock in a shady spot, a pillow under one's head, a glass of iced tea, and a good book to read, these make for a perfect summer day! Cleopatra the Cat followed me out and lay on the large, flat rock just beyond the hammock. She quickly fell fast asleep. Squeaks the Squirrel bounced over and joined us. She found a comfortable place on the limb of a small tree just to my left and stretched out on it. I was glad to have her company. I put my book aside, lay back on my pillow, and asked Squeaks what was going on around the yard.

"Oh, about the usual things," she said. "Don't know if you can see him from where you're flopped, but away over there behind that pine tree, I see Mopey the Squirrel doing what he always does when he's not doing something else. Can you hear him?"

I acknowledged that, while I could hear some squeaking and chirping, I could not make out what it was about. "I'm too comfortable to sit up or listen hard," I said. "Why don't you just tell me about it?"

Squeaks stared hard in the direction she had indicated and responded, "He sees a few old acorns up there. They're caught in a crack between a limb and the tree trump about half way up to the sky. He wants 'em but is sure he can't get 'em. He's just sitting there on the ground looking up at 'em and moaning. Says they're too high up, probably can't reach 'em, somebody else will beat him to 'em, and probably rotten by now anyway. Says he might slip on the slick bark, flail, and break a leg.

"There comes another squirrel up to the tree. He's talking to Mopey. Says he'll boot him up so he can reach the first limb. Mopey is politely defusing. Says somebody might get their back hurt. Big lie-ability suit! Courts! Lawyers! Judges! Banging gravels! Hung juries! Too big a chance to take. Other squirrel is climbing the tree. He has the acorns. Bringing 'em down. Hmm. He threw them down on Mopey's feet and stomped off. Mopey is looking at the acorns. Says if they were any good the other squirrel would have kept 'em. He is going off and just leaving 'em lying there. Oh, well. As the saying goes, you can lead a squirrel to water but you can't make him think."

I offered that I thought the saying was about a "horse" and making him "drink."

Squeaks said, "Hmm. Never seen a horse around here. And why would you make it drink if it wasn't Thursday?"

I did not answer.

Squeaks said, "Mopey is what I think you call a 'pestimist.' If an opera... uh, opportunity were to knock down his door, he would fuss it up for making too much noise. He looks on the bark side of everything. Never sees delight. Can't see roses for the horns. Can't see the lawn for the dandy lions. Wears a belt AND 'spenders. Never flails 'cause he never tries. Gets along OK 'cause others feel sorry for him and give him things. Might as well. He'll take your stuff if you're not looking. Doesn't bother him. Says it's probably stuff you stole from him when HE wasn't looking. You've heard about a snitch in time saves time! Well, that's him."

I said I thought that was a "stitch" and saves "nine."

Squeaks looked puzzled and said, "Really? Ohhh. I knew he stitched a few hickory nuts from me but I didn't know he stitched NINE of 'em. Ohhh." I did not comment.

Squeaks sat there awhile scratching her head and twitching her tail. Then something off in the other direction caught her attention.

"Over there," she said. "It's Scampy the Squirrel. Over by your big, round flower bed. He's stalking around the outer edge of it." Squeaks head went up, left, down, right, up, left, down, right as she followed Scampy's progress. She continued, "He's going round and round and round and round and round. Can you hear what he's saying? He says he wants to see where it goes. Says everybody knows there's a pot of gourds at the end of the rainbow, so there must be something good at the end of your bower garden. Says he is going to be resistent, deadfast, determined, and tenacious. Says he'll never give up. Gets an idea and sticks to it. That's him. What do you call his kind? An optometrist? Yes! That kind finds roses on thorn bushes. Doesn't wear a belt OR 'spenders! Finds silver clouds back of every black lining. When some ask, 'Any milk?' he says, 'Pass the cream!'"

41

Squeaks stopped looking and stretched out flat on her tree limb, hung her front paws over the edges, rested her chin on the limb, and seemed to be in deep thought. As she swished her tail back and forth, she continued, "Pestimists and optometrists! Swish is right and swish is wrong? How do you know when to give up; how do you know when a nuff is a nuff? How do you know if you ought to keep on running when you're so tired you've forgotten whether you're running to or running fro? I can tell you, but I'll bet you won't like the answer.

"The truth is, you don't know 'til after the sun goes down! Then you can look back and see how things trimmed out. If Scampy bumps his nose on a big pot of gourds, everybody will say, 'Told you so! See how sticking to your glue through flim and flam always plays off? But, if he just ends up going round and round and round until his tail falls off, everybody will say, 'What a dummy!' If he quits early and somebody else finds a pot of gourds around there somewhere, they'll all say, 'He gave up too soon! He just didn't have the courage of his conflictions.'

"And what about Mopey? If he'd climbed that tree and flopped off and broken his ear, everybody would be saying, 'Stupid thing to do! Got his just berserks, he did! Never should have climbed that tree!' And if I go over there after I leave here and find nine good nuts in that bunch Mopey walked off and left, everybody will say Mopey is a quitter who preserves all the bad luck he gets. So, do you want to know when you should keep crying and when you should give up? Well, I'll tell you! But wait 'til the sun flops down and I can look back on how things turned up. That's the only time you can chew for surety."

Squeaks gets very serious sometimes, and this was one of those occasions. As though thinking something through for the first time, she spoke as if she were talking to herself as much as to me. She said, "I think pestimists and optometrists are extremish, and that's bad. Mopey and Scampy are always getting themselves in pickles, jams, and hot tamales. I think that's 'cause they're so extremish.

"Mopey thinks most everything about life is bad, and that the things that aren't bad are worse. He's got very low selfish steam. Doesn't think he is worth mush. Keeps his head down so he can't see his face. Others always try to jeer him up by telling him things are worse than he thinks. Doesn't do him any good though. He seems completely remitted to gloom and doom. I worry that he might go try to hang himself, but... nah! He'd be afraid of a flop from a loose noose or broke rope. You want to know how he got the way he is? I think I know. Started when he counted the toes on his back paws and found he has only five on each paw. He's reformed that way, you know. All the other squirrels have six. And, anyway...."

I stopped her there and said, "Wait a minute. That's not true. All squirrels have only five toes on their back paws."

"What?" said Squeaks, as she pulled her back paw around in front of her nose. "Let's see. One. Two. Uh. What comes after two? Ohhh! I think I'm reformed too. Is that bad?"

"And, then, there's Scampy," continued Squeaks, seemingly forgetting her deformity. "Why do you think he's so optimistical? I bet he has low selfish steam, too. Or maybe it's too high. Anyway, I bet he's afraid to look at what's real and submit there are things in life that rub the wrong way. I bet he's afraid to stop laughing 'cause he'd start crying and couldn't quit."

Squeaks paused here for a minute, gave her ears a good scratching, tried again to count her toes, gave up, and continued her discourse. "They're both extremish 'cause they caught low selfish steam. Ohhh. Bet it's going around. Bet I'm going to catch it too. Can I take a pill or get a shot for it or something?"

Cleopatra, apparently aroused by Squeak's moaning, stood up, arched her back, stretched, yawned, padded over to a shady area next to the hammock, checked out a spot on the grass, sat, cleaned her front paws, looked up at Squeaks, and joined the conversation. "Low self esteem is not something you catch," she said, speaking directly to Squeaks. "I do not think you need to worry about it. You seem to be adequately secure, reasonably realistic, and of sufficiently low intellect to avoid both low self esteem and extreme behavior. You seem to see yourself as you really are and accept what you see. How you manage to do that is, of course, beyond my comprehension. If I were you, I simply would lie down and die of sheer mortification."

"Ohhh," said Squeaks in an awed voice, "you are just chuck full of wise slayings and generous-osities."

Cleopatra yawned out of boredom and continued, "Intelligent creatures cannot stand the thought of not being something very special. So, because most are quite ordinary in most respects, they do not like themselves very much. And, while it is true that their low self esteem is based on how they feel about themselves, that is not all there is to it. A major factor here is how they feel about the Creator and themselves as part of the Creator's creation."

Squeaks, bounced up and down in excitement, almost slipped off her limb, recovered, and shouted, "I know! I know! I know all about that Cremator! All! All! All!"

Cleopatra frowned, twitched her tail, shook her head, and said, "The word here is 'Creator.'"

"Swat I said," argued Squeaks. "Preacher Possum told me all about Him. This Cremator gets you burned to gnashes if you don't pay up and fly right."

Cleopatra's frown deepened as she continued. "As I was saying, a major characteristic of those with low self esteem is their inaccurate thinking, such as seeing everything as black or white, making mountains out of mole hills and mole hills out of mountains, filtering out what they do not wish to see, assuming the worst—or the best, and assuming others are out to get them when others actually have not even noticed they are there.

"Low self esteem, believing one is of little or no value, comes from believing the Creator's creation—and we as part of it—is of little or no value. Such negative beliefs probably result from having been treated with disdain rather than with respect. What can they do about this? Well, they can at least try to assume control of their thinking. They can refuse to allow negative and inaccurate thinking to become a habit. But how can they recognize that their thinking in inaccurate? Well, for one thing, inaccurate thinking often results in ideas that are either dazzlingly positive or bleakly negative. Accurate thinking more likely will leave them in the gray area between those two extremes. And perhaps they can try to keep their eyes open, be alert to outside happenings, be aware of inside feelings, and be less resistant to ideas that may go counter to their wishes. Also, they can make opportunities to put themselves around those who will provide the kind of keen insights and genuine affirmation I so generously have been providing here. What else can they do? I do not know and, if the truth be known, I do not particularly care."

Squeaks again bounced up and down in her excitement and cried, "I know! I know! I'll tell you how I fixed things. I got all optimistical about learning Latins and Greeks so I could depress that old crow who caws in six languages. But, then, I got all pestimistical when I tired so hard my head hurt. I derided to take a good look at myself. First, one day when I was feeling brave, I took just a little peek. Then I checked to see if I got any busted legs from it. I didn't. So, since I still was feeling grave, I took a longer peek. And checked again for busted bones. Gradually jerked myself up to taking a good, hard look. Saw lots of things I didn't like. But looked around and saw nobody else was looking. Decided to try to change things I didn't like about me but to be real-istic about it. Decided to dump the Greeks and just learn Latins. Didn't completely recede. But I learned.... What did you say comes after two? Yeah, I learned three words. Don't remember what they were, but I learned 'em. After that, I liked myself better just 'cause I had tired so hard. I like myself! I really AM special! After that, I didn't sorry too mush whether I was pushing too hard or giving up too soon. I just did the best I knew to do, checked when the sun went down to see what perked and what didn't perk, made any 'justments that seemed seasonable, and got on with my life."

Squeaks paused to catch her breath, took a good grip on her tree limb, hung her head down so she could look straight at Cleopatra, and asked, "Wasn't that 'bout the wisest stuff you ever heard? Don't I know just about EVERYTHING?"

Cleopatra moaned softly, rolled her eyes, and answered, "While this seems to be one of those times when you, surely by accident, stumbled onto some truths, I can assure you that you absolutely, positively, definitely, indubitably, unequivocally do NOT know everything."

Squeaks looked puzzled and said, "Sure glad I don't know everything 'cause I think it would make my head hurt again. She turned around, stretched and scratched a bit, climbed down the tree, and continued, "Well, got to get back to doing nutting, which is what I was doing when you came out here. See you again yesterday or the day before!" And she was off.

Cleopatra shook her head, swished her tail, looked after Squeak's retreating figure, and moaned, "There, except for the grace of I, goes God!"

She growled softly and strode purposefully back toward the house. I lay back in the hammock, took up my book, stretched into a more comfortable position, and relaxed for the first time in several weeks.

VIII. Merlin the Magic

"You like my shoes, my shirt, my tie?
He asked, with gun held to my ear.
"Of course I do!" was my reply,
For words are cheap when choice is dear.

42

I have a bird feeder in the back yard that I keep filled with sunflower seeds. The chickadees, titmice, and goldfinch, in particular, love me for this, so I like to think. I have had a great deal of trouble keeping squirrels and raccoons away from the feeder. The "keep out" signs simply did not work. At first, the feeder was mounted on top of a ten-foot plastic pipe. I tried putting grease on the pipe so that, when large animals tried to climb the pipe, they would slide off. But the plastic was soft and they simply dug their claws deeper and climbed anyway. Next I attached a wire to the limb of an oak tree twenty-five feet in the air and hooked the feeder to the bottom end of the wire. The squirrels and raccoons climbed the tree, walked out on the limb, and slid down the wire to the feeder. It had been time for desperate action, so I had taken it.

I purchased a ten-foot galvanized steel pipe and bolted one end under the eves of the house. The pipe stuck straight out with the far end about fifteen feet above the ground. I used a piece of wire to suspend the feeder from the end of the pipe. I put grease on the pipe and a metal baffle on the wire between the pipe and the feeder. Even if the squirrels and raccoons did not slide off the greased metal pipe, they would never be able to get around the baffle. It had been a week now and nothing but birds had been able to get to the feeder. So, last night, I went to bed and dropped off into a deep sleep, secure in the knowledge that human intelligence and ingenuity had prevailed and that no wild creature was going to outdo me.

My pleasant dreams came to an abrupt and shattering end when a loud crash from the direction of the kitchen pierced the stillness of the night. Burglars! Tornado! Tree falling on house! Earthquake! These were thoughts that flashed through my sleepy brain as I groped for my eyeglasses, turned on a light, and rushed to the kitchen. The kitchen light showed everything to be in its place. A sleepy Cleopatra raised her head, yawned mightily, and asked why in the world I was shining lights in her eyes in the middle of the night. Obviously, the source of the noise was outside the kitchen window where I had fastened the pipe for the bird feeder. I went back to the bedroom for my slippers, turned on the outside floodlights, and went outside. And there it was!

The weight of an animal had been too much for the bolts that held the pipe under the eves. The pipe, feeder, and part of a board from the edge of the roof were lying in a heap on the ground. Apparently, in falling, the pipe had struck the window sill and gouged a small rip in its outer edge. The ground was covered with sunflower seeds. Sitting on top of the destruction, with her paws and mouth full of seeds, was none other than Jimmie the Racketycoon.

She seemed startled by the sudden flood of light and by my indignant approach. But she thought quickly and apparently decided the best defense was a strong offense. She glared at me and roared, "Just where were you when this happened? Why weren't you here to look after things. Good thing I came along when I did or they would have torn down the whole house. There were fifteen or twenty of them, all armed with guns, axes, and long teeth. They were orange and green and had red, glowing eyes about this big!" She held out her front paws to indicate a circle about twelve inches in diameter and, then, continued her story. "Flames came out of their mouths when they breathed, and they burned up everything within half a mile. All fifty or sixty of them started after me at the same time. Good thing you were not out here! They would have scared you to death! When they saw me, they got scared and ran off in every direction, all two hundred of them. Now, just what are you going to do about all this mess? Why don't you just go back in and let it go until morning? I volunteer to stay here, watch, and make sure they don't come back."

I didn't say anything. I stared at the damage and then gave my full attention to Jimmie. She winced at my angry glare, knowing she had not fooled me. She tried a different approach. Her voice softened to a low whine and she said, "I bet you think I had something to do with this, but I was just an innocent bystander. I slept soundly all night and didn't know a thing about it until tomorrow morning. Uhh. You may think I'm Jimmie, but I'm not. I have a sister that looks just like me and she does all kinds of bad stuff. So, before you start blaming me for things, remember I am just a poor, innocent, helpless, little creature who never did anybody any wrong."

Here, she stopped talking, sobbed an appropriate minute or two to emphasize her innocence and helplessness, and then continued, "I can't help it if I have a bad sister that looks like me. It's just not fair that I get blamed all the time." She sobbed another minute before abruptly turning off the tears and trying another approach. "Tell you what we will do, you and I," she said in her usual pert and chummy voice. "We will track down my cruel sister and make her pay. We will make her come back here and fix everything back the way it was. You can lock her in your workshop where you keep all those cans and bags of seeds. You can keep her there until she starves to death and promises not to cause any more troubles. Do you want to start first thing tomorrow, or do you want to wait until maybe next year when the weather is better? It is all up to you now. I have done everything I can do to be helpful to you."

I had not yet said a single word. But, now was the time to speak, and I said a single word. Shaking my finger in her face, I shouted, "GO!"

She opened the bag she always wears around her neck, stuffed it half full of seeds, and raced off into the darkness. I went back to bed and dreamed of ways to get revenge on unruly raccoons.

This morning, I repaired the window sill and the eve of the house, strung a tight wire thirty feet in the air between two tall trees that grew about seventy feet apart, and hung the bird feeder from the wire with a nylon string. In the afternoon, I sat in my chair on the porch and read my latest book from the library, a book on hypnotism.

It was almost dark when Rosie the Raccoon came in for a snack. She was almost two hours later than usual. I asked her why she was late. She said, "Well, I guess you know I have three new little ones. And the little nippers are at the awkward age: too young to be intelligent and too old to be cute. I can't take them with me and I can't leave them by themselves. And you know how hard it is to get a sitter! Finally got one but, as you can see, I'm running late."

I had some slices of stale bread and some chicken bones I had saved for her. I brought these out and she took them one at a time to the bird bath, climbed into the bird bath, dipped them into the water, and wolfed them down. Between trips, she checked me out to see what I was doing. She asked me about the book I was reading. I said, "It is a book about hypnotism. That's when you put someone to sleep and ask them questions and tell them to do things. The book says you can hypnotize somebody and tell them they do not like sugar, for example. And, then, after you wake them up, they will not be so keen on eating cakes, pies, and other things that have lots of sugar in them. Sounds kind of doubtful to me, but that is what the book says. It does say, though, that you can't get a person to do something that goes against their basic beliefs. Maybe that's the secret of it. Maybe you can only get people to do things they want to do anyway."

And then I had an interesting thought. I said, "I suppose you know about all the trouble we had here last night. What if this book is correct and I could hypnotize Jimmie and make her stop lying and stealing! Do you think it's worth a try?"

Rosie had finished most of her snack by now and was lying on the brick floor at the corner of the porch. She was thoughtful for a moment and then replied, "No! I don't think that would be a good idea. It never works to try to MAKE someone what she is not. You really cannot MAKE anyone be good. You might make her ACT good, but you can't make her BE good! If you just want her to ACT good, maybe your idea would work. But, that way, you would never know what Jimmie is really like. You would have a robot. If that is what you want, go ahead. But you might just as well strangle her and go buy yourself a robot. That would be easier."

"If," Rosie continued, "you want an intelligent creature, one that can make choices, you should let her be. You might tell her what you wish were different about her. You might tell her you wish she would change. But that probably will just make her defensive. The only constructive thing you can do to encourage her to change is tell her how her attitudes and actions leave you feeling. That might motivate her to change—that is, if she cares anything about your feelings. But she has to do the changing for herself. There is no other way. That's the way the system is set up and you can't beat the system. Did I ever tell you the story about Merlin the Magic? I didn't think I did. He tried to force someone to change, somewhat the way you are thinking about forcing Jimmie to change. I want one more piece of that bread and then I will tell you about him." She grasped a slice of bread in her front paws and, staggering on her two hind legs, made her way to the bird bath. She threw the bread into the water, climbed up, lay in the water, and leisurely finished off the bread.

43

The raccoon, or *Procyon lotor*, is certainly one of my favorite animals. It is a small furry animal that is related to the bear. The common raccoon, when full grown, is about thirty-two inches long from nose to tip of tail and weighs from twenty to twenty-five pounds. It has a stout body covered with long, coarse hair. It has a bushy, grayish-white tail with black rings. The nose is sharp and delicate. Each eye is surrounded by a patch of black within a circle of white hair. This gives it the cunning look that fits its mischievous nature. It has a keen sense of smell and sensitive, prehensile paws that are shaped much like the human hand.

While a raccoon will eat almost anything, some of its favorites in the wild are frogs, crayfish, other fresh-water animals, berries, other fruit, and bird eggs. Our resident raccoons seem to have a strong preference for chicken, dog food, peanuts, watermelon, and corn. While most of their foraging is at night, our resident raccoons quite often visit as early as noon.

The raccoon usually lives in a hollow in a tree anywhere from ground level to sixty or seventy feet in the air. However, it sometimes lives in a cave, under large rocks, or under a house. While it always is an avid eater, it has an insatiable appetite in autumn. Before winter sets in, it builds a layer of body fat to keep it healthy over the winter. It does not hibernate in the winter. One winter I told our neighbor's child that I had not seen our raccoons for several days. His response was, "Yeah, they've done gone doormat." He was almost correct. Actually, they go semi-dormant. They prefer to curl up in their dens and sleep for long hours during the winter. They prefer to avoid cold wind and snow.

The male raccoon usually is polygamous. However, the female is very choosy about a mate and often will reject several males until she finds one to her liking. The mother raccoon rears the young with no help from the male. A baby raccoon weighs about two ounces at birth and is blind and helpless. However, it is a lusty feeder and grows rapidly on its mother's rich milk. Litters usually consist of two to seven babies. Our resident raccoons always bring in either three or four little ones.

The raccoon is one of the more intelligent animals and, as with all intelligent creatures, presents a range of personalities. The raccoon also is one of the most articulate animals. It has thirteen to fourteen distinct calls with many nuances of each. These calls include trills, screams, grunts, churring, and purring. The range of sounds helps the mother communicate with the young and keep her family together during their nightly foraging trips.

Rosie had finished her snack. She climbed down from the bird bath, checked the surrounding ground for stray sunflower seeds from the bird feeder, and slowly moseyed back to the porch. She settled herself solidly into her place on the porch floor and told me the following story.

44

"Merlin the Magic was the oldest raccoon in the forest. Some said he was four hundred years old; others said he was at least that old when he was first born. Anyway, he lived in the hollow of an ancient oak. He lived alone. He had no friends. In fact, animals rarely ever ventured into the part of the forest where he lived. They were afraid to go near him for they were afraid of his magic. The few animals who did, on rare occasions, go near, were wanderers who were strangers to the area and did not know of Merlin's magic. Stories were told of animals who ventured into Merlin's edge of the forest and were never seen again. Stories were told of the loud-mouthed duck who, because he awakened Merlin out of a sound sleep, had his beak turned into a turnip, and of the deer who, because he sharpened its horns on Merlin's tree, had his horns turned into carrots. Merlin was thought to be able to conjure up spells, put hexes on anyone who annoyed him, turn bushes into bears and bears into bushes, and fry eggs well done without scorching the edges. In short, Merlin was a fearsome creature, the very thought of which caused babies to scream in the night and adults to shake in fear and look the other way.

"But, as usual, the truth was somewhat different from the rumors. The truth was that, while Merlin could cast a spell or lay a hex when he was in the mood, he rarely was in the mood. In fact, he was a very sad and lonely raccoon. He missed not having friends, companionship, and someone to love him. He tried very hard to make friends. He would go to the edge of his part of the forest, sit on a low-hanging limb until some unsuspecting animal came by, and drop down on their head and scream in their ear, 'Hello! Good morning! Let's be friends!' The poor recipient of this invitation would scream in fright, shake Merlin off its head, run for its life, and tell all the other animals how it almost had been gobbled up by a big, gray demon. And Merlin would go back to his tree, climb up into his den, curl up, and weep.

"One dark and stormy night when he was unusually lonely, Merlin journeyed through the forest to the den of Sylvia, the widowed Raccoon who he thought would make him a wonderful mate. He sat peering through the front window of her den wondering how to get her attention. He saw her pet canary singing in its cage and her cat curled up on the rug in front of the fireplace. As a way of introducing himself, he cast a very small and insignificant spell on the canary. The canary growled, ripped through the bars of its tiny cage, swooped down on the unfortunate cat, and devoured it alive. This greatly displeased the widow Sylvia. She screamed for help, dialed 911, and beat Merlin over the head with a broom. Poor Merlin, immensely puzzled over what could have gone wrong, ran back to his tree, hid under his bed, and did not come out again for two hours or fifty years.

"And then one day, Merlin, while he was deep in thought about his need for friendship, conversation, and love, realized that he needed to define exactly what he wanted. Being very intelligent, this was easy for him to do. First, he wanted someone who would love him. Well, maybe not just love. He wanted someone who would worship and adore him, someone whose heart would skip a beat at the mere sight of him, someone who thought endearing thoughts of him all her waking hours and dreamed sweet dreams of him when she slept. That was part of what he wanted. And then, there was something else. He wanted a friend with whom he could discuss things, important things, like why it always rains on golf days, what spells worked best on elephants and tadpoles, the relationships between hexes and hiccups, and why, when you put ten socks in the washing machine, only nine come out. This would need to be a different animal because he wanted this one to be able to think of things other than how much it worshiped and adored him. While thinking these long thoughts, Merlin had what seemed to him a most wondrous idea. He would cast a spell on an animal and MAKE it into someone who would love him, and he would cast a spell on another animal and MAKE it into someone who would be his friend!

"The very next day, Merlin combed his hair, put on his best suit and silk necktie, took up his walking cane (which also was a magic wand), climbed down his front steps, and started through the woods. He reasoned that, if he walked quietly and far enough, he eventually would come upon a couple of animals whom he could MAKE into what he wanted. And, sure enough, very soon he spotted, right at the edge of his part of the forest, right next to the crooked creek that marked the boundary, sitting on a dead log, half in the sun, just above the laughing waters, a fat female frog. It was an idyllic setting: the frog sitting on the log, the flowers scattered across the landscape, the trees wearing their brightest green, birds singing as they partook of the ripened blackberries, the air cool and sweet. What a place for romance!

"Merlin hid behind a patch of blackberry bushes, reached in his hip pocket, pulled out his book on magic, thumbed through the index, found the correct page, and read quietly and quickly

about how to turn a frog into a beautiful raccoon who unfailingly would worship and adore Merlin the Magic. He carefully followed the rules of hexism spelled out in the magic book. He marked three parallel lines on the ground with his cane (which also was a magic wand), looked first to the east, then to the north, then to the west, and then to the south, repeated this seven times seven times, almost fell down from dizziness, picked up his hat which had fallen off, pulled himself loose from where his britches had caught on a brier, walked silently to where the unsuspecting frog sat, eased up behind her and, before she could croak or jump out of the way, planted a big kiss squarely on her mouth. The magic was instantaneous. The frog went 'poof' into thin air and, in its place, there appeared a lovely female raccoon who looked up at Merlin with love-stricken eyes, clasped her dainty paws together, batted the long lashes of her beautiful green eyes, and began to ooh and ahh over the very sight of Merlin the Magic.

"Merlin was delighted, but his day's work was not yet finished. He took his new love by the paw and lead her to his den. Here, he moved his set of incantation encyclopedias from their prominent position in the center of his bookcase and placed his newly-created love on the shelf in their stead. Here she would be out of his way but still be where he could look at her and easily pull her down when he wanted her. And, then, he headed back to the edge of the forest.

"It now was time for Merlin to MAKE a friend. He would use the first creature he could find. He went first to the idyllic spot where he had found the frog. The setting no longer was idyllic! The log seemed to have shriveled and sprouted with harsh-gray fungus, the flowers were wilted and dead, the trees hid behind ghastly, knobby, evil limbs, the birds were gone, and the blackberries had rotted on the wilted, briar-strewn bushes. The hot, dank air hung heavily over the putrid brown waters of the stream. Merlin walked past this desolate place into the deep woods. All was silent and ominous. The clouds lay close and the sun hid its face. The distant rumbling of thunder warned of storms and destruction. Merlin walked on looking for some sign of life. And at last, just when he had almost given up hope, he spotted his quarry.

"Sitting on the ground, twitching its antennas, thinking of nothing in particular (since it was about as bright as a rotten cucumber) was a large, green hopgrasser. Merlin had planned ahead and he knew just what to do. He pounced on the hapless hopper, banged it on the head seven times seven with his cane (which also was a magic wand), and said the appropriate four or five or nineteen thousand magic words. The effect was immediate. There was a flash of lightning, and the hopgrasser disappeared in a cloud of smoke. Merlin stood back and used his hat to fan the smoke away. And there, sitting in the very spot was... well, a hopgrasser! Not the very same hopgrasser, of course, but a very wise, knowledgeable, educated, literate, congenial hopgrasser, the perfect friend and companion for Merlin the Magic.

"Merlin introduced himself to his new friend, sat and conversed with him for a few hours or fifteen or eleven-hundred years just to get the feel of good company, and then took him by the antenna and led him home. He put him in the cupboard where he could close the door on him for, as you know, good friends are not necessarily pretty to look at. Here Merlin could open the door and pull him out whenever he wanted learned conversation or congenial companionship. And then Merlin curled up in his chair, slept soundly, and dreamed sweet dreams.

"From then on, for the next five or six months or ninety-seven years, Merlin was a happy raccoon. His love loved him—constantly, persistently, and passionately. His friend was the perfect companion and intellectual associate. Merlin needed nothing else to make his life perfect and complete. Or so he thought.

"One day, when Marlin was a bit bored with being worshipped and adored, a bit tired of listening to the cooing and sighing of his love, and somewhat weary of seeing the pinning and passionate creature sitting on the book shelf, he managed a short reprieve by putting her out in his side yard where she could get a bit of sun which might make her just a little less clingy and dependent. He also closed the cabinet door on his friend and companion and put earplugs into his own ears so he would not have to listen to continuous charming and entertaining talk. Sometimes it is nice just to be alone with one's own thoughts. In this mood, he fell asleep and slept for some five minutes or twenty or thirty years. And then he awoke. But, perhaps he did not awaken just yet. Perhaps he dreamed. Who can tell? Or, is there really any difference?

"In any event, it seemed to Merlin that he was rising from his chair, putting on his sunglasses, and going out to get his love before she got so much sun that he would have to slather her with sunburn lotion. He went to the spot in the sun where he had left her. She was not there! Well, it was all right for her to move around a bit. She could worship and adore him from one place as well as another. He looked around the edges of the yard and found them empty. And then he thought he heard a faint voice coming from the vicinity of the creek. He walked a short distance in that direction, and there she was. She was sitting on a stump, weeping softly. Merlin hid behind a tree and peered around it to see what was happening and to whom she had been talking. And then he noticed, sitting near her under the shade of a toadstool, a large, warty frog. Merlin's love was weeping and talking to the frog!

"Merlin listened as she said, 'I love him dearly! He is wonderful! I can't live without him! Being away from him and sitting out in the sun was more than I could bear! I want to be near him every moment of every day! I want to feel the touch of his dear fur, hear the sound of his tender voice! I don't have any choice. I MUST love him dearly! But... but... I want to be a frog! I was meant to be a frog! Please kiss me so that I will turn back into a beautiful frog!'

"Was Merlin still asleep and having a bad dream? Did this really happen? Does it make any difference? All this was too much for Merlin to bear. He returned to his den and waited. Soon his love returned. While her eyes were still red from weeping, she welcomed him joyously, even ardently, and clung to him passionately when he put her back in her place on the bookshelf.

"Merlin avoided his love for the next few days, or the next four-hundred and fifty years. He was not so sure he liked being worshipped and adored by someone who had no choice in the matter. He spent more and more time with his friend and companion in an attempt to get his help in figuring out what life was all about. But his friend, Merlin found to his surprise and disappointment, was no help at all.

"His friend, Merlin discovered, had a fatal flaw. Merlin's magic had made him so wise, knowledgeable, educated, articulate, and congenial that the friend could not conceive of the idea that everyone was not equally wise, knowledgeable, educated, articulate, and congenial. As a result, the friend made all kinds of mistakes. He told his banker he should quit the bank, give away all the money, and be a philosopher; the banker followed the advice and ended up in jail. Next, Merlin's friend took an opossum's last few coins and bought the opossum a chemistry set and a microscope; the opossum looked at an ant through the wrong end of the microscope and died of fright. Later, the friend told a wren how to correct her flight patterns so as to get more miles per grub worm; the wren tried it, went into a spin, crashed, and lost her tail feathers. Merlin began to realize that one could not be truly wise unless he had once been unwise, that wisdom is learning from mistakes, and that true wisdom comes only to those who recognize the possibility that they also can be very foolish.

"At this point, Merlin awoke from his deep sleep and bad dreams if, indeed, he had been asleep and had been dreaming. He began to see things clearly that he had not realized before. First, he realized that having someone who worshipped and adored him because she had no choice was not very fulfilling. He could have hired an actress to play the part, or he could have built a robot and programmed it to act that way. If she did not worship and adore him out of her own free choice, it was not worth a great deal. And the same thing was true of friendship and companionship. If the friend did not act out of his own free choice, his friendship was worth nothing.

"Second, Merlin learned the importance of the PROCESS of becoming. He realized that, while the final product may be the only thing of any importance for inanimate objects such as automobiles and rocks, or unintelligent life such as trees or weeds, there really is no such thing as a final product when considering intelligent living creatures. He recognized that what we are today is an accumulation of our past behaviors, experiences, thoughts, and feelings; that our current operating data are the data accumulated from our past interactions, awareness, and choices. We ARE our past. To deny our past would be to deny the very essence of our present and future! And, then, there was another thing Merlin learned that might have been even more important. He learned there must be an interdependence between two lovers or two friends, mutual giving and receiving, a sharing and merging while retaining individual boundaries. Without these, love and friendship become antagonistic relationships between slave and master or between the pretender and the gullible, or they become a drama acted out by two desperate clowns who are afraid to stop smiling.

"After taking up his cane (which also was a magic wand), Merlin gently lifted his love down from her place on the bookshelf and opened the cabinet door and took down his hopgrasser friend. He marched them straight to the places where he had originally found them. Without a word, he cast an unhex on both, thus returning them to their original conditions. Without even a glance backward, he walked back to his den.

"What he did later is not known for certain; there are several versions. One story is that he had had his fill of lovers and friends and spent his remaining forty, or six hundred, years enjoying the peace and quite of living alone in his otherwise deserted edge of the forest. The other version, which all but the most cynical accept as being the more likely one, was that Merlin built a fire in his stove, ripped all his magic books into tiny pieces, and tossed the pieces into the fire. He then phoned the florist, the candy store, and the card shop and had posies, bonbons, and a lovely card sent to the widow Sylvia. Later in the week, he sent her a bright yellow canary in a shiny new cage, and a brown and yellow kitten who already was house broken. Still later, he put on his best suit and new silk necktie and made a proper call on the delighted widow. After a long and tender courtship, she came to... well, not exactly worship and adore him, but to love him tenderly for being the earnest, caring creature he had become. Merlin the Magnificent, as he now was called, also went out of his way to be helpful to those who needed help and kind to those who did not. He was delighted and surprised when fifty, or nine thousand, of his friends attended the ceremony when he and the widow Sylvia were wed."

45

Rosie yawned, stood up, and stretched. She said, "Telling stories uses up so many calories that I really get a hunger on. I surely would like to have a few more pieces of that bread or, maybe, some drumsticks."

I went in and brought out a few more scraps and held them out to her. She took them in her paws and sat down to eat. She was silent for a while and then said, "Don't know if you've thought about it but the GREAT RACCOON that created all things might have had some of the same thoughts Merlin had. Maybe SHE thought about creating animals who would always do and be just what SHE wanted. But SHE was smart enough to know they would only be robots. And one can get very lonely with just robots around. You can't really love a robot. And there are never any surprises, because a robot will do just what it is programmed to do. But, I think you are wondering how we can relate positively to others without making at least some effort to make them be just what we want them to be. Hmm. Maybe only the GREAT RACCOON can manage that."

I can't say Rosie was through eating because I don't think she would ever stop eating if the food didn't run out. But she was through for now because I didn't have any more scraps. She started her head-down, rear-up walk back to the woods. Her last words were, "Bet I owe that sitter a fortune. Have to pay dear because they don't like to come to that part of the woods because Jimmie will pick their pockets. You really MUST do something drastic about her!"

IX. Teddy the Toad

The peacock hung her lovely head
And furled her feathers in despair.
She'd heard the buzzard when he said
What ugly plumage peacocks wear.

46

I usually wear just socks in the house. Well, I mean, on my feet. Otherwise, I dress quite modestly or, maybe, even prudishly. I have a pair of old boat shoes on the porch that I slip into when I intend working in the yard. I used to just throw the shoes on the porch floor when I came in but, when our neighbor adopted a shoe hound, I started putting them on top of the barbecue grill where the shoe hound could not kidnap them and hold them for ransom. But recently the shoe hound made a bad slip somewhere and got caught, convicted, and thrown in the slammer. So, I don't have to worry about him any more, and I have gone back to just tossing my old shoes on the porch floor.

We have a porch toad named Teddy the Toad. Teddy enjoys lying on the cool, brick floor on hot summer days. He also likes to snack on the minor insects that run into a dead end when they meet the inside corner of the porch. They just sit there and wait for Teddy to hop over and take them in. The results are that the insect population on the porch stays within comfortable limits and Teddy has a bit of a weight problem. While, so it seems to me, there is nothing wrong with a toad being fat, Teddy thinks otherwise. Each evening before retiring for the night, he carefully measures his waistline to make sure he is not getting fatter. He vows that, if his waist ever measures more than six inches, he will go on a starvation diet until he is, again, under six inches in girth. Teddy also has a thing about being tall. He sits on his haunches as all toads do. But, unlike other toads, he holds his front legs almost straight out so that his head is as high in the air as he can get it. He is two inches tall and wishes to be taller. He knows that my lawn mower is set to cut the grass to two inches, so he checks his height every day by hopping down into the lawn grass and seeing if his head is at least even with the tallest grass. Sometimes he cheats a bit by standing partly on the grass instead of flat on the ground. When I have been slow about mowing the lawn, he goes into a panic because he thinks he is shrinking. And then he is a joy to behold when I mow the lawn anew and he, again, can almost see over the top. Teddy doesn't hurt anything, hopping around on the porch the way he does. He actually doesn't particularly help anything either. That is, if he decided to locate elsewhere, I think we could manage fine without him. We do have to step over him sometimes, and he gets fussy when I wash the porch down with the garden hose and wash him down in the process.

That morning I got up at the usual time, pulled a robe on over my pajamas, brushed the hair out of my eyes, and put on my socks. Then I went out to the porch, slipped my feet into my boat shoes, and walked out to pick up the newspaper. I had a vague feeling something was not quite right but could not put a finger, or a foot, on it. I thought the new gravel on the driveway might be just a little rougher than I had noticed before. Anyway, when I returned, I sat on the porch with the newspaper in my hands and kicked off my shoes. The left one seemed to quiver a bit, and then Teddy crawled out and flopped on the floor. I had worn him all the way to the street and back. He had not worn well.

As I said earlier, Teddy has a real thing about keeping his waistline under six inches and standing tall. But when he climbed out of the shoe, he appeared to be as big around as a saucer and only about a quarter of an inch tall. Other than that, he was in fine shape. He looked up at me kind of solemn like, checked out his new shape, let out a low moan, and went into a deep funk. This was the first time I realized that what I thought was his concern for his dimensions was, in fact, an obsession. Apparently he had been taking great pride in being the tallest and slimmest toad on the porch. Now he was the shortest and fattest. Of course, he also was the ONLY toad on the porch, but that didn't seem to enter into his calculations.

Anyway, I was sitting there with my shoes off, an unread newspaper on the table, and a funky toad at my feet. And I had not yet even had my first cup of coffee. That is a bad way to start a day.

Enters Squeaks the Squirrel! "Did you by any chance notice that you have not yet put down seeds for me?" she asked. "I try to keep a good altitude in the mornings but it's hard to do when I don't get fed. What's that?" she asked, pointing toward the low-lying toad. "Didn't know you had taken up frisbee throwing. Go ahead! I want to see you toss him!"

This kind of talk did little to lift Teddy's spirits. He just lay there glued to the floor and moaning softly. I told Squeaks what had happened. She sat there with her head cocked to one side, listened carefully, and then said, "I thought I heard somebody let out a plaintiff whale. "Must have been him. Bet you unconsciously did it on purpose. Bet it was a Freudian slap. Don't think you ever really took to him. Looks all right to me, though. What difference does an inch here or an inch there make? And you don't have to step around him any more 'cause, if you ran a truck over him, you wouldn't be able to tell the difference. Now, how about some 'flower' seeds?"

"I think you mean SUNflower seeds," I suggested.

"Swat I said," she replied, "someflower seeds."

I did not respond. I could hear Cleopatra the Cat wandering around in the house looking for me. She was awake and screaming for her breakfast. "You can wait," I said to Squeaks. "Let me go in and feed the cat. Then I'll come back out and take care of you."

"What? Feed the cat, did you say?" Squeaks asked. "Feed her to WHAT? Didn't know anything ate cats. Well, push it along will you. I will keep an eye on that toad and see that he doesn't slip into a crack somewhere."

I went in, rubbed Cleopatra between the ears, and asked her what she wanted for breakfast. She said she preferred half a can of fat-free rendered rat. I found half of a can of low-sodium minced mouse in the refrigerator and raked it into her dish. If she noticed the difference, she didn't say anything. She's like that. Doesn't talk much in the mornings before she's eaten once and had at least one nap. I went back out to feed the squirrels and birds.

Squeaks was jumping up and down with anxiety. She wanted to eat and get on with her day. She was fussy the way she usually is when her stomach is grumbling. She said, "You're always canning cats, racking coons, and quacking ducks when you should be squeaking squirrels! Why do I have to come last? I always think of me first, so why don't you do the same?"

I spread her sunflower seeds on the ground and, while she scarfed them down, went back into the house, poured my first cup of coffee, and brought it back out on the porch. Squeaks finished her seeds and came up and joined me. She looked at the forlorn figure of Teddy the Toad and asked, "Is he going to sit there all day and sulk? He does seem to have an altitude problem, doesn't he? Hmm. Well, maybe not. Let's just say he sure looks low. He says it was not your fault this time. Says it was his own foolishness. Says he just can't seem to do anything right. Says he is the stupidest blockhead on the block. Says he can't find a mate because he's warts all over. Says his ears are too short and his legs too long. Well, actually, I've never heard him say a single word. But I asked him and he didn't say 'no.' Why do so many animals seem to go into a flunk on these steamy, hot summer days? Is it just the heat, or is it the humility? Same thing with Ribbit the Rabbit. He's been deplaining about his ears being too long and his tail being too short. And Phoebe the Finch is all up in the air over her yellow-gold feathers. Wants to be blue like Jenny the Jay. At the same time, Jenny the Jay is blue over being blue and wants to go red like Carrie the Cardinal. Guess if I asked Carrie, she'd say she wants to turn yellow, or grow horns, or swap her feathers for fur. When they grow up and leave home, they seem to want a mommy-back guarantee that they can have everything anybody else has. But, snuff about that. What are you doing for this poor creature? I think you have a moral de-lemon here. Even if it wasn't your fault this time, you can't just leave him this way."

"I think you mean moral dilemma," I offered.

"Swat I said," she replied. "I also think we have a pair of 'doxes' here. The only way to get him DOWN to regular size is to blow him UP. Think you could use your tire pump and sort of puff him up a little? What about feeding him one of those firewhackers you had last July. Then you could light a match to him and maybe blow him up. If those don't work, I have about eleventeen more ideas."

I had had enough of this. "Look, Squeaks," I said, "please just go away and come back tomorrow. I'll figure out something and tell you tomorrow how it worked out. OK?"

"Can tell when I am not wanted," declared Squeaks. "Just wait 'till I get in trouble. Will I listen to you? Will I let you help me out? Will I ever ask you for anything? Will I ever accept even a crumb from you? Hmm! Uh! Say, do you have any idea what we are talking about here? If it's all right with you, I'll snunk over here tomorrow, snack out on some seeds, and sneak a new look at that toad. Then, maybe you can tell how you squeezed the old moral de-lemon." Squeaks was gone and, for once, I was glad to see her go.

47

Twelve of the world's two-hundred species of toads may be found in North America. Teddy the Toad is of the specie *Bufo americanus*, the predominant toad specie in eastern North America. Also known as a hoptoad, the *Bufo americanus* is similar to the frog in that both are amphibians that hatch from eggs and go through a tadpole stage before becoming a toad or a frog. The primary differences are that the toad has dry, warty skin, lives on dry land, and hops on short legs, while the frog has smooth, wet skin, lives in wetlands, and leaps on long legs.

The toad may measure up to four inches from nose to rump. Its topside is mostly a drab shade of brown, although females sometimes are brightly colored. Its white belly is spotted with black. It has bulging eyes, a wide mouth, and gold-flecked eyes. Warts cover its back and its hind legs. These warts stay with the toad; humans can handle the toad without any danger of picking up any of the warts. When threatened, toads can secrete a toxic fluid from their skin glands. This fluid is harmless to humans unless they rub it into their mouth or eyes. Even then, it causes only temporary irritation. The toxin can, however, be sufficiently poisonous that most predators who try to eat the toad will cough it up as soon as the toxin touches their mouth and throat. Snakes, alone, seem to be immune to the toxin; they continue to swallow toads with impunity.

The toad has excellent vision, and the circular drums that serve as ears record vibrations that warn the toad of approaching danger. Despite the fact that the toad looks like a... well, a toad, it is surprisingly intelligent for an amphibian. Since most amphibians are dumber than a post, this is not saying a great deal. The toad reacts quicker and learns faster than other amphibians such as the frog. It can figure out a maze, learn that it cannot walk through a glass barrier, and estimate distances before leaping off high objects. The toad is a gentle creature with an easy going, nonaggressive personality.

The toad lives a solitary life except during spring mating. It prefers to live in woodlands where there is cover, moist soil, and food. It digs a burrow with its hind legs and lurks just inside the burrow entrance to await its prey. It also hides in the burrow when threatened. During exceptionally hot or dry conditions, it lies dormant under a rock, in loose soil, or in a rotten log. During the winter, it works itself a foot or more underground and hibernates.

The adult toad eats insects, snails, slugs, hopgrassers, caterpillars, beetles, earthworms, and spiders. A single toad will eat up to ten thousand insects in a single summer without a hint of high cholesterol or high blood pressure. To make sure its food is fresh, the toad refuses to eat anything that does not move. To catch its food, it mostly sits and waits. It does not bother its potential prey until the prey moves to within six inches or less of the toad's nose. Then, if the prey stops moving, the toad sits and waits. When the waiting game ends, that is, when the prey is moving and is within the correct range, the toad acts with incredible swiftness. Its sticky tongue lashes out as much as two to three inches, nabs the prey, and whips it back into its mouth. This all happens faster than the human eye can follow.

The toad has little need to communicate, so it doesn't. The only exception is that the male toad sings for sex during breeding season in the spring. It blows up its throat like a balloon and forces the air through its vocal cords to produce a trill that lasts from fifteen to thirty seconds. Female toads apparently get thrills from these trills and come hopping in to see what else the male toad has to offer. The toad can breed only when it is in water; not just any water though, it prefers the same pond or water hole where it was hatched. The mating game is a prolonged activity. The male toad attaches himself to the back of the female and stays there while the female lays strings of black eggs in the water and he secretes sperm into the water to fertilize the eggs.

The female may put out as many as twelve thousand eggs before she has finished. The pair of toads then part company and each heads back to its own part of the woods where it will remain until spring comes again.

From the moment the eggs are laid, their number begins to be reduced as they are eaten by fish, water beetles, crayfish, and dragonflies. Only about five percent of the eggs survive. This is fortunate; if all of them reached maturity, we would be neck deep in toads. In about a week, the surviving eggs turn into tadpoles. These have adhesive organs that allow them to cling to any available surface for a day or so until they begin to grow and develop. The tadpoles then swim around, eat algae and particles of soft plant tissue, and are slowly metamorphosed into toads. The change into toads takes about two months, after which the tiny toads crawl onto land and begin behaving the way toads behave.

48

Cleopatra finished her morning snack and antiqued the wall next to the door to indicate that she wanted out to see what all the talking was about. I opened the door and let her out. When she saw Teddy the Toad, she stopped in her tracks. "So, I see you finally backed the car over him," she said. "But what is the problem here? You did not damage our automobile, did you?"

I told her what happened, how upset Teddy seemed to be, and the "fixes" suggested by Squeaks the Squirrel.

She jumped onto the glass-topped table and began cleaning her front paws. I was pretty sure she was not through talking about Teddy, and I was correct. She took her own time, but finally finished licking her paws and carrying out her usual quality control inspection to make sure the level of cleanliness met her stringent specifications. Then she stretched out into her lecturing position, and began.

"From my position of power, prestige, and perfection," she began, "I can see that I am the only one around here who knows what to do in a situation like this." She looked me straight in the eyes, and said, "I think I have said before that clumsy is as clumsy does. But, enough about you. We must give our full attention to this toad that you have so cruelly injured. What we have here is a toad who is overly concerned with his looks. His looks, however, have absolutely nothing to do with how well he eats, hops, or hibernates. The only way his looks could possibly make any difference is in his choice of a mate. And is there even a shred of evidence that a pretty toad makes a better mate than an ugly one? No! If anything, the evidence shows the opposite.

"If this toad were the only creature on earth, he would never give a thought to his looks. So, obviously, he is concerned about how he looks to others. In plain words, he is vain! He wants others to think he is quite a bit better than he really is and at least a little better than they are. The only way he can feel important and worthwhile is to get reinforcement from others. He does not care much what he REALLY is so long as he thinks others think he is OK. This is why human males wash their cars. Washing them does not make them run any better or last any longer. They do it so others will look at them, think what nice, clean, shiny cars they have and, thus, think they are OK. They get their hair cut, mow their lawns, rake their leaves, and wear neckties for the same reason. Human females are as vain as males. They wear those stilt shoes with the pointed toes, have their clothes fit just right, and I heard one say she would simply dye before she would let her hair go gray. If all humans were blind, ideas about what is important would change considerably. To talk about a vain human, however, would be redundant; vanity is their middle name. Some of this vanity rubs off on some of the other animals. Only cats are completely immune to it. Now, if you will sit back and watch, I will show you how my superior intellect deals with a down and out hoptoad."

Cleopatra jumped down onto the porch floor, picked up my crossword puzzle pencil that had rolled off the table onto the floor, and eased up to the low-lying Teddy the Toad. She spoke to him in a whisper. "Teddy the Toad," she said, "It is I, the Wizard of Memphis on the Nile, come to set you free." She held the pencil over Teddy's head and continued. "When I wave this magic wand, say the magic words, and touch you on the head, you will become completely invisible. You will be invisible until the next time it rains and the magic washes off. Until then, you can go where you please, do what you please, eat what you please, and look as you please. No one will know the difference because no one will be able to see you."

Cleopatra waved the magic wand over Teddy's head, mumbled some words that sounded to me like, "Hocus poke, on this porch floor, may we see this toad no more." She then touched Teddy on the top of his head and said, "Done! You now are completely invisible."

Teddy raised his head and asked, "Am I really invisible? How can you tell?"

Cleopatra answered, "I cannot see you. I hear your voice coming from over by that empty spot on the floor. But I do not see a single toad."

Teddy turned to me and asked, "Can YOU see me?"

I stared hard at the ceiling and assured Teddy that I did not see any toads. Teddy then began to perk up. He lifted his oversized body off the floor, danced a little jig, and began looking for snack bugs. All the while, he sang, "Can't see me! Can't see me! Can't see me!"

Cleopatra turned to me and whispered, "I suppose now he will want us to throw a big party for him so all his friends can come over and admire his invisibleness. Now you go find your squeaky little friend and tell her what is going on here. If you do not, she will come in here and spoil everything."

Squeaks was easy to find. I told her how Cleopatra had made Teddy invisible, and I warned her not to do or say anything that would cause Teddy to think otherwise. I went back to the porch to see what was going on with Teddy. Squeaks followed close behind.

Squeaks jumped onto the porch, looked around, and said, "I see a cat and a, uh... hu... hu... human on this porch. That's all I see if you don't count chairs and tables and all the other things I see. But I don't see any toads anywhere. Not a single toad! Who said anything about toads? Does anybody see any toads around here anywhere? See, nobody sees a toad. If there is a toad around here anywhere, he must be invincible, because I definitely do not see any toads." Squeaks pointed at the supposedly invisible Teddy and continued, "Sitting right over there on the floor is just an empty spot on the floor. I don't see a single toad sitting there. If Teddy the Toad is sitting there, he must be invincible, 'cause I don't see no toad nowhere!"

This must have convinced Teddy the Toad. If no one could see him, he could afford, for once in his life, to look exactly the way he really looked; short, fat, wart covered, bulging eyes and all.

Squeaks paused on his way back to the woods and yelled, "Got to go build a new nest. Have to flee from fleas. Old nest's full of 'em. Lots of work, so got to get started. Unless... wait a minute. Maybe I don't have to build a new one." She walked over to the supposedly invisible Teddy, tapped him on his warty head, and asked, "Teddy, old butter ball, by any chance, do you eat fleas. If we can just figure out some way to get something as fat as you off the ground, we can... oops. Uh oh."

Squeaks held one paw over her mouth, slipped on the edge of the porch, fell flat on her face, got up, gave us an embarrassed grin, and dashed for the woods. Cleopatra gave me a disgusted look and said, "It would have worked if you did not associate with such unsophisticated creatures. I have no more time to waste on fat toads." And she climbed onto the roof, jumped onto the top of the fireplace chimney, and curled up for a long overdue nap. Teddy the Toad lay an the floor moaning softly.

I was not sure quite where the latest turn of events left me. What ARE my obligations in life? Am I responsible for every Tom, Dick, and Teddy? My first thought was to go into the house, slam the door, and forget the whole affair. My second thought was that I certainly was not going to tell fairy tales to a toad just to make him feel good. And then I decided to squander a few minutes trying to use simple logic to tell Teddy the simple truth. I should have known better; logic always is wasted when pitted against emotions.

First, I tried to assure Teddy that his current corpulent condition was temporary and that, in a matter of hours or days, he would regain his former form.

This did not please Teddy. He said, "Doesn't matter. Former shape just as bad."

I said, "But I thought you liked your usual tall, slim shape."

"Didn't," Teddy replied. "Too short and fat."

"What makes you think that?" I asked.

"Television," responded Teddy. "You had it out watching golf. Saw three minutes golf; twenty-seven minutes commercials. Said use Raspy Razors, Wetdog Deodorant, Goo Shampoo, and Bear and Bottomly's Better Bath Bars. Said wear Gene's Jeans,

Phew's Shoes, Noose's Neckties, and Pincher's Pantyhose. Said eat Putrid's Pizza, Grease's Pieces, Saltlick's Subs, and Lardo's Congealed Crunchies. Said drink Catnip Cola, Loada Soda, Burpee's Beer, and Tinkle's Tea. Said brush teeth with new, whiter-white Grime, chew Chompin Gum, drive Itsy Bitsy auto, and wash clothes with new, improved Fade. Said, if I did all that, would be tall and slim and all girls go mushy on. Got to be tall and slim. Can't deny. Said so right there. But, can't do. Can't afford. No money. Not win lottery, not play professional ball, not be matinee idol. Doomed! Nobody like!"

"But, that really is not the way it is," I argued. "Those on television are just trying to sell things. And, they can sell better if they don't get sidetracked by having to tell the truth. The trouble with you is you spend so much time worrying about what others think of you that you have no time left to think about what you really are, what you really wish to be, and what you have a realistic chance of becoming. So, what if you don't look exactly the way you think you want to look? Who cares? I don't care. Cleopartra doesn't care. Squeaks doesn't care. Nobody cares. The only way you can really grow... uh, improve your mind and disposition, is to accept yourself as you really are, work at changes that make sense, and feel good about yourself for being a unique individual and doing the best you can with what you have."

"But I try to think positively," whined Teddy.

"Don't try to think positively; that is polliwog stuff. Think REALISTICALLY! And realistically you are a toad. A T-O-A-D toad. Being a toad has its advantages and its disadvantages, just like being anything else. You can observe what kind of toad you are now, what kind of toad you would like to be, and what kind of toad you are capable of becoming. And then you can decide if you are willing to put forth the effort to make the changes necessary to close the gap between what you are and what you might become. Or you can worry yourself sick trying to be something you are not. But, those are about the ONLY choices you have. So, why fret about things that you can't do anything about?"

Teddy was beginning to look a bit more alive. I thought I must be doing something right. This time, I was succeeding where both Squeaks the Squirrel and the Wizard of Memphis on the Nile had failed. I should have let good enough alone, but I was blinded by my brilliance. I should have remembered that an intelligent animal knows WHAT to say, but a wise animal knows whether or not to say it. For the moment at least, I was not wise. I continued with, "I think all of us have some need to be liked by others. But we have to be careful that we don't pay too high a price to be liked. If others like us for what they THINK we are instead of what we REALLY are, the relationship is a false one and not really worth anything. But the really important thing is whether or not WE like ourselves. If we do, we have control of our own destinies rather than being at the mercy of the whims of others who have their own agendas and needs."

Teddy looked thoughtfully up at me and asked, "You like self?"

"Well, yes I do," I responded.

"Why," Teddy asked.

"Hmm. Well. Uh, well, I like myself because, for one thing, I tell the truth."

"You tell truth," echoed Teddy. "Then tell me, if all over you have warts, if have pop eyes, if be short and fat, what do?"

Without thinking, I replied honestly, "I think I would hop over to the nearest cliff and plunge over the edge."

Teddy moaned, "Thought so. Which way to cliff?"

X. The Benevolent League for Aid to Animals

You gave them bread, you gave cheese,
You gave them cause for thanking you.
But what they needed more than these
Was knowing they were needed too.

49

This story began about a year ago. As I often do on pleasant afternoons, I was lying in my hammock, which was swung between two trees in the side yard. My head was propped on a pillow and I was reading a novel. I think I had read the same page four or five times and still was not sure what I had read. I kept getting distracted by the rays of light that were breaking through the overhead limbs and bouncing back and forth as the soft breeze moved the leaves. The woods were alive with the peeps, cheeps, chirps, coos, caws, and clarion calls of birds and the rustle and chatter of squirrels. I read page 137 one more time, concluded that I finally had focused sufficiently to have followed the words, and turned to pages 138 and 139. That was as far as I got that day. Some books, and some days, are that way.

The slight rustle in the grass behind me indicated the approach of something bigger than a box turtle but smaller than a bear. A raucous "meowarl" let me know it was Cleopatra the Cat even before I felt her weight shift the hammock as her flying leap deposited her in the rope webbing at my feet. She has never liked walking on the webbing, but she has no qualms about walking on me. She used my right leg for a balance beam, made her way along my stomach, heavy-footed across my chest, and came to rest with her nose shoved into my face. She likes my beard. In her more generous moments, she concedes that I have reasonably acceptable face fur and that, if I would discard my ungainly body from the neck down and grow a long tail in its place, I might at a distance, on a dark night, pass for some distorted form of a cat. After rearranging my beard to her satisfaction, she settled on my chest, yawned, and half closed her eyes for a nap. I disturbed her half sleep with a question.

"Where have you been," I asked. "If you've been down to the road again, I'll put a collar on you and chain you to the fence."

"Tacky! Tacky! Tacky!" she responded. "I know the facts of life. You do not have to tell me about the busses and beeps. I know about roads and cars and getting flattened. That is part of what we were discussing."

"Who is 'we'?" I asked.

"I just came from a BLAA meeting," she replied. "Their talking about how the road splits the neighborhood was what got them started with their big plans to fix everything that needs fixing."

"Uh, I don't want to appear stupid here, but what is a BLAA meeting?" I asked.

"That is the Benevolent League for Aid to Animals. Its membership includes all kinds of animals except, uh, humans. Humans have their own branch called BLAH, the Benevolent League for Aid to Humans. I think BLAH probably would suit you better than BLAA suits me. I just go to keep up with what is going on around here. I rarely ever say anything or do anything. Today they were getting ready to vote on a huge benevolent project to help animals who have been put in distress by traffic on the road or by not being able to cross the road to get at whatever is on the other side. The vote was almost unanimous. I did not vote."

"Well, aren't you the courageous one!" I said. "I'm surprised at you. You usually fight for what you think is right, and you do lots of fighting even when you know you're wrong."

"This was different," she said. "I do not think their plan will work. So, if I voted, I would have voted against it. But, I did not want to discourage those who think it will work, and I think voting against their plan would have discouraged them."

"So," I said, "you decided not to vote and just let them take their lumps when things don't work out?"

Cleopatra yawned a toothy yawn and turned her head. "Sometimes I do not know why I bother to try to talk to you," she said. "You do not seem to understand even the simplest things. It is not a matter of their taking their lumps. There is something here they need to learn. And the only way they are going to learn it is to try their plan. It is not as if it were going to kill them or anything. It simply will cost them some time, energy, resources, and agony. And that is a cheap price to pay for learning something important."

"Well, why didn't you say that in the first place? What is this big plan?"

"Actually, it is not a very big plan," Cleopatra responded. "At least not at first. They intend to start off very small and then expand after they have had more experience. To begin, they are going to select four families that might have been adversely impacted by the road. These have to be needy families for whom most of the members have a great deal of pity. The plan is for the Benevolent League to go all out to fill these families' pitiful needs. What they want to do, ultimately, is to take the animals on the bottom half of the socio-economic scale and move them up to the top half. I am not sure who this leaves to pick up garbage and pluck chickens, but they do not seem to be concerned about that. They say, with this plan, there will not be any poor, mistreated, or overworked animals. The long-range plan is to do the same with education. If they can take the young ones who score below the fiftieth percentile on the standardized tests and educate them to the point where their score goes up, they can, according to the plan, have everybody functioning above average.

"But, back to these four families with whom they wish to begin. They already have selected them. First, they picked the Byrd family. I think you know them. There is the mother, Cathy Wren, the father, Wren Tin Tin, and their four new ones. Their names are Wrender, Wrenegade, Wrenounce, and Wrenovate. And then they picked Homeless and Hopeless, the Box Turtles; Rancid and Raunchy Rabbit and their twenty-five little ones; and Deer Dominique and her three daughters, Siren, Vixen, and Temptress. The Benevolent League decided to be pragmatic, take each family as a separate case, and develop an assistance plan specifically tailored to that family's needs. Let me take these families one at a time and tell you what they are going to do for them."

I said that I would like to hear about them but that I wished she would shift over to the right side of my chest. Her weight on my left side had caused my arm and shoulder to go numb. She shifted, and continued.

"First," she said, "is the Byrd family. Cathy Wren, the mother, as I think you know, is into sour mash. She is smashed most of the time. She, by the way, was at the meeting today, but left in a huff. The Benevolent League advertised an alcohol-free meeting, but she thought they meant a free-alcohol meeting. The father, Wren Tin Tin, has not quite been right in the head since he got caught in the middle of that badminton game back a few years ago. The Byrd's roof is leaking, one side of the nest is falling in, the floor has holes in it, and if you cleaned out all of the leaves and straw, I understand there would hardly be anything left. They are down to their last bug. After it is gone, they will be hungry. I do not know much about the little ones but I understand they are hopping around in unpreened feathers and no shirts or shoes. They are skipping school and hanging around the pool hall. They are learning foul language and habits when they should be learning fowl language and habits. They are missing all their school classes, and they hardly know a worm from a caterpillar.

"So the plans for them are quite simple. The Benevolent League is going to put the little ones in a foster home where they will be cleaned up, fed wholesome bugs and slugs, and made to go to reform school every day. They will be flogged every morning and made to read fifty pages out of the Good Book every evening so as to make sure they grow up to be solid citizens and a credit to the Benevolent League. The mother will be sent to the local BB meetings. You know, of course, about the BB organization. The Boozing Birds is a fine group. They have a twelve-stomp plan where they stomp you down if you do not give up on the sour mash. They are going to put the father in a job training program where he will learn marketable skills such as modern worming methods and insect technology. When the little ones get cleaned up, smartened up, and beaten up, Mrs. Byrd gets sobered up or stomped down, and Mr. Byrd gets trained and placed in at least a minimum-bug job, they will put the whole family back together in one of those nice public nesting projects where they can keep an eye on them and sort of whack them back in line if they do anything other than show what fine, upright, productive citizens they have become.

"Now, let me see, who was next? Yes, that pair of box turtles, Homeless and Hopeless. You found Homeless stranded in the middle of the highway, remember? He could not remember which side of the highway was home, so he just kept plodding down the yellow line in the middle. He said he thought it was the turtle lane. And then a couple of weeks later, you found Hopeless right on that same yellow line all scrunched down to keep from getting tumbled or sqished by the heavy morning traffic. You brought them both home in the back seat of the car, in a cardboard box. That is why they are called box turtles. Their problem is that they do not seem to have any ambition. They do not seem to be going anywhere, and they have never learned any social skills. They just keep to themselves all the time and, when they do move around, they seem to just wander aimlessly about. So the Benevolent League wants to get them to open up and come out of their shells and to learn to be goal-oriented. Their plan is to get them jobs, maybe as jet pilots or elevator operators. This will give them incentive, direction, and get them out with other animals. The idea here is to turn them from worthless recluses who are taking up valuable real estate, with no return on investment, into productive, tax-paying, civic-minded citizens.

"The Rabbit family probably is the most needy of the four. They are what you would call profoundly impoverished. Not only are they going hungry but also they are getting beat up on by some of the other animals. They need safety and they need food, lots of it, and immediately. The plan for them is simple. The Benevolent League is classifying rabbits as an endangered specie and will put up signs warning molesters to stay out of their edge of the woods. Also, they are giving the rabbits guns so that they can defend themselves against hunters. And, to take care of the food problem, they are beginning a massive food lift which will bring in food from places far and near. They are going to distribute the food through what they are calling their 'Carrots on Chariots' program. This program will ensure that the food is fairly distributed so that no bunny goes hungry.

"Now, the Deer family is another problem altogether, a very DELICATE problem I must say. The mother and daughters are,

173

how shall I say it, free spirits, VERY free spirits. The terms wanton, dissolute, promiscuous, fast, and loose come to mind here. If something is not done immediately, we are going to end up with some illegitimate, illicit, misbegotten, outside-of-matrimony deer on our hands here. And then, so the Benevolent League says, 'There goes the neighborhood!' There was a great deal of heated discussion about this one. Several bucks walked right out of the meeting. Said they had urgent business elsewhere. Ideas were presented that involved education, counseling, contraception methods, nunneries, and scarlet letters. Finally, it was decided that the best plan is to get them married off fast. So they are going to start immediately taking applications, checking references, matchmaking, and making travel arrangements for honeymoon trips. They hope to have all of them married off and on their way before the season begins.

"So, that is what happened today at the Benevolent League meeting." Cleopatra gave a low sigh, dropped her head, and covered her eyes with her paw as if to signify the end of the conversation.

"Those seem like perfectly wonderful plans to me." I said. "How could you possibly be opposed to them?"

"As I said," responded Cleopatra, as though she had not heard my question, "I do not think the plans will bring about any great improvements, I do not think they will make this a better world, and I do not think anybody is going to be helped except the Benevolent League members who will feel all warm and fuzzy inside for having done such good and noble deeds. Of course it is a fine thing to help others! But I am not sure one is really helpful when the primary motivation is pity rather than compassion. Acting out of pity causes the other fellow to feel belittled. Acting out of compassion is practicing tough love. It is letting others know you care about them enough to allow them to make their own choices, rather than trying to force your values on them. It is doing what you can to help them become self-respecting, self-confident, self-reliant, self-sufficient, self-assured, and self-propelled."

"That sounds a bit cold hearted to me," I said. "What if there were a famine in the land and animals were starving. And suppose you had adequate food for yourself. Would you feed the hungry ones?"

"Depends," she answered, "on what caused the famine. If it were the result of something entirely outside their control, I would feed them all—after I fed any hungry cats, of course. But if it were the natural consequences of their own foolish actions, well, I would just let them... let them... hmm.

"Aw, go ahead and invite them over for dinner! I just hope we do not make them so comfortable they do not learn anything from their mistakes. Maybe you can encourage them to smarten up if you refuse to give them a second helping. But leave me out of this, please. I cannot stand to see an animal hurting. You brought up the subject, so this is your problem. I just hope you have learned about tough love. Tough love is standing by and watching those you care about hurt as they accept at least some responsibility for their behavior.

"But now it is quite late. You have kept me up way past my nap time and have completely ruined my day. And you know how that makes my claws want to dig into something."

Since my past threats to have her declawed had seemed to fall on deaf ears, I simply lifted her gently from my chest, gathered her limp form in my arms, moved to the porch, and deposited a sleeping cat onto her favorite porch chair. I would find out, in time, how the grand plans of the Benevolent League turned out. But, for now, I would let sleeping cats lie.

50

While noble plans play themselves out and cats sleep, let me tell you some things you might not know about three of the categories of animals that Cleopatra had been telling me about. I have already told you about rabbits; remember, they are basically the same thing as hare bunnies.

Our wrens are Carolina wrens, or *Thryothorus ludovicianus*, of the family *Troglodytidae*. Wrens are small, hyperactive birds with slender bills, curved and rounded wings, and dull brown or grey feathers. They like to live near the ground and seem always to be on the move. Watching a pair of them flit and jump around looking for bugs can lead you to physical exhaustion. They eat insects, hopgrassers, and beetles. Their songs are beautiful. Our male wren sits in one tree and sings, "She's weird, she's weird, she's weird." The female wren sits in another tree and answers with, "HE'S weird, HE'S weird, HE'S crazy." Wrens can, however, be a royal nuisance when they run out of songs and get in a chattering mood.

In the spring, the male wren's fancy turns to nesting. He goes bonkers and works himself into a nest-building frenzy. He builds nests everywhere: in the barbecue grill, mailbox, porch ceiling fan, coffee can half full of roofing nails, on top of the trim in the corner of the carport, and in various parts of the underside of your automobile, if you don't move it every few hours. After a few weeks of this exhausting activity, the female finally makes her appearance and, as with females everywhere, checks out his two weeks of hard labor and tells him he has done it all wrong. She selects one of his nests, usually the one that will require the most reworking, and lays down her plans for his rebuilding it. So, the poor fellow follows her belated specifications and rebuilds. At least, that is the way wrens are supposed to behave and usually do behave. This past spring, however, our wrens did something entirely different. He made her pick a nesting site FIRST. And, then, he put all his energies into that one nest, which was under the eves at one corner of our back porch. He built and built and built until he ended up with a nest that was almost as large as a basketball. Once he finished, she cooperated by laying down her usual six or seven eggs. She incubated them until the little ones reached hatchhood and then let him know that she had done her part. He responded by stuffing every insect on the block down the gaping mouths of his hungry offspring.

The eastern box turtle, or *Terrapene carolina*, is a reptile that can easily be recognized by its shell. This shell is colorful and dome shaped and usually measures, on a full-grown turtle, four to eight inches across. The turtle has been around for about one hundred and seventy-five million years so it must be doing something right. Probably what it is doing right is having a strong suit of armor that protects it against most predators, and a slow pace that does not cause it to burn itself out. The turtle is at one with its shell. Its top shell, or carpace, is made up of its backbone and ribs joined into a solid mass by a number of bony plates. Its bottom shell, or plastron, includes its breastbone. Broad hinges divide the plastron into moveable front and back sections and allow the turtle to close its shell to protect itself. The shell closes so tightly that even a knife blade will not go through the cracks. The shell will support a weight of two hundred times the turtle's weight. Unfortunately, for the turtle, automobiles weigh much more than this and, thus, are one of the turtle's worse enemies. While turtles in the wild often live sixty to eighty years, and some are thought to be over one hundred years old, it would take them longer than that to get anywhere. Even with all these years to travel, a turtle rarely goes more than three hundred to four hundred feet from where it was born. No turtle has ever been known to work itself or run itself to death.

The turtle's day usually is not filled to the brim with excitement and thrills. It spends the night alone in a shallow recess in the dirt or leaves and, then, since it is cold blooded, does not emerge until the sun has time to warm it up. It then spends virtually all the daylight hours searching for food. This search includes a slow, haphazard shuffle across its limited domain. It turns, doubles back, criss-crosses its path and, occasionally, almost by accident, bumps into something to eat. It eats ants, earthworms, moths, beetles, larvae, crayfish, small frogs and toads, leaves, grass, buds, berries, and fruit. While it has no teeth, it can use its hooked beak and sharp ridges of bone in the edges of its mouth to bite, cut, and tear its food. The box turtle has keen senses of smell, sight, and touch. While its hearing is poor, or nonexistent, it can feel vibrations. It is a quiet creature. The only sound it makes is a swoosh of air when it snaps its shell shut.

The box turtle is not noted for its social skills. It is a loner. Sometimes, during its haphazard meandering, it happens upon another box turtle. They look each other straight in the eyes. A male has whisky-red eyes; the female has brown eyes. When the eyes turn out to be the right combination, the two turtles may mate. Mating is sort of a one-day stand, particularly for the male. While the female simply sits still, the male has to stand in a near-vertical position for their parts to fit together in any productive manner. He must maintain this position for at least three hours. No one ever said turtles are fast! As with humans, mating can be hazardous for the male box turtle. The female turtle, after getting her due, simply moves forward, leaving the male to fall back into a horizontal position. Sometimes, the male accidentally falls on his back. When this happens, he can't get up. His legs are too short. If he is fortunate, he will be able to grasp something and turn himself over. If not, he lies there on his back until he dies. Either way, he never sees the female again unless by sheer accident.

The female does all the remaining work of producing a family, and she doesn't exactly work herself into a frenzy. After a few weeks of putting it off, she finally digs a hole in the ground and lays four to six leathery, pink eggs that are smaller than ping pong balls. She covers the eggs and goes about her business of shuffling aimlessly around. She never returns, unless by accident, and never sees her offspring. After about three months of being heated by the sun, the baby turtles break out of their shells, dig themselves to the surface, and go their separate, random ways.

The white-tailed deer, or *Odocoileus virginianus,* is the most common and widely distributed hoofed wild animal in North America. It also is the largest animal to frequent our neighborhood. An adult deer stands about forty inches high at the shoulders and weighs about one hundred and fifty pounds. A buck (male) weighs more than a doe (female) and may weigh as much as four hundred pounds. When a deer is alarmed, it usually will give a "snort" or "blow," raise its white tail, apparently as a signal of danger to other deer, and bound gracefully away. The deer also communicates in other ways. It stomps the ground with one front foot, apparently as a signal of aggressiveness intended to warn molesters to stay away. It communicates with other deer with bleats, blathers, and whistles. It has excellent hearing. It seemingly can rotate its antenna ears in any direction to pick up sounds. It appears constantly alert to warning cries from other animals such as birds and squirrels. The deer also has a keen sense of smell and acute eyesight. It can see clearly at great distances and can spot movement that indicates potential danger.

The natural enemy of the deer once was mountain lions and wolves. Since these enemies have been decimated in most parts of North America, humans have become the deer's worst enemy. Hunters and automobiles destroy millions each year. Packs of free-running dogs, winter starvation, and disease also take their toll. These leave the deer with an average life expectancy of only about three years. The buck deer grows a set of antlers every summer and sheds them following the fall breeding season. The antlers are used to fend off other bucks so as to gain breeding privileges. Combats between bucks can result in serious injury to one or both from sharp antlers or cutting hooves. The buck deer is not monogamous and does not maintain a harem; it simply breeds as the opportunity presents herself.

Once bred, the doe gives birth in about two hundred and five days. It produces a single fawn, twins or, occasionally, triplets. A Whitetail fawn weighs about five to six pounds at birth. The mother introduces the newborn to life by giving it a vigorous licking with her rough tongue. Initially, the fawn has difficulty making its wobbly legs obey its command to stand up, but it soon gets the knack of it and, after an hour or so, can walk a straight line. The mother then leads it to a new place because odors from the place of birth might draw natural predators. The spotted youngster knows how to lie perfectly still and blend into its surroundings. The mother may leave it alone for hours at a time while she forages for food so as to maintain her milk supply. When the fawn reaches the ripe old age of two or three weeks, it goes along with the mother on grazing trips. It nurses for perhaps three months and then quickly becomes a part of the adult world. The doe begins to breed at about eight months of age; the buck does not breed until its second autumn when it is about eighteen months old.

The population of deer in North America exceeds twenty million and is increasing rapidly. In many parts of the country, particularly in suburban areas such as ours, the deer has become an outright pest. Its natural diet of buds, twigs, shrubs, trees, grass, herbs, mushrooms, and roots often is supplemented with landscape shrubbery, flowers, ground cover, birdseed, and garden vegetables. Although we try to keep our deer at bay by putting out mothballs and human hair and spraying plants with deer-ban, nothing seems to stop them in the winter when their natural food is in short supply. By the end of winter, our shrubbery and ground cover usually are virtually destroyed. I have looked at my carefully-tended plants lying in ruin, grabbed up a golf club, and threatened bodily injury to the next deer who comes into the yard. And then, when a hungry doe appears and looks at me with her huge, luminous, innocent, brown eyes, I sheepishly put the golf club aside and spread out another can of birdseed. Some of our more practical neighbors have suggested that the deer population be kept under control by reintroducing some of the deer's natural enemies. Others have objected that bringing in mountain lions and wolves might also reduce the human population. Some have said that would be an acceptable tradeoff. I still tend to favor controlling the deer population by simply teaching the little does to say "no."

51

Almost a year had passed since Cleopatra first told me about the Benevolent League's grand plans. The morning seemed like a good time to put my hammock back in its usual place. I had taken it down to give it a good washing to get rid of the mildew. I then hung it in the workshop to dry. Since we had had several weeks of rain, I had not needed it, but now the rain had ceased and it was time, once again, to string the hammock up between the trees. The problem was that the two trees I had been using had grown too large, threatened the house with destruction, and been cut down for use as fire wood. Fortunately, there is an ample supply of trees surrounding the house at a safe distance. I selected two of them that were the right size and the correct distance apart. These stood just at the edge of the gravel driveway and, thus, were easily accessible. I drilled a small hole into the trunk of each of the two trees and screwed in hooks to hold the ends of the hammock. In less than twenty minutes, I was in business again and lay stretched out on the hammock with a pillow under my head. This new spot was a definite improvement over the old one. Here, the sun did not shine in my eyes and I had a better view of the house, driveway, and animal feeding area.

As I lay there with my light cotton jacket spread over me for warmth, the trees reached majestically skyward and swayed gently in the morning breeze. It was a lazy day—if one would permit it to be so—a day for resting, thinking, and dreaming. As I watched the birds flitting about in the trees and the white clouds coasting smoothly through the pale blue sky, I almost dropped off to sleep. Then, as I had the previous year at hammock-hanging time, I heard a slight rustle in the grass behind me that indicated the approach of something bigger than a hoptoad but smaller than a cow. I thought, "Uh oh! Cleopatra is going to jump up on me again." I shifted my body to accept the impact of her full weight on my stomach and turned my head to get a better idea of when she would crash down onto me. But it was not Cleopartra. It was a raccoon, the raunchiest, dirtiest, scrawniest, most miserable-looking, tattered, and ragtag raccoon I have ever seen. I raised my head from the pillow, turned toward him, and asked, "Who in the world are you? And what rock did you crawl out from under?"

The raccoon eased up closer to the hammock, looked up at me with innocent eyes, and replied, "Well, Sir, my proper legal name, assigned to me at birth and on record down at the county courthouse, is Rags. But my friends all shorten that up and call me Ragamuffin. As for the rock that I crawled out from under, there is a large pile of rocks over in the woods there. If you go straight down the side of the road and turn right, you will find them. It's about two miles if you go down the road. Or, you can take a shortcut down a trail across the creek and through the woods. That way, it's only four miles. When you get to the rocks, go clear to the other side and look off toward the trees by the creek. There, you will see just one big rock out there all by itself. Well, that is the one I just crawled out from under. That is home. That is where I spend most of my time when I am not out working. Come by any time. I will show you the whole layout, except that I don't think you can see much because, and I hope you won't take this as criticism, you are not built right for crawling under there. Anyway, Sir you asked me the questions and I hope I have answered them to your satisfaction."

He stood there, shifting his weight back and forth from one foot to the other, and awaited my response. What can you say to a raunchy, dirty, scrawny, miserable-looking, tattered, ragtag raccoon who answers your questions precisely, accurately, and in detail? I gave careful thought about how to respond and finally asked, "Uh, What are you doing out this time of day?"

Again, his answer was precise, accurate, and in detail. He said, "I am on the way to the BLAA meeting. You surely know about BLAA which is the Benevolent League for Aid to Animals. I never miss a meeting. They sponsor bingo once each week and, sometimes, they serve free lemonade. I hate lemonade but I drink it anyway because I don't want to hurt their feelings. Since they had to cancel their big aid programs back a few months ago, they seem to get their feelings hurt easily. All they do now, other than playing bingo and giving free flu and distemper shots and, sometimes, free lemonade, is plant trees and put up signs. So, Sir, I hope I have answered your question to your satisfaction. If not, just say so, and I will answer with considerably more precision, accuracy, and detail."

I assured him that his answer was quite sufficient. I was prepared to ask him for more information about BLAA but was sidetracked by an odor that I could not identify. So I asked him if he noticed a strange smell. He hung his head and held a paw over his face so that I could see only one bashful eye shining between his fingers.

"Well, Sir," he responded, "I hoped you would not notice that. The truth is that the redolence that you detect may well be wafting from my direction. You see, I met a strange little fellow named Aromatic on my way over here. Aromatic, in case you don't know him, is of the skunk persuasion. He was feeling lonesome so I stopped to chat with him. He said most of the animals don't much take to him. Said he rarely gets invited out to any parties or to join in any games and that no one ever stops by his place for tea. Said he had his fur all brushed up and looking shiny but no one had said it looked good. I kind of got up close to him, maybe too close, and took a good look at his fur. He was right; it did look pretty good. So I told him his was the finest fur coat I thought I had ever seen. He liked that; saw that I was sincere, which I was. He insisted on my sitting for tea. The tea was awful! But what do I know? I don't like tea even when it's good. He is a shy and gentle fellow. Told me about how he found his house, which is a clean and orderly hollowed out stump, and how he ate mostly buds, berries, and grass but, sometimes, snacked on insects. We had an agreeable time together. He shook my hand when I was leaving and invited me back if I ever happen in that part of the woods again.

"I suppose I will stop by again, but maybe skip the tea and maybe maintain a slightly more discreet distance between us. Fine coat of fur there, that's for sure. Never seen better. I stopped by the creek and sponged off some. Something about him got to me, if you know what I mean. Positive feelings; negative feelings! Not sure exactly how to balance them out. Been thinking of telling him the honest truth, which is that we have some things in common that it would be nice to share and, also, we have some differences that might just as well be left alone—be close without getting TOO close, if you know what I mean. Each of us letting the other one be, without either of us trying to make the other over in our own image. So that, Sir, hopefully will explain about the strange incense you asked about."

I assured him that his answer was more than sufficient and then finally got around to asking him the two questions I had intended to ask earlier. I asked him what he meant by stating that BLAA had canceled their big aid programs, and what kind of signs they were putting up.

His response was, "Well, they started off small with an aid program to help four groups of animals. I don't know what happened. No one will talk about it. I think the programs did not work out as they envisioned. Anyway, they canceled the programs and announced that they, henceforth, were into 'caring and compassion' and out of 'fixing.' I don't know what that means but I am sure you know and will explain it all to me. I do know about the signs, though. That is clear and simple. They are putting out signs that say, 'Have you hugged your animals today?' And, speaking of hugs, I'm feeling kind of unloved, and unwanted, and unneeded, and unappreciated, and disaffirmed, and unvalidated, and disesteemed, and uncherished, if you get the drift here."

What can you say to a raunchy, dirty, scrawny, miserable-looking, ragged, ragtag, smelly raccoon who wants to be hugged? I reached out a tentative arm and sort of hugged, and he sort of hugged back. This was not one of my better moments. I recognized my feelings of superiority and my dread of getting my hands and clothing soiled by contact with such a miserable specimen. I also felt pangs of guilt for turning away from such an innocent and honest creature. I struggled with myself and, finally, either lost or won the struggle, I'm not sure which, and got up from the hammock and took the vile but wonderful little creature in my arms and gave him a genuine hug. I backed off from him and said, "Ragamuffin, you are one neat little fellow. I am glad to have made your acquaintance and hope we will meet again."

Rags upset me even more by wiping a tear from his cheek and saying, "Isn't this a wonderful day? Did you ever see the sky so blue and the clouds so white? Isn't it wonderful just to be alive? Got to go now. Can't afford to be late for BLAA bingo and miss out on all that delicious free lemonade. Was good to meet you kind Sir. I hope our paths will cross again." And the Ragamuffin was gone.

52

I lay back in the hammock, watched a woodpecker above me hammering on the trunk of the tree, and almost went to sleep. I was aroused by Cleopatra's silky voice calling from where she had just positioned herself on a large oak stump some twenty feet away. She said, "I do not know any polite way to tell you this, but you need a bath. And who, pray tell me, was that mangy creature that just left?"

"That," I replied, "was Raccoon Ragamuffin. He may be a little strange, but he is a kind and compassionate creature. You shouldn't put him down just because he's different. He needed a hug and, maybe, a little of him rubbed off on me. Well, maybe a little of me rubbed off him, too. Anyway, if you don't like it around here, go back in the house and check out your litter box."

"Oh, I see!" Cleopatra said. "He was telling you about BLAA and those stupid signs. Most undignified thing I ever heard. Can you imagine a sophisticated creature like me getting involved in anything like that? Hug your animal! The very idea! Hug, indeed! All right for them to hug each other, but if anybody even tries to lay a paw on me, I will call the police! I told you that Benevolent League bunch were not very bright. I do not know why I keep going to their meetings. Can you imagine a cultured, refined creature like me playing bingo and drinking lemonade?"

I told her to keep her distance if that would make her feel more comfortable, but that I would like to hear about what had happened over the past year to the grand plans the BLAA organization had for rehabilitating the four groups of animals.

Her response was, "If you will lie still and not even breathe in this direction, I will tell you all about it. Actually, I could have told you about it last year before it ever happened. Clever creatures like me know how things like that will turn out. If I had been crude enough to lay down some bets, I would be a wealthy feline by now. I would have won back all your coin collection that I lost last week betting on the horses."

I sighed over the loss of my carefully-hoarded collection of pennies but, realizing it was a small price to pay for the company of such a sophisticated, cultured, refined, clever creature, I said nothing.

"So, listen up, I am going to tell you this only once," she threatened, "and if you want all the details, ask somebody else. If you remember, the first family was the Byrds. They were going to sobber up the mother, train up the father, and beat up the little ones; i.e., shape up the whole family. To make a short story even shorter, the little ones escaped from reform school, got jobs as bug boys, saved their money, and bought out the pool hall. They converted one end of it into a neighborhood bar where Mrs. Byrd is the bartender and the old man sweeps the floor. Mrs Byrd is off the sour mash. Says she would not touch the stuff after seeing what fools it causes her customers to make of themselves. As for Mr. Byrd, apparently he just sweeps and drinks and sweeps and drinks. The little ones gave the business to their parents and moved on to better things. One heads up the local numbers racket, another is a drug lord, and the third is a television evangelist.

"Next, the box turtles. The Benevolent League's plans to get them settled in as jet pilots just never got off the ground. Next, the League tried their backup plan of making elevator operators out of them. That failed because, in spite of months of training, the poor creatures simply could not learn the route. One requirement of both jobs was that the turtles improve their communication skills. The only thing the turtles had to say about this was, 'Anybody who knows anything about turtles knows that turtles will not talk, cannot talk, and do not talk. Turtles are solid citizens who keep both feet on the ground. Turtles stay at home, tend to their own business, and wish everybody else would do the same. Thank you, over and out!' That was the end for them. As far as anybody knows, they are out there somewhere wandering aimlessly around in the woods the way all box turtles do.

"As for the deer family, there really is not much to tell. The Benevolent League put a great deal of energy into trying to find proper mates for the four does. They could not find any. The bucks all said the whole idea went against their nature and probably also was against union rules. They pointed out that deer have never been of the monogamous persuasion. Neither were they bigamists. If they fitted into any such classification, they would have to be considered pigamists. After months of searching, the Benevolent League finally came up with a few old great grandfather types who were willing to contribute if the dowry was high enough. Unfortunately, by the time all the details were worked out, and the Benevolent League thought their expectations finally were realized, they found the does' expectations already had been realized—all four were expecting. The Benevolent League has taken no further action concerning the expectant mothers and has marked deer morality off their list of concerns to be addressed.

"The rabbits were the most embarrassing failure of all. Remember how they were declared an endangered species, given guns to protect themselves, and subjected to massive food donations? Well, the Benevolent League wanted the rabbits to learn to be productive, and they got results! With all that free food and protection, those bunnies had nothing to do except be productive. There were twenty-seven rabbits at the start of the program; in two months, there were four thousand, nine hundred, and twelve. The Benevolent League had to open up a new section of the forest to resettle four thousand of them. By the time they got those resettled and took a recount in the original settlement, the reduced population there already had increased to twelve thousand, four hundred, and fifty-one.

"And that was not all. You would think there would have been a lot of contented, happy bunnies there. But, no! There was constant grumbling, and the only thing that kept the population from getting even more out of hand was that they started shooting each other out of spite and boredom. A mob of young rabbits declared their refusal to accept any more food handouts from the 'Carrots on Chariots' program. Said it was beneath their dignity, they did not need charity, and they were perfectly capable of looking out for themselves. And I suppose you heard about the Clark Creek Carrot Caper. The bunny mob captured two chariots of food and dumped it all in the creek. Actually, they were right. They did not need help. Remember, they had guns. They simply robbed the local business establishments and took whatever they wanted. And not just food. At one time, for example, they seemed to have had an average of two television sets, two VCRs, and three automobiles per family.

"Well, the Benevolent League was forced to take drastic action. They took the rabbits off the endangered species list and canceled the 'Carrots on Chariots' program. But the most effective thing was that they passed a law that declared that all rabbits should turn in their guns and any rabbit caught carrying a gun could legally be shot by any other rabbit. This led to big change. All the bunnies except two turned in their guns. These two shaved their front legs to demonstrate what they claimed was their constitutional right to bare arms. Then they had a fight over a little female rabbit and had a big shoot-out at high noon. They winged each other and their guns were confiscated.

"Now, the Benevolent League has given up and pulled out. All the rabbits are on their own. After about six weeks back to the normal give and take of life, the population was back down to twenty-seven healthy, alert bunnies. These twenty-seven may not be particularly pleased with their lot in life, but no one has heard a great deal of complaining out of them either. So, there you are. If they had just listened to me, none of this would ever have happened. We would have, as I urged them to do, used all the resources to start a shelter for homeless kittens. Then the whole world would be a better place in which to live. But what can you do when you are dealing with a bunch of selfish animals who can only see the world from their own warped, twisted, distorted viewpoint?"

Cleopatra was silent. I looked over and saw that she was asleep. At least now I was permitted to move from my position on the hammock. I got up, stepped gingerly past where she lay coiled on her tree stump, went into the house, burned my clothes, and took a long and vigorous shower.

XI. The Blue J.

The thunder did not waken me;
Through rain and hail I snored.
But the softly dripping faucet
Just could not be ignored.

53

I was in a downright nasty mood that morning, mostly as a result of my experiences the day before. On the morning of the day before, I left home to drive over to Nice Nellie's Knicks and Knacks to purchase a table I had looked at earlier in the week. We needed a new table to set next to a thirty-six inch square table we already had. We were going to cover the two with a single table cloth so as to end up with a six-foot table that would comfortably seat six people. My route to Nice Nellie's happened to take me right by Cheap Willie's Furniture Emporium. So, I decided to stop off and see if he might have the same or a similar table. If he did, this would save my driving another four miles and might even save me a few dollars.

At Cheap Willie's, I found what appeared to be the perfect table with a tag on it which listed it as a thirty-six inch table, exactly the size we needed. And, to my delight, it was five dollars cheaper than the one at Nice Nellie's. I purchased the table, looked carefully at the shipping carton to make sure it was the correct thirty-six inch size, laboriously loaded it into the trunk of the car, and took it home. There, I struggled to get it unloaded and into the house. I ripped open the box, cut the box into small pieces that would fit in the trash bin, and laid out the pieces to the table. I read the assembly instructions and, after a considerable struggle, screwed on the four legs. It was only then that I pushed the new table over beside my old table and discovered that the new one was, in fact, only thirty-two inches square. I phoned Cheap Willie's Furniture Emporium and asked them what to do. Their response was that, if the table were carefully disassembled and put back into the original carton exactly as I had found it, they would refund my sixty-five dollars, less their usual ten dollar restocking charge. I told them I had destroyed the carton but that I could find the piece of it that indicated the table was supposed to be thirty-six inches. They said they were not responsible for what was printed on the box; that was done in Hong Kong where the table was manufactured. And they could not accept returned merchandise that was not packed neatly in its original container. They suggested that my only recourse was to take the problem up with the Hong Kong manufacturer or with Cheap Willie himself. I asked to speak with Cheap Willie. I was told he would return my call as soon as he returned from his two-month vacation in Hawaii.

I did not react gracefully to any of this. The fact is my prudent selection of choice words and phrases represented a masterpiece of skirting around the use of outright profanity. Also, I may have threatened to write the Attorney General's Office, contact the Chamber of Commerce, complain to the Better Business Bureau, and write to my congressman and senators. There is even some possibility I might have promised to paint a sign and march back and forth in front of the store in an attempt to warn others that Cheap Willie's was a den of iniquity that should be banished from the face of the earth. My mild admonitions seemed not to bring about any noticeable contrition on their part and did little to keep my blood pressure from hitting the ceiling. I was livid with rage. I gently eased the telephone back into its cradle and gave the table a gentle nudge with my foot. All in all, I probably could not claim this as one of my better moments.

And that was not the end of it. I brooded all night, hardly sleeping at all. The next morning, I was a pitiful sight, with puffy eyes and grumbly face. I drank extra strong coffee in an attempt to ease my headache. I read the morning newspaper and noticed that the stock market was down. Our stocks had lost more than a thousand dollars in one day. I did not even blink an eye at that. The market goes up and the market goes down. Everybody knows that, so why worry about a mere thousand dollars. But, what to do, what to do, what to do about my potential sixty-five dollar loss on that stupid table? It was then that the bird crashed into the glass pane of the kitchen window.

I rushed out to see if there was any hope for the poor, unfortunate bird. He was lying flat on his back under the Golden Bell bush next to the bird bath. He was shaking his head from side to side and counting the stars in the clear morning sky. I realized at once that the accident was not fatal. His collision with the window had crossed his eyes and dotted his T's but, with a little rest, he would recover. He introduced himself. Said J. Wellington Witherspoon was his name and being a blue jay was his game. I rung my hands and fretted over him. After all, if my window had not been there, he would not have been hurt. I had put stick-on decals on the windows to help the birds see the glass but, obviously, I had not done a very good job of it. I helped him, as best my trembling hands would permit, to bend his wings back into position, straighten his beak, and smooth down his feathers.

After he recovered a bit, he reached over with his good wing, patted me on the head and said, "Now, now! Slow and easy does it. Calm and quiet is the way to go. If you don't ease up a bit, you'll give yourself a stroke. We're not talking lawsuits here. Wasn't your fault. I just wasn't looking where I was going. I saw it at the last second and turned so as to hit it a glancing blow. Do it all the time. Can't afford to molt over the little stuff. There are enough REAL problems in life to fret over. Don't ignore the crocodile and then let yourself get nibbled to death by a duck. Advice time here! Don't ever hit anything head on if it is bigger than you are. Start off by hitting a glancing blow. Then stop to check if the dent you made in your head is bigger than the dent you made in the obstacle. If so, don't be afraid to give up on breaking down that barrier and go find one that is more your size. Works well for me, on all kinds of obstacles." He gave his wings a few trial flaps and found them functional, said something about the crash into the window being an interesting experience, and flew off into the morning sky.

54

The blue jay, or *Cyanocitta cristata*, is the common jay east of the Rocky Mountains. It is a boisterous, colorful, bold, gregarious bird who does not always get along amiably with smaller birds. It is omnivorous, which means it will eat practically anything. I can attest to its enjoying bird seed, suet, peanut butter, and, apparently, acorns. It also seems to take in its fair share of worms and bugs. Jays often nest near houses and seem to have a particular preference for nesting in vines. Their nests are bulky collections of leaves, twigs, and bark. The male contributes his genes, helps with the nest building and, on rare occasions, egg sits while the female is out grocery shopping. But these are about the extent of his contributions to family life. The mother incubates the three to five eggs and accepts the primary responsibility for getting the little ones off and flying. Many blue jays migrate in autumn. When migrating, they fly just above the tops of trees in loose flocks. Some blue jays, however, like where they live and choose to stay home all year.

55

A month had passed since J. Wellington Witherspoon's encounter with my window. And, then, one morning he was back picking over what was left of yesterday's bird seed. He saw me come out of the house and asked me if I was about to put down some fresher stuff. I told him that was why I came out and that he was welcome to breakfast there. I put out the feed and he ate while I sat in one of the lawn chairs. I asked him where he had been for the past month. His response, given between gulps of satisfaction as he scooped down the seeds, was, "You probably would say I have been wasting my time. You likely are right, but I think I have had a most interesting look at how the business world functions and how the human types react to exceptions to the rule."

"Uh," I said, "if it's not too personal, what do you mean by all of that?"

"Been trying to open a bank account," he said. "Had extra worms and a few choice bugs. Thought I would deposit them in the bank for safe keeping and earn a bit of interest. Worked at it the whole month. Didn't work out. Just wasted my time. But did I ever have a great adventure! Do you want to hear about it?"

I said I would, so, apparently having eaten his fill, he perched on a low limb in the small tree next to my chair, peeped around to make sure no one else could hear and, in a soft voice, launched into the following tale.

"My name, as you know, is J. Wellington Witherspoon. Want to know why I use an initial for a first name? Well, I will tell you if you will cross your heart and hope to die that you will keep it a deep, dark secret. The truth is my mother named me when I was still in the shell. She wanted girls. She named me Josephine after her sister, Wellington after her mother's family, and Witherspoon after my father. Well, when I broke out of my shell and she saw I was a boy, she just about fainted. But she never changed my name. I didn't pay much attention to it at first. My friends all called me Wellington. If any of them heard my mother call me Josephine, I simply told them she was nearsighted and took me for one of my sisters. But then, one day, when I was in the full bloom of my young manhood, I sent off the top of a corn flakes box to get a free prize. The prize promised to be a cardboard airplane that I thought would be a big help in getting me ahead in the flying department. Instead, it was the beginning of trouble and inconvenience for some of the animals with whom I have dealt, and the beginning of a multitude of interesting experiences for me.

"When the prize arrived, delivered airmail by the U. S. of A. postal service, the package was address to MISS Josephine! I was mortified. I hid in a dark corner of our nest for two days or, maybe, seventeen years. When I came out, I took one of those big felt markers and marked out all but the first letter of that despised name; marked it out in the family book, on my sociable security card, and on my flying permit. After that, my name was J. Wellington Witherspoon. And it will take more than the U. S. of A. army, marine corp, and infernal revenue service to get me to change it."

His voice rose as he talked. He seemingly did not care who heard the balance of his tale. His eyes were bright and his feathers glistened as he continued. "Well, like I said, I went down to open an account with our friendly neighborhood bank. Should have known they would have trouble. Happens all the time. But, do I ever learn? Of course not! But that is another story. Went into the bank and this nice lady came up and asked me what I wanted. Told her about having extra worms and a few prize bugs I wanted to deposit. Told her I needed to open an account. She was all gushy and sweet and explained how I would get a free toaster as soon as my wealth had been on deposit for thirty days. She said how wonderful it was that I was the thrifty type and had chosen their bank. She assured me I always would find her and the others at the bank trustworthy, loyal, helpful, and friendly.

"Then, she pulled out the application form and we got down to business. First, she wanted to know my name. I told her it was J. Wellington Witherspoon. She started to write that down but paused and asked me what the J. stood for. I asked her why she wanted to know. She said the bank had to have my full name. I said my full name was J. Wellington Witherspoon. She asked again what the J. stood for. She said the bank needed to know my full first name because the application form asked for a first name, middle initial, and last name. I asked her why that was so. She said the computer system was set up that way. I asked WHY it was set up that way. She was getting a bit edgy and green in the gills by now and replied that they might have two customers named J. Wellington Witherspoon and, if they did not know the full first names, they might get the two accounts mixed up. I asked her how they would keep them straight if they both happened to have the same first name and middle initial. She said that, in such a case, they would use the address to keep the accounts straight. I told her my name was J. Wellington Witherspoon and that we should move to the next line and be sure to get my address straight so they would not get me mixed up with somebody else with the same name. She said, between clinched teeth, that she absolutely must have my full first name.

"I gave up. I said she could put my full first name down as 'Jentle jay who refuses to give the trustworthy, loyal, helpful, friendly lady the information she does not need and is too short in the smarts department to recognize she does not need.' That was when the poor thing came unglued and started biting her nails, clutching her throat, and screaming. She rushed out of the room and sent her supervisor to get me straightened out.

"The supervisor was a portly, bald-headed gentleman with lovely manners and a calm demeanor. I was sitting on the counter by now with my worms in a pile and my bugs neatly lined up in a row. The courteous gentleman asked me what he could do for me and I explained about wishing to open an account. He said that was wonderful and that he was adding on a month's free supply of bread to go with my free toaster. He assured me I would always find the bank personnel to be courteous, kind, obedient, and cheerful.

"And, then, he whipped out a new application form, stuck the pencil in his mouth to dampen the point, and asked me my name. I told him I was J. Wellington Witherspoon. He said something about what a fine name that was and that he needed to know my full first name. I told him I didn't know how to pronounce it. He scratched his head and asked if I would please spell it then. I told him I didn't know how to spell it either. He then asked if I had a copy of my birth certificate with me. I reminded him that blue jays don't have birth certificates; they are not born; they are the result of what you might call a lay-hatch operation. It was then that the courteous, kind, obedient, and cheerful gentleman gave me a blank look and said he probably ought to get the bank president in on an important account like this one. He left, and out came the president of the bank.

"The president was a mousy little lady with her hair cut short and her tail cut long. She had huge, thick eyeglasses and was dressed like a man. I told her I wished to open an account, and she said that was wonderful and that she was adding free butter and jelly to go on my free bread that I would toast in my free toaster as soon as my wealth was on deposit for thirty days. She said she was sure I would find all the bank people to be thrifty, brave, clean, and reverent.

"She also told me an interesting thing that the others had failed to mention. She told me that my deposit absolutely would be one hundred percent guaranteed by the U. S. of A. government which, at the time, was only one hundred zillion dollars in debt. And, then, she asked for my full first name. I looked her straight in the eye and said my full first name was Jaulquesting-flumberzammerston. She puzzled over that for a few moments and said, 'Why don't we just put that down as the initial J.' I said, 'Lady, I can tell why they made you president of the bank.'

"She seemed pleased enough and said, that to be sure there would be no confusion about my first initial, she was putting me down as J. (only) Wellington Witherspoon. We completed the application on friendly terms, and she paged a clerk to come out and measure up my worms, weigh up my bugs, and box them all up in a neat carton. Then, while the clerk was hauling the whole mess off to stash away in their big, safe safe, she was busy writing out my deposit receipt. She said the bank would let me know as soon as my checks were printed so I could come by and pick them up. She said, if I wished to save a trip, I could just wait thirty days and pick up my free goodies at the same time. And then the thrifty, brave, clean, and reverent bank president thanked me again for my patronage and sent me happily on my way.

"Some three weeks later, I received a notice in the U. S. of A. mail that my checks were printed and I could come down and pick them up. I flew over immediately and told the young lady at the counter what I wanted. She found my newly printed checkbook, handed it to me, and told me to look it over and make sure everything was correct. I looked it over and, you guessed it, they had my name down as Jonly W. Witherspoon.

"I ripped out one check and stuck it under my wing to keep as a souvenir, ripped out a second one and used it to write a check for my entire bank balance, and tossed the checkbook into the trash bin that they apparently had there just for that purpose. The young lady looked over my check, examined her records, and very efficiently reached into a drawer under the counter and counted out a pile of worms and collection of bugs. I measured the worms and weighed the bugs to make sure I was receiving my due. The bugs weighed out right on the ounce, but the worms measured one worm short and three worms long. I asked the young lady about the discrepancy and she said I had to pay one worm for having checks printed and that the extra worms were interest for the twenty-eight days that my account had been open. She said if I had waited two more days I would have gotten a free toaster, a month's supply of bread, peanut butter, jelly, and cheese to put on my toast, and a case of fine wine with which to wash it all down. I allowed as how I would not suffer much from the loss since I had plenty of worms and bugs."

His story told, he sat there for a minute, and then asked, "Don't you think that was an interesting experience? I still have that souvenir check. I'm using it to line one side of my nest and to remind me of some of the interesting people I've met. Do you think I handled the situation with common sense, dignity, aplomb, composure, poise, and savoir-faire?"

I told him he obviously was a model citizen and that I did not know how he had kept his temper under control. His response was that, "Most animals are not big in the temper department. Mostly, just humans and dogs need distemper shots. After all, what difference will it all make in a hundred years, in one year, or just tomorrow."

J. Wellington Witherspoon hopped down from his perch, sampled a few more seeds, thanked me, and told me he was leaving. I asked him where he was going next.

"Ha!" he said. I'm going to work on two big projects. First, I'm joining in a big protest march to protest protest marches. After that, I'm joining a campaign to conduct telephone solicitations to garner support for a campaign to outlaw telephone solicitations. Then, I don't know. May go down to the post office and try to get myself sent to Miami Beach by first class mail."

XII. The Homosaps

Intelligence, they say, is in his genes;
He has the wits to conquer sea and land;
Can shrewdly blow the earth to smithereens,
And leave himself, alas, no place to stand.

56

I was pretty sure I heard something scratching on the back door. Probably was Cleopatra again, either wanting in or wanting out for the zillionth time that morning. Whatever it was, it could wait until I finished my unenthusiastic efforts to unload the dishwasher and put away the clean dishes. It was almost noon of what seemed, in many ways, a mostly wasted day. I was not in a good mood and the dreary, sodden weather did nothing to lift my spirits. With the dishes out of sight in haphazard stacks on the wrong shelf, I moved on to other chores. I pulled a frozen container of something or other out of the freezer, shoved the container into the microwave, and punched in some random numbers on the timer and power buttons. While the microwave did its thing, I pulled cheese from the refrigerator shelf and crackers from the pantry. I then sat down to eat. The soup was lukewarm with small chunks of ice in the center, but I didn't care. I again ignored the persistent scratching on the back door and methodically ate my lunch. The rain continued to come down steadily and the dark, brooding clouds matched my mood. I had been trying, of late, to do a better job of getting in touch with my feelings. And this morning I was succeeding wonderfully well.

I think my down mood started yesterday morning. As on most Sundays, I ate breakfast out. Doing this gives me an opportunity to wake up gracefully and to observe life from a spectator perspective before moving on to a more active involvement in Sunday school and church. Yesterday I ate breakfast at the local fast foodery. As I sat there with my grease biscuit and coffee, a dejected-appearing young man came in and sat down at a nearby table. His clothing, while appearing clean enough, looked as though it had been slept in. His face showed evidence of a careless shave and his hair of a half-hearted brushing. He held his coffee in fidgety hands and stared at the floor through lack-luster eyes. Two or three times each minute, he glanced nervously at his watch, the foodery entrance, and back to the floor. He was not a happy person.

Soon a young woman with two children came through the door. They lined up at the counter, ordered and picked up their food, and looked around until they spotted the man. The children, a boy about seven years old and a girl about five, came over and sat with the man. The woman dumped her ample figure heavily into a chair at the adjacent table. She did not speak to the man and was careful not to look in his direction. Her hands trembled as she toyed with her breakfast, and her face showed the affects of stress and suffering. The boy sat straight and still and stared out the window. He seemed to carry the weight of the world on his young shoulders. The little girl squirmed in her seat and splashed out part of her orange juice. The woman made a motion as though coming to her aid, but stopped herself and settled back to her solid seat in the chair. The man wiped up the juice with a paper napkin. The damp napkin slipped from his fingers, fluttered to the floor, spread out flat with the spot of juice showing through, and lay there as if resigned to the brevity of it useful life. The little girl continued to squirm and, finally, looked up at the man and asked, "Daddy, why don't you and mommy like each other any more?"

The man mumbled an answer in a voice so low I couldn't hear. The girl frowned and twisted her shoulders as though to indicate that she had asked the same question before and received the same disheartening answer.

Outdoors, just on the other side of the plate glass window, another scene played itself out. Near the outdoor tables, two juvenile boys and two adolescent girls stood in the uncertain rays of a sun that barely broke through low-hanging clouds. The boys strutted around in their new sneakers, tight trousers, garish tee shirts, pimply faces, and caps that were on backwards. They were trying to impress the girls and, apparently, were succeeding. The two girls, who wore their hair long and their makeup heavy, were whispering secrets to each other and giggling. Their trousers and sweaters accented figures that had flowered early in the spring of their lives and likely would lose the bloom with the first hot, arid days of summer. The music vibrating from the store carried to the outdoors. When one of the girls took her biscuit wrapper over to the trash bin, she swiveled her hips and bounced with every beat of the tune. The boys watched with eager but uncertain eyes as the girls giggled nervously and uncertainly at the edge of the unknown.

From inside the foodery, the man and woman could see the two young couples. And what they saw, so it seemed to me, was a reflection of what they had been ten years before. The little boy and girl also could see, and what they saw reflected what they would be like seven or eight years in the future.

The sun outside the window disappeared behind the darkening clouds and a cold wind blew. Faces and shapes changed as people came and went, and my focus on individuals was lost in the blur of the hoards of spirits hurling through time and space in earthly forms.

57

"I really should see to that cat," I thought. She had been scratching on the door long enough asking either to be let out or to be let in. She is that way on rainy days. But I was wrong; it was not Cleopatra. It was my good friend, Squeaks the Squirrel.

Squeaks stood on her hind legs, stared up at me, and asked, "Can your cat come out and play tag with me?"

That was when I remembered that Cleopatra had finally settled down in the house and was piled up in the middle of the guest room bed fast asleep. I stepped out onto the porch and closed the door behind me. The rain was coming down in torrents. Squeaks was soaked. The water dripped off her and formed a puddle at her feet. I was glad to see her. She knew what good care I took of all our neighborhood animals. She knew I was helpful, generous, and kind. She had learned from me that at least some humans have their head on straight and have a reasonable understanding of what life is all about. I knew Squeaks would tell me how great humans are and what a wonderful guy I am and, right then, I had a strong need for approval and praise regarding the human race and myself. In short, I was down and I was sure Squeaks would pump me back up. "What are you doing out in the rain?" I asked.

"Rain?" Squeaks said, looking at the sheets of water rolling off the roof and splashing into the Ajuga beds. "So that's what that is! My! My! The things you can learn when you keep an open mind." She stood there for a minute watching the deluge, and then said, "You have not answered my question. I asked if your cat-type can come out and play."

I told Squeaks the cat had finally settled down to sleep and could not be disturbed. Her response was, "That cat should be exorcised. That's what she should be."

I replied that "exorcise" meant "cast out devils," and that I thought she meant "exercise."

Squeaks backed up to the edge of the porch, scratched her head and said, "Why in the world would anybody exercise a cat? I am talking about your thermos cat here, the one you said stayed on the wall in your hall and auto-magically conjures up heat for your den in winter and cools it off in summer. That's the one that I think needs to be EXORCISED!"

I decided this was going to take awhile, so I eased myself down into a porch chair and watched as Squeaks flopped down on the porch floor. "I don't know what you are talking about," I said. "My thermostat is right in there on the hall wall where it always stays."

"Don't think so," said Squeaks. "I'm pretty sure it is up and around. I'm sure I have been seeing magic out here. I've been sitting over there on the ground where I had a good view, and I watched this place. And strange things are going on here, that's for sure."

"What, specifically, are you talking about?" I asked.

"Well," Squeaks said, "I watched you letting a cat in and out of that door. Every time you let it out, I made a short scratch in the mud, and every time you let it in, I made a long scratch. And according to my palpitations you have let it out thirty-three times and back in forty-seven times. So, either your house is getting filled up with cats or there is some voodoo, sorcery, wizardry stuff going on here. I may not always be right, but I'm NEVER wrong. You can go over there and count those shorts and longs for yourself if you don't believe me."

I sat up straight in my chair and said, "I'm impressed with your mathematical expertise and deductive reasoning, but you're wrong."

This appeared to make Squeaks angry. She shouted, "And I'm depressed with your extensive, comprehensive, majestic, awesome vocabulary, but I saw what I saw, and that's that!"

"Front door!" I said. "Sometimes, on wet days, I let Cleopatra out the front door. She sneaks around under the eves where it's dry and comes back inside by the back door."

"Oh," said Squeaks. "Wasn't your thermos cat? Was Cleo Patrick all the time? Hmm. Are you so ashamed of being a full-time doorman for a cat that you spring her out the front door part of the time so nobody will see you do it? Why didn't you tell me in the first place that it was Cleo Patrick? Well, answer my question, can she?"

"Can she WHAT?" I asked.

"Can she come out and play. That's what this conservation is all about, isn't it?" Squeaks said.

"Already told you," I answered. "She's asleep and can't be disturbed."

"Oh," replied Squeaks, "That's what I thought. But, no harm in my asking, is there? Thought she might like to see my marks in the mud over there. Thought she might like to know that she isn't the only one who can draw."

"What do you mean, 'draw?'" I innocently asked. "She can do almost everything, but one thing she absolutely can't do is draw."

"You mean you never heard that all cats draw lightning?" Squeaks said. "And, if she can draw lightning, she must be able to draw all kinds of things."

I did not respond directly. Instead, I said, "You really don't know much about cats, do you?"

Squeaks said, "Of course I don't! How could I? They're the other kind. All I know is she plays a fine game of tag when she's awake, which isn't very often. And she always wants in when she's out and out when she's in. Other than that, all I know is that she's a 'kept.'"

"She's a WHAT?" I asked.

"She's a 'kept,'" insisted Squeaks. "Other than your type, there are just two kinds of animals in the hole, wide, world: the kept ones and the unkempt ones. And she, definitely, is one of the kept ones."

I was puzzled. Squeaks, in spite of the fact that she occasionally gets her tang toungled, is a pretty straight thinker. So I tried a simple question. "What makes her 'kept'?"

"Because YOU are the reprehensible... uh, responsible one there," Squeaks said. "She's kept 'cause you keep her. She doesn't accept responsibility for anything. You feed her, brush her, house her, litter her, and vet her. She doesn't do anything for herself. She's a kept cat for sure. All she has to do is act cute and sleep a lot. 'Kepts' usually are cats, dog types, gerbubbles, cold fish, or birds like cannards or a pair-o-keets. Other animals, other than your kind are, like I said, unkempts."

"Do you, perhaps, mean unKEPT?" I asked.

Her indignant reply was, "I've got a nexcellent vocabulary and when I say unkempt I MEAN unkempt. Discordant to my dictionary, 'unkempt' means disheveled, untidy, uncombed, unbrushed, ruffled, rumpled, tousled, no nail polish on your toes, and no ribbon in your hair. We unkempts have no time for such jibble jabble. Outdoor animals are all unkempts 'cause they have to take responsibility for themselves and for each other. They have to make it on their own and don't have time for primps and preens. You are not unkempt, 'cause you're not an outdoor type. On the other paw, you don't quite make it as a 'kept.' You, in your weird way, show lots of reprehensibility... uh, responsibility. You do all kinds of work like carrying in groceries, carrying out garbage, mowing lawns, blowing leaves, washing and waxing cars, weeding gardens, watering plants, cleaning and filling bird baths, refilling bird feeders, and laying out seeds for doves and an occasional hungry squirrel."

I was feeling all warm and fuzzy inside over Squeak's assurance that she considered me to be responsible. I was sure I had always treated the animals fairly. I was sure all of them thought highly of me and that I had their eternal gratitude for being such a good friend and neighbor. The kind of reassurance I was getting from Squeaks was just what I needed to heal my pride which was wounded by my recent doubts about the human condition. Squeaks stretched out on the floor, rested her chin on her folded front leg, and began to relax. I knew this was going to be a long conversation that likely would include additional assurances from Squeaks that all of the animals considered me to be a hard-working, responsible, paragon of virtue. I settled down even further in my chair and eagerly waited for her to continue.

Squeaks said, "Actually, I'm more knowledged up on your kind than I am on cats. All the animals know about Homosaps. Learning about them is one of the first things we have to do to keep from getting killed down. But, there's lots we don't understand about them. Like, we don't understand how such unstable creatures stay alive. We don't understand where all of 'em come from and why anything that matures so slowly breeds like a rabbit. But we know for sure that Homosaps are peculiar, irrational, and dangerous creatures."

I asked, of course, if she could, by any chance, be referring to Homo sapiens.

Squeaks responded, "Sure. Homosaps. Swat I said. I think that's the scientific name for your kind, and I was using it so you wouldn't get refused. Actually, most of the animals defer to your kind simply as sapheads. No defense intended here, but true is true and you are the one asking the questions. Some of the animals around here remit that you may be a little less reprehensible than most sapheads. But they know better than to trust your kind and they keep their guard up around here."

If I had not been so puzzled, I would have been angry or devastated. I told her that, because I had proven to be her friend and I had never harmed any of the animals, I didn't understand how she could say such nasty things about me. I suggested that she really didn't know anything about Homosaps... uh, Homo sapiens, and I asked where she had gotten her information.

She said, "Don't know much about most of them. I'm lucky that way. Know about your good friend and neighbor down the street that shoots down dead any animal that comes near his vegetable garden. And know about those who drive cars on the road without looking at who they're running over. Heard, too, about how sapheads leave their pets in hot cars with the windows all rolled up tight while they go shopping or off to lunch. And about how they go on vacations and leave their poor 'kepts' locked in the house without any company to speak of. Know they take animals to the vet and have needles punched into 'em. Face to face, though, I only know about you. And I listen to the other animals and I know what they tell me about you."

I sat there in my chair and counted off the seconds, and then the minutes, while I waited for Squeaks to ask me if I wanted to hear what the other animals had told her about me. This time, I outlasted her.

Squeaks raised her head and shouted, "Well, do you or don't you?"

"Do," I responded.

"Well, it's this way." she said as she stretched back out into a comfortable position. "First off, they say you came in here one day and starting whomping down a bunch of our trees. Cut down seventeen squirrel dens, six flicker nests, and homes of twenty-seven other bird families. Dug up or otherwise misrupted thirty-six doves, forty-three voles, twenty-six moles, thirty seven field mice, eight box turtles, forty-two hop toads, eighteen rabbits, and thirty-three lizards. And then there were the mislocated insects and other things that are too numerous to mention. You came in and built this big, oversized monstrosity of a den right in the middle of our homes without even asking if you could live here or giving any warning that you were going to throw everybody out of their homes and mess up our whole neck of the woods. And you never said 'thank you,' 'I'm sorry,' or nothin'.

"The hickory nut trees you chopped were supplying nuts to ninety-two squirrels. Thanks to you, most of these have had to move clear out of the county. The two persimmon trees you pushed over kept ninety-seven miscellaneous birds and twelve opossums in fruit. And I won't even think about the acorns, berries, and other things you destroyed. Have you noticed hungry deer around here every winter? Well, they are hungry because you cut into their supply of shrubs and acorns. Now let's talk about your den. We've calculated out the 'proximate cubic feet in it and figured out how many animals could live comfortably in that amount of space. It comes out to about eight thousand squirrels, with room left over for all the voles, moles, field mice, rabbits, raccoons, and opossums in this end of the county. We could even squeeze in a few deer on rainy days. And what lives in there now? Two sapheads and two stupid cats, if you count the thermos cat."

Squeaks paused to catch her breath and then continued. "The animals around here also are onto the things you let other sapheads do. The animals say you just watch bad things happen all around you and you don't do anything to stop it. The only deception, if you can call it one, was when your neighbor shot down the raccoon in cold blood. Some of the animals say you told him you didn't think it was a nice thing to do. You should have gotten a gun and shot him, that's what you should have done! And don't say you don't have big guns, 'cause last week I heard you with my own ears say you were on the way over to a fiends house to shoot pools. And you must hunt golfs, too. You came home that day bragging to everybody about how you made a hole in one, and that you shot an eagle and three birdies.

"And you haven't done anything at all about sapheads who drive by here and drop off dogs just because they don't want them any more. Those sapheads just leave the poor, stupid dog types to starve or sorrow to death or get run over by a car driven by another speed-crazy saphead. Don't tell us you take care of homeless animals, 'cause we've seen what you do. Any dog wonders by here, even if he's just out for a walk, like he's got a perfect right to do, you put a fuss on him. You're so afraid he might be astray and you might have to put him up for a few days or twenty years that you yell at him and ruin him off. So, don't conflaberate things even more by saying you like dogs! Also, don't say you don't do animal sacrifices. We've seen you burn dead cows, pigs, chickens, and fishes on your grill. And don't say you don't eat up on animals. You've been heard to say you ate a turkey for Thanksgiving and, I can't believe this, your mate has been heard to mention squirrel stew, tracking rabbits in the snow, and four and twenty blackbirds baked in a pie."

Squeaks got more and more excited as she talked about my wrongdoing. She stood on her hind feet and shouted at me. "You try to make up for all your blatant grimes," she went on, "by throwing down a few seeds whenever you happen to think about it. Well, the animals have had enough. Last week, they had a vote on whether or not to run you out of the county."

"You mean they actually wanted to get rid of me," I asked incredulously.

"Well, not all of 'em, I guess," Squeaks replied in a softer voice. "Some of them wanted you to stay because they're afraid, if you left, somebody even worse might come in. They said you've already done about all the harm you can do and that a new family probably would have all kinds of new ways to lay torture, plunder, and destruction on us. If it will make you feel any better, you didn't lose. The vote was a tie. Four hundred and forty 'for,' four hundred and forty 'against,' and one animal chose not to vote. That was I. I restrained."

I was puzzled and a bit angry. This was not doing much for my ego. "You say you abstained?" I asked. "Why? If you had voted, at least I would have had a clear victory."

Squeaks settled back down to her spot on the floor and responded. "No," she said, shaking her head from side to side. "That's why I restrained. I'm your best friend, remember. If I had voted, you would have lost."

58

The gray squirrel, or *Sciurus carolinensis* is a clever, curious, capable, comely, determined, dogged, destructive, disturbing member of the rodent family. Its natural habitat is hardwood forests with nut trees, river bottoms, and wooded suburban backyards. Gray squirrels may be found throughout the United States and southern Canada, east of the Rocky Mountains. The squirrel eats nuts and large seeds in fall and winter and fruits, berries, mushrooms, and insects in the spring and summer. It is particularly fond of hickory nuts but is too impatient to wait for them to ripen. Usually it cuts them down and eats them green. It needs water at least twice a day. Our squirrels seem to have no objection to drinking water that has been used by dirty birds for bathing purposes. Thus, our bird bath appears to be their primary source of drinking water.

The gray squirrel's ears are cut short and its tail cut long. The squirrel is sixteen to twenty inches long, and about half of its length is tail. This tail is a multi-purpose tool. As a communication tool, it is used to communicate alarm, dominance or submission, and readiness during breeding times. As a "fifth leg," the tail helps the squirrel maintain balance during its frequent acrobatics and serves as a parachute during too-rapid descents from tree limb to ground. The tail also is used as a muffler and top coat in winter, a sunshade in summer, and an umbrella in wet weather.

The gray squirrel communicates by chattering, clucking like a hen that has just laid an egg, screaming, mewing, purring, barking, buzzing, and quacking like a not-too-sober duck. Our squirrels sometimes are so noisy that I have to tell them to shut up or buzz off. They pay no noticeable attention to this, but telling them off makes me feel better. The squirrel also has a keen sense of smell and excellent vision. The squirrel squirrels away nuts in the fall. It does not approach this task lightly but, rather, devotes long hours and much digging and patting down of dirt to the endeavor. Contrary to popular opinion, the squirrel does not draw up a treasure map showing the locations of its hoard. Neither does it devote mental energy to remembering the exact locations of zillions of buried nuts. How does it find the nuts? Simple! It scrunches up it nose and sniffs them out, even from under several inches of dirt and snow. How does it know it is getting its own nuts and not somebody else's? It doesn't know and, presumably, doesn't care.

The gray squirrel produces two litters each year. When the female comes into heat, she is pursued energetically by every male squirrel on the block. This chase is essential to the reproduction process in two ways. First, the female cannot ovulate unless she is chased. And, second, unless she is chased, and caught, copulation cannot take place. Apparently only the male squirrel knows when enough is enough. He plugs up the newly-impregnated female with a wax-like plug to keep her from continuing to mess around.

After about forty-four days, the female gives birth to from three to five little ones. They are helpless, naked, and blind, but apparently have no trouble locating the milk supply. In about five weeks their eyes open. During this period, their weight increases from one-half ounce at birth to three to four ounces. They soon are weaned and start nibbling whatever solid food they can find which, in the beginning, is mostly insects.

The life of the gray squirrel in the wild is quite short. The average life span is one year. Under more favorable conditions, it may live six to twelve years. Its natural enemies are hawks, owls, snakes, bobcats, and foxes. Many also die from accidents, disease (mostly mange) and parasites. Human hunters apparently do not kill enough to have a significant impact on the population.

The squirrel does not clean house. When the nest becomes too unkempt to suit its fancy, it simply abandons it and builds a new one. The primary reason the nest becomes unsuitable is that the squirrel is a flea bag. The nest gets so full of fleas that there is hardly room for squirrels. When it is time to move, the mother squirrel picks up her babies one at a time with her mouth and moves them to a new den.

The squirrel usually has a home range of less than an acre to perhaps ten acres. However, this range may overlap with the ranges of a number of other squirrels. Within these overlapping ranges, there is a well defined social hierarchy. Squirrels establish dominant and subordinate positions that lead to reasonable order and the avoidance of serious fights. While most youngsters are permitted to establish their own local ranges after they are weaned, some are rejected and have to pack their bags and seek their fortunes elsewhere.

In most of the squirrels' habitat, the population currently is kept reasonably stable by the high mortality rate. This has not always been the case. In the first half of the nineteenth century, numerous mass migrations of squirrels were observed. Lack of food and overpopulation appear to have led thousands, or even tens of thousands, of squirrels to join in mass migrations. Since no sudden and dramatic increases in the squirrel population was noted in the directions in which the squirrels were traveling, it is assumed the many of them died during the migration. While this migratory phenomenon is not clearly understood, it appears to be a mechanism by which the squirrels kept their population within sustainable bounds.

59

I left Squeaks standing in the rain and came back indoors. Squirrels, as you know, are of low intelligence and unstable emotions. It is better to pay no any attention to them, particularly on dreary days when you do not wish to hear the truth. As I walked down the dark hallway to my study, I failed to see the cat who was stretched out on the carpet right in the middle of the floor. I tripped and fell flat on my face.

Cleopatra yawned, stretched, and said, "Clumsy, clumsy, clumsy! You ought to be more careful. Now, go away and keep quiet so I can finish my nap."

I went into my study, sat at my desk, and stared out the window. My mood was as dark as the hovering clouds. I was depressed by the dreary day, doubly depressed by my encounter with Squeaks, and annoyed with my arrogant cat.

Cleopatra's nap was short. She soon came into the study, jumped onto the table by the window, and began washing her face and ears. "I saw you out there with that squirrel," she said. "You were merely frowning when you went out but were scowling when you came back in. So, my guess is that she really cheered you up. Right?"

I did not respond, so she continued. "The trouble with you is that your opinion of yourself is too dependent on what others say about you. Most humans are that way it seems. Actually, you should never listen to the truth about your kind. I think you have just enough intelligence to listen, half understand, and go slit your wrists."

"I know a lot about cats," I replied, "but I wonder if you really know anything much about humans."

"I know considerably more than I wish to know," she said. "I know pretty much what your squirrely little friend told you this morning. She has said it all to me a dozen times. She has a very narrow view, if that is any consolation to you. Humans have a great deal of difficulty trying to understand humans. I, and most other cats, have no trouble with it at all. That is why we are so aloof and why we are the only intelligent creature that can live in close proximity to humans without getting ulcers. So, what I am going to do for you today is share some of my infinite wisdom with you. I will tell you about humans."

60

I knew better than to deny her or interrupt her when she was on to something like this, so I kicked off my shoes, curled up in my chair, and prepared for a long discourse.

Cleopatra, warming to her subject, continued. "Your kind is of the genus *Homo* and the specie *sap*, which means 'stupid.' Homosaps, when referring to themselves, often omit the term, '*sap*' and substitute the term '*sapien*,' which means 'wise.' This says a great deal about their arrogance and ignorance. Actually, they are not born wise and but few of them ever grow to be wise. Not only are they born without wisdom, but also they are born with very few instincts. In fact, their primary instinct is the instinct for survival, without which they likely would lie down and die as soon as they matured enough to realize what miserable creatures they are. Homosaps seem to forget they were born with but few instincts and that they are the only animal who, literally, has to learn how to do everything it needs to do to stay alive. This being short on instincts but long on the capacity to learn is both the Homosap's primary drawback and its primary advantage. If it does not wish to learn, it can remain dumber than a dog, but if it wishes to and tries hard enough, it can learn all kinds of wonderful things. But learning is hard work and Homosaps are lazy. So, most of them choose to end up about half way between the two extremes of completely stupid and somewhat wise. To help you understand Homosaps, what we are going to do here is compare and contrast you, a rather typical Homosap, with your friend Squeaks, a rather typical non-cat and non-Homosap."

"Squeaks," Cleopatra continued, "is a bright little girl, for a squirrel. She definitely can learn some things. She knows your face and connects it with sunflower seeds, for example. Also, she has outsmarted you a hundred times when you have tried to put bird feeders where she cannot get to them. But she has definite limits. She is not as smart as you think she is. You read all kinds of things into her that simply are not there. Sometimes she scratches long marks and short marks on the ground and says that helps her count. She has done this for me a dozen times. But when I ask her what the marks mean, she has forgotten the difference between long and short. And she cannot really count. In fact, she does not even know the meaning of the word. The concept of numbers is past the limits of her mental ability. But you are different. You have known long from short and how to count since you were forty or fifty years old. On the other hand, Squeaks has been able to feed and house herself since she was six months old. She does it without really having to think much about it. She just does what comes naturally. Again, you are different. You still do not know how to get your own food. But you have learned how to earn money and buy most of the things you need. Squeaks would never understand the relationship between money and food."

Cleopatra paused to scratch her ear and then continued. "Squeaks is a good mother. She knew everything she needed to know about mothering as soon as her first one was born. All her offspring have turned out to be stable, contented, productive members of their kind. And while she knows exactly how to deal with newborns and exactly when to push them out of the nest, she does not have the slightest idea how many children she has had. You, on the other hand, as a parent, you... well, let me talk about Homosaps in general; I still have to live here, you know.

"Since Homosaps are short on instincts and have to learn to do everything, their developing years are crucial to their success. If they do not have wise parents, they are doomed. But here is what happens. Their most important product, baby Homosaps, are produced by completely unskilled labor, usually by children who are old enough to hanky-panky but not old enough to humor Junior. The parents seem to have some sort of instinct that says, 'make babies,' but they have zero instinct that tells them how to rear children. And, actually, they usually do not give it much thought. They are much too busy growing up themselves to take much notice of their offspring. So, they either rear them the way they were reared by their parents or, if they did not like the way they were reared, they do just the opposite. Either way, it usually is a disaster. Only after they are a hundred years old and have learned from their failures do Homosaps know enough about child rearing to make good parents. And by then they are far too old and decrepid to make babies and, probably, are too wise to do it even if they could.

"Another major difference between you and Squeaks—well, actually it is the same thing we have been talking about, but you are more likely to think of it as a completely different thing—is that Homosaps can contemplate. By contemplate, I mean Homosaps can think about their condition. They can choose how aware they wish to be. Actually, the word 'aware' is misleading. All creatures are more or less aware. But only the Homosap is AWARE that he is aware. Squeaks is quite aware of lots of things. If I ask her if she knows she has fur, she will pat herself on the chest and respond with something like, 'You thought maybe this was a vinyl raincoat?' And, if I ask her if she is aware of the tree in front of her, she will say, 'Of course! Did you think I thought it was a hole in the ground?' But, if I ask her if she is aware that she is three years old and probably has maybe five or six more years to live, she will stand there and stare at me until her eyes glaze over. She is aware that she is a squirrel, but she is not aware that she is aware of it. She never thinks about it, never wonders what it would be like to be a chickadee instead of a squirrel, never wonders about the meaning of her life, and never gets a headache or ulcers from worrying."

"So, there you have it," said Cleopatra. "That is what Homosaps are like. Now, do you understand them?"

Cleopatra really had not told me anything I didn't already know, but I didn't want to hurt her feelings by telling her so. The rain had stopped and one edge of the sun was trying to peep from behind the clouds. Cleopatra had not been outdoors for almost an hour and seemed to be in the mood to go out. I decided to join her. She slithered about the porch, walkway, carport, and yard to make sure everything was in order and finally, in spite of the wet ground, settled on one of her favorite spots, a small, flat boulder several feet in diameter that she referred to as her pet rock. I pulled a wet lawn chair up beside her, sat down, and tried to ignore the dampness I could feel soaking into the seat of my trousers. I decided to push the last conversation a bit further.

"So," I said, "you think humans are hindered by their lack of instincts and by their awareness."

"What?" Cleopatra responded, "Is that what you thought I said? You picked up some of the words, but you failed to pick up the meaning. Remember this: all things are true; all things are false; and meaning is found only in the context. Yes, Homosaps are hindered by their lack of instincts. They make a zillion mistakes they would not make if they had instincts instead of intelligence. And, NO, Homosaps are NOT hindered by their lack of instincts for, if they operated by instinct, they could not operate by learning. And learning allows some wondrous things to happen in the world. Also, awareness is a blessing in that it is part of experiencing and learning; it is a plague in that it also can result in a great deal of pain. Homosaps have the capacity for becoming the best or the worst, for building or destroying, for respecting self or despising self, for being happy or being sorrowful, for being kind or being cruel, for feeling delight or being depressed, for killing or caring, for thinking or repressing, for knowing or denying, for confronting or retreating, for living for the moment or living according to long-term priorities, and for saving life on this planet or destroying it."

"Most Homosaps," she continued, "operate like a go-cart with a two-hundred horsepower engine. Their intelligence is too much for them. There is no road map for an intelligent creature. Each is different and each lives in a different world. While they can learn from each other, they must adapt what they learn to their own unique situations. Intelligent creatures are 'becoming' creatures and nobody knows what they can and will become. So, of course they are concerned! Of course they are uncertain! Of course they are frightened!"

Cleopatra's head was sinking lower and I knew she soon would be asleep. I was not sure if she had cheered me up or cheered me down. I was not even sure she had any idea what she was talking about. She raised her head and I could see that she had a few more words to say.

"I have this good friend," she continued, "who never makes a mistake, never has any regrets, never worries about tomorrow, and never breathes an unhappy breath. Do you think you would like to exchanges places with my friend? I think not."

She knew, of course, that I was curious to know to whom she was referring. She reached down with one paw and gingerly patted her pet rock.

XIII. The Demise of Sam the Serpent

He's featherless and has no hair,
Or legs to take him anywhere.
And, yet, for him, do not despair.
His blood runs cold; his fangs lie bare.
He slithers here and slithers there
Without a tear, without a care.

61

It was a hot, lazy, late-August afternoon. I had been sitting most of the day in my favorite living room chair with a book in my hand. My back was beginning to ache from sitting in the awkward position forced upon me by having to hold the book above the sleeping cat curled in my lap. I thought of getting up and stretching a bit but was fully aware that Cleopatra the Cat would not take kindly to having her nap interrupted. And besides, I was as deep in thought as she was in sleep. I was reading a popular book about the earth environment and how it well might be too late to save ourselves from our own folly. The book warned about global warming, changes in the earth's protective ozone layer, trashing of the world's oceans, damage to the underground water supply, destruction of the rain forests, depletion of nonrenewable resources, the accumulating mountains of garbage in our cities, and the permanent loss of vast numbers of the earth's species of plants and animals.

These potentially catastrophic outcomes of the dominance and destructiveness of the human animals, along with the explosive increases in the earth's human population, seemed to me to be very real reasons for concern and concerted action by all intelligent creatures. Hard choices, so it seemed to me, were going to have to be made between, for example, worldwide population control and individual freedom. Who among those in positions of power had the courage to face such hard choices?

Who among the citizens had the courage and foresight to support leaders who struggled with such issues? Would we all go our selfish ways and leave a world in which our great grandchildren would have no chance for survival?

Thinking about the condition of the world and the potential for both the caring creativity and wanton destruction possessed by the human animal left me with a sense of dread, feelings of guilt, and an anxiety that I could not quite identify. I tried hard to get in touch with the anxiety and, finally, realized what was causing it. The simple truth was that I did not have the faintest idea what I could do to make any more than a token bit of difference in stopping the trashing of the earth. What could one person do? Even if all the people in this country united in a concerted effort to fix the problem, what could we do that would make more than a token difference? If I suddenly found I had been crowned King of the Earth, what action could I take that would result in a real beginning toward repairing the damage that has been done?

As I sat there and reviewed the pitiful options that seemed to be available to me, my initial feelings of helplessness and hopelessness evolved into anger and cynicism. My wife and I could, of course, trade in our automobiles for bicycles, burn down our house and live in a brush arbor, and eat only what grew naturally in the woods. The only significant result likely would be that we would die a few years sooner and, thus, reduce the world's population by two. It seemed to me that simply slitting our wrists right then would be more effective. We could and would, of course, recycle our garbage, turn out lights when we leave a room, keep the windows closed on winter days, use fewer chemicals on the lawn, turn off the water promptly when we finished showering, and write an occasional letter to our congressional representatives and senators. While such steps appeared unlikely to make any significant difference in the world environment, at least they might make us feel better.

As I sat there and pondered, the thought came to me that, in a real sense, as creators of most of the environmental problems, humans simply will be reaping the natural consequences of their shortsighted actions and of their choosing not to be aware of the damage they are doing. I had little sympathy for myself or others of my generation, or for the cockroaches that likely will survive us if we continue on our present course. Rather, my sympathies were for those yet unborn who will suffer the final agonies of a destroyed civilization knowing their ancestors could have prevented the cataclysmic disaster. My sympathies, too, were with the innocent victims: the animals that have been driven into small and ever-shrinking domains where they are dominated and harassed by humans. While I did not know of any way to react positively to the overall ecological concerns, perhaps I was in a better position than some to recognize and react constructively to the destruction of our animal population. I remembered the idea suggested in the book I had been reading that we accept all earth's creatures as our friends and neighbors and treat them as we would want to be treated. I remembered words in the book about the value of maintaining a sense of community with all living things, understanding the interdependence of all of creation, and recognizing the sacredness of all life. These seemed to me to be words of truth. These, perhaps, were suggestions that could guide my thinking and my actions. At least, this seemed a place for me to begin to discover a meaningful role. If I could not understand and react positively here, I feared, I likely would remain a part of the overall disease rather than a part of the cure. My new resolution was that I would begin at once to be a better friend to all creatures. I saw this as a simple and straight-forward idea; however, I recognized that I was not sure exactly how to convert the idea into actual practice.

62

My reveries were rudely interrupted by the sound of the doorbell and of someone banging frantically on the front door. I jumped to my feet, noticed that cats do NOT always land right side up and, ignoring Cleopatra's scornful wails, dashed to the door. It was Nancy the Neighbor who lives just down the street. She was pale as an opossum's tail and trembling with fear. "Snake!" she said. "There's a huge snake right on my front steps. What... what am I going to do? Oh! I'm so scared. Its head is as b-b-big as a grapefruit and it m-m-must be t-t-ten feet long. Horrible, horrible thing. Please! Can you do something?"

I went out, closed the door behind me, took a side trip to the workshop to pick up a hoe, and encouraged Nancy the

Neighbor to follow me over to her house. "Over there!" Nancy shrieked as we approached her front steps. "Oh. Look out! It will bite you for sure. What am I going to dooo?"

Sure enough, there in the flower bed by the side of the steps was Sam the Serpent. Sam was a Copperhead, a poisonous viper common to our area. He had the distinctive copper-colored, hourglass markings and was about thirty inches long. His head appeared to be exceptionally large for such a small snake. I looked closer and saw the reason why. He was holding Tammie the Toad firmly in his jaws. Nancy the Neighbor was screaming, "Kill him! Kill him! Please kill him! Oh! Oh! What am I going to do if he gets away? I'll never be able to come out of the house again. He'll bite me when I'm not looking! We won't be able to live here! We'll have to move."

I stood there scratching my head and trying to ignore the screaming. What WAS I going to do? Sam had spotted me and, possibly thinking I might try to take his dinner guest from him, stared coldly at me through the narrow slits of his eyes. I could feel my skin crawl as I thought about how I might handle him. I trembled slightly as I noted his swift movements and seeming aggression. I backed off a few steps, looked in Nancy's direction, and said as softly and calmly as I could, "Well, maybe I'll just try to scoop him up and move him out back in the woods away from the house."

"No! No!" Nancy shrieked. "He'll just come back and bite me when I'm not looking. I read somewhere that if you just take snakes away, they always come back. I'll never come out of the house again as long as he's alive."

And there was Tammie the Toad to consider. She looked up at me with her sparkling eyes and asked, "You just going to stand there and watch my civil rights being violated? He intends to swallow me right down, you know. Has already pumped me so full of poison that I am numb all over. I think if you swack him a lick or two with that hoe, he might just turn me loose and let me hop along to my business, if I can remember what it was."

"Well, let's see here," I thought. "What did I just read in that book about all the creatures of the world being my friends and neighbors? What did I just read about a sense of community, the interdependence of all creation, and the sacredness of all life?

Had I not just vowed to treat all creatures as I would wish to be treated?" In my mind, I went over my current options. I could walk away and say the whole thing was none of my business. This would leave one fat snake, one eaten-alive toad, and a poor Nancy who probably would die on the spot from fear and anxiety. Or, I could slay poor Sam who was only doing what came naturally for him. This would free up little Tammie, who might die anyway from the poison. And it would greatly relieve poor Nancy. I had to make a quick decision; Tammie was fast disappearing down Sam's throat and Sam was eyeing me and slowly slithering away. I reluctantly raised my hoe and chopped poor Sam in half. As Tammie popped loose, I smashed in Sam's head, picked up the pieces of his torn body, and started to deposit them in the trash can.

Nancy the Neighbor screamed, "No! No! Sometimes, they come back alive! Please, please take the horrible thing away."

I took a plastic garbage bag from the trash can, dropped poor Sam into the bag and, with the bag in hand, headed for home. Tammie the Toad, seemingly unharmed, hopped happily away. Nancy the Neighbor thanked me and pranced merrily into her house. I went home, deposited the plastic garbage bag on the porch for future burial, went into the house, and sobbed.

63

Three days had passed since the untimely demise of Sam the Serpent. I had buried him deep and there had been no resurrection. By now, all the animals in our woods had heard what happened. But, somewhat to my surprise, there had been no lynch mobs gathered on the porch, no tar and feather advocates massed at my door, and no threatening or unfriendly remarks from any of the neighborhood animals. The only acknowledgment of my role in Sam's demise came from Squeaks the Squirrel. As I headed out to pick up the mail, she circled around in front of me and stopped at my feet so that I either had to stop or step on her.

She stared up at me with curious eyes, and said, "Show me how you swung the hoe. Did you use both hands? Did he splash mush blood? Heard he was a hot-blooded viper until you cut him down in gold blood. How does it feel? To be a killer, I mean. Did you wash your hands good? Did you wash them before, or after, you did the deed? Tammie the Toad told me how she wasn't feeling any pain, until you came along and went 'chop, chop.' Then, so she said, she started having aches, pains, and fevers all over. She said if you had let nature take its course, she wouldn't be having aches, pains, and fevers all over, and she would get to be the guest of honor at the memorial service this afternoon. I think she's just jealous, though, 'cause she's never been able to get carried around in a plasticated garbage bag and get somebody else to dig holes for her."

I asked Squeaks what she meant about a memorial service. Her reply was, "Heard you buried old Sammy over there back of your workshop. That's where we're holding the memorial service. You're coming, of course. I invited you yesterday, remember? Well, I was supposed to entice... uh, invite you yesterday but I forgot about it until I saw you just now. But, anyway, NOW you're enticed and you have to come 'cause, like I forgot to tell you yesterday, you've been chosen to deliver the eulogy for Sam the Serpent. It's at three clocks right out there under the big popular tree back of your workshop where you packed him in. You're bringing a big deathday cake with candles and nicecream and paper hats and nose makers and everything. Remember? That's part of what I forgot to tell you yesterday."

It was almost three o'clock already, so I completed my trip to the mail box, went in the house, popped a large bag of popcorn and, with the bag of popcorn under my arm, walked out to the place under the poplar tree where I had buried the pieces of Sam's broken body. Cleopatra the Cat had followed me out but refused to join in the memorial service. Instead, she climbed onto the workshop roof and lay where she could be a silent observer.

"We are all here and waiting," cried Squeaks as I walked up. "Did you bring the berserks and other goodies?"

I told her the only deserts I had was popcorn, and I asked where were all the animals that were supposed to be there.

Squeaks could barely contain her disappointment. She said, "Just whompcorn? Need more than that to keep ME awake at a wake. Thought you were bringing nicecream and stuff. I just invited these five 'cause didn't want all the goodies to get chomped down. Besides, these are all who would come. Nobody cares about old what's-his-name any more. He's history!"

We sat on the ground in a half circle. To my right were Squeaks the Squirrel, Rackets the Raccoon, and Ribbit the Rabbit. On my left were Chicken Dee the Chickadee, J. Wellington Witherspoon (the Blue Jay), and Daphne Deer. Our half circle faced Sam's grave behind which stood a crude monument the animals had erected in memory of the deceased. On the monument were engraved these words: "Here lies Sam the Serpent. May he rest in pieces."

My refreshment bag was passed from paw to paw and wing to wing, and we all sat silently in our neat little circle munching on popcorn. Squeaks finally spoke up and said that, since this was my party, I should get the show on the road. I was not sure what was the right thing to do so I suggested we begin by going around the half circle and each of us telling the good things he or she remembered about Sam the Serpent. We would begin with Ribbit the Rabbit.

Ribbit spoke up immediately. "Great suggestion," he said. "Great idea to go around and have each one of us lay some good stuff on, uh..." He looked over to the new monument, focused on the first line, and continued, "On Sam the Serpent. Knew him well, I did. He was a pennyhead. A viper type, *Agkistrodon mokeson* of the family *Crotalidae*. Uh, let's see. He, uh, ate stuff, I think. Yeah, he ate bugs, wizards, and toads. If not for him, we would be crowded out by bugs, wizards, and toads. Know lots of other good stuff about him, but that's all I can think of right now."

The circle was quiet for a while and all heads turned toward Rackets the Raccoon. Rackets blushed and tried to hide his eyes with his paw. He finally spoke up. "We are supposed to... Uh, tell me again. What is it we are supposed to be doing? Oh, yes, that's what I thought. Well, old Snake Eyes was a fine, upstand-ing... Uh, upstanding? Well, low-lying, creepy, crawly, slinky, slithery... Uh, what? GOOD stuff, did you say? Hmm. Wait! Got it! Got it! It's this way. I always thought old Snake Eyes would go far. And he did! All the way over to this side of the street in a plastic garbage bag!"

It was Squeaks turn and she spoke up immediately. "Sam was a copy head, one of the four types of poisonous snakes around here. The other three are the rattle and shake, the cotton mouse, and the quarrel snake. Good thing about Sam's type is that he was quieter than a rattle and shake, didn't squeak like a cotton mouse, and didn't fuss you up like a quarrel snake."

It was my turn and I did the best I could. I said, "I didn't know Sam very well but he certainly never did me any harm, and he wasn't doing anything wrong when he met his end. He was only doing what snakes are supposed to do. I'm sorry he's dead. I wasn't sure at the time I was doing the right thing by killing him, but I didn't know then, and I still don't know, what I should have done."

Chicken Dee was next in the row. She said, "Snakes eat birds and that particular one ate either me or my sister, I'm not sure which. But he was a good snake 'cause he never ate both of us."

J. Wellington Witherspoon was next. He said, "Snakes also eat other snakes. I hate snakes and I'm glad Sam was around because I'll bet he ate lots of them."

Daphne Deer was last. "Lots of times, when someone leaves, they leave a vacancy. Sam didn't leave one. Wasn't that considerate of him?"

All was quiet for several minutes. All of us were thinking our own thoughts and going over in our minds what we knew of the deceased. Also, several of us probably were wondering what we were supposed to do next. A voice from the edge of the workshop roof broke the silence. It was Cleopatra. "Did any of you," she asked, "by any chance, notice that not one of you really said anything good about Sam? I think perhaps you are avoiding the truth which is that all of you are a great deal more concerned with yourselves than you are with the deceased. His demise reminds you of your own mortality. You are here because you wish to be remembered kindly when your body ceases to live. I think Sam was a slick and slithery creature who never did anything but follow his instincts. He did not want to get killed, but he did not KNOW he did not want to get killed! He was not outstanding in the intelligence department; he did not will to do anything either good or bad. So, I think you are going to have a difficult time thinking of anything good, or bad, to say about him. I do not care if he is dead or alive. I have eaten a few snakes in my lifetime and I can tell you for a fact that I have eaten better things and I have eaten worse things. Now THAT is the truth!"

Again, there were several minutes of silence. This was the most unusual memorial service I had ever attended. The very idea of someone telling the truth at a memorial service! At last Squeaks spoke up. "Glad you said that," she said. "I agree with you. Actually he was a sneaky, snaky character. But this is a memorial service and the rules say we've got to find something good to say against the miserable creature. But, we ought to be honest. I think we should sit here for an hour or a hundred years until somebody actually does thinks of something good about the no-good bum."

There was a nod of agreement from most of us and we sat there in deep thought. At last Chicken Dee jumped up, flapped her tiny wings, and shouted, "Got it! Got it! Got the good stuff! Sam the Serpent was ecologically correct! He didn't use nonrenewable resources, didn't trash the earth, packed neatly into the hole you dug for him, and would have been biodegradable if you hadn't used the plasticated bag. And, he didn't mess up anything; didn't even leave a slither print. What other animal in the whole world and Massachusetts can say that?"

There was a buzz of excitement as all the animals acknowledged their agreement. Daphne the Deer spoke up and said, "You are exactly right. He really was deep in environmental stuff, wasn't he."

J. Wellington Witherspoon looked over at Sam's grave and said, "Not as deep as he is now."

I sat there with my head bowed. Squeaks looked at me and asked, "Swats the matter with you? Are you going to be difficult and disagree and make us sit here forever or two hours?"

"I think you told the truth," I said, turning toward Chicken Dee. "It seems to me that the fact that Sam spent his short life on earth without doing the slightest damage to the ecosystem is an admirable thing. I think what I am sad about is that I must admit that ALL animals are ecologically correct. Except for humans! We are the ones who do all the damage. If we didn't interfere with nature, nonrenewable resources would not be destroyed, natural selection would continue in force, and everything would be in balance."

Cleopatra cannot resist a good discussion, except at nap times. She climbed down from her perch, joined our circle by sitting on Sam's grave, and said, "I think I just heard you say the natural world is the way the world would be in the absence of intelligence. Are you saying the earth stays in ecological balance only when it is left undisturbed by intelligence in action? And, how could you know that? If there were no intelligence on the earth, how would anything be known about the condition of the earth's environment?"

Squeaks added, "Yeah. Good questions. I don't understand what we are talking about here. I think our saphead fiend... uh, friend is trying to work himself into another one of his moral de-lemons. I'll remit the main reason I don't goof up the earth is that I don't know how. If I could, I would cut down all the pines and populars and telephone poles and fence posts and plant all hickory nut trees everywhere. I would fill in the ocean and other ponds and there would be hickory nut trees all over. I would get into, uh, generics and alter up the jeans of the hickory trees so they all would plunk down nuts as big as pumpkins. I would put down all animals that eat nuts, except for squirrels, of course. And I would put them down, too, if they got in the way of my nuts. Deer would have to go; they mess up trees, raccoons got to pack it in; they would rack some of my seeds. Rabbits got to go; they might nibble up little trees. Birds, well, I don't know. If I knew how to do it, I'd get rid of 'em too, just in case. Sapheads? Well, you chunk me out some sunflower seeds and sometimes bring me a golf bag full of hickory nuts from over at Reedy Creek. I guess you are the only one I would keep. Trouble is, I don't know how to do all that stuff. Sapheads are the only ones who can do much good stuff or bad stuff."

I ignored Squeaks and addressed Cleopatra's question. "Well, yes," I said, "The world DOES stay in ecological balance without sap... uh, humans. Humans have damaged the earth from their beginning and do so more and more as they get more numerous. Without humans, nature works things out in most wondrous ways. For example, in the world of nature, wolves destroy the weak and sick deer, which keeps the population within reasonable limits. Even without wolves, if the deer population gets too large, disease and starvation take over and regulate the numbers. All of nature is interdependent and works in harmony. Without humans, that is."

Ribbit the Rabbit chimed in. "Put yourself down too low, I think. Or up too high. Maybe sapheads, too, are a part of the natural world. Maybe you worry too much about ecological problems. Maybe the natural order of things is that if sapheads mess the world up so much they can't live in it, they will disappear and turn the world over to the alligators."

"Alligators?" shrieked Squeaks, "That's a crock of diles! Squirrels are IT!"

Cleopatra ignored Squeaks and addressed the questions and comments about intelligence. "You are all wrong about intelligence," she said. "I am living proof that intelligence is a wonderful thing. I never say anything about myself because I am very modest and I like for others to find out for themselves how wonderful I am. But intelligence is, indeed, part of the natural world. Intelligent creatures are subject to the same rules of adaptation to the environment, natural selection, and survival of the fittest as are rocks, trees, and opossums. Homosaps are not messing up the earth BECAUSE of their intelligence. Their intelligence merely is helping them do a better job of messing it up. If they chose to clean up the mess they have made, their intelligence would help them do a good job of that, too."

"Well," I asked, "if all of you know so much about ecology, tell me what can be done about just one relatively simple problem. Tell me how we can keep from having the county dump get bigger every year."

"Nothing to it," said J. Wellington Witherspoon. "Just increase the cost of garbage collection to ten zillion dollars per month. The extra fees could pay for cleaning up the dump. Only, there would be extra fees for only about six months. By then, there would be such a reduction in trash that the whole world would be different. The reason you throw your television set into the trash dump and buy a new one is that it's CHEAPER to buy a new one. If it cost you ten thousand bags of bird seed to get rid of the old one, you would get it repaired and use it for a thousand years. And, when the county dump starts getting so big you don't have anywhere to stand, the price of garbage collection WILL be ten zillion dollars. So, stop worrying. Sapheads are a part of the world of nature, and nature can deal with you. The earth got along fine before your kind got here and, if you do yourselves in, the earth will do just fine after you are gone."

Daphne Deer added her opinion. "I think that, from the beginning of time," she said in her soft voice, "life on the planet has evolved in the direction of intelligence. It seems strange to me that the more-or-less end product of evolution could be the cause of the destruction of the very environment that made intelligence possible."

"Good point," said Cleopatra. "Maybe Homosaps eventually will get their act together. I heard somewhere that we can only fix things we care about, and can only care about things we know about. Maybe Homosaps have just recently started to know about the damage they are doing to the earth, and have just started thinking seriously about what they can do to stop the destruction."

"Are you saying," I asked, "that everything is turning out all right and that I should not be so concerned about the trashing of the earth by humans?"

"You sapheads surely do ask ridiculous questions," said Chicken Dee. "Of course you should be concerned. The only way anything worthwhile ever gets done is through concern."

"Right!" added Rackets the Raccoon, "But sapheads are the only animals who can never afford to tell the truth about anything. If someone asks you, 'is the sky going to fall in?' and you tell them the truth and say 'no,' then they will go on their merry way and do everything as they have before. And, as a result of their actions, or inactions, the sky WILL fall in. But, if you tell them what is NOT the truth; that is, you answer 'yes,' they will do all kinds of things to keep the sky from falling in. And they will succeed and prove you were wrong when you said 'yes.' What I am saying here is that you MUST tell everybody how bad everything is and that it probably is too late to save the earth. Otherwise, they will not get scared enough to do the things they need to do to save the earth. If you tell the truth, that the saphead is a very ingenious animal and always has done what it had to do to survive, they will do nothing and your kind will be destroyed."

"Well," I said, "Maybe what you are telling me is that humans will start fixing things only when they start being so inconvenienced that fixing things is the easiest way out for them. I think my worry is that I'm sure it would be so much easier if we started fixing now instead of waiting until things get even worse. But I have to agree with you that humans don't seem to work that way."

Squeaks was beginning to yawn, Ribbit was tapping one foot on the ground, Chicken Dee was preening, and Daphne seemed to be asleep. The memorial service clearly was moving toward closure. But I wanted one other thing from the others before we parted. I put it to them bluntly. "Do you think I was wrong to kill Sam?" I asked.

"Would have been all right if you had eaten him," Rackets answered. "Nothing wrong with killing what you eat. Only other way would be to eat it alive or die from starvation. Well, nice party. Got to go." And he was gone.

"Don't have to eat it for it to be all right," declared Daphne, shaking the sleep out of her eyes. "Sometimes you have to kill things to keep them from hurting or killing you. And I've got to go find some water to wash down that popcorn." And she dashed for the woods. In her rush, she knocked over and destroyed Sam's monument. No one noticed or, if they did notice, seemed to care. After all, as Squeaks had said earlier, Sam was history.

"Yeah," added J. Wellington Witherspoon as he flapped his wing in preparation for takeoff, "It's NEVER right to kill anything. But, sometimes, you don't really have any alternative. In cases like that, you just do what you have to do. Besides, he's already dead. So why worry about it?" With a whir of wings, he was gone. He was followed by Chicken Dee on wing and Ribbit the Rabbit on foot.

"I'm not so much worried about this time," I said, "as I am about what I should do if the same sort of thing happens again."

Squeaks was the only one left. "Well," she said, "you could just curl up and let the next serpent swallow you down. But, then, who would put out seeds for me? Good thing, though, to worry some about what you did. If you didn't fret some over it, you would get callouses all over. But I think you did right to whack him down. That way we got to have this memory service. Next time, though, wish you would freeze up some hickory nut nicecream and bring it 'stead of this whompcorn." And she, too, was gone, leaving me very much alone, except for Cleopatra who was sleeping soundly on the loose soil that covered the final resting place of Sam the Serpent.

XIV. The Golden Ruler

Before you complain about my frown,
There's something you should do.
Consider the possibility
I caught it from you.

64

I had not noticed that Pearl was ailing until Squeaks the Squirrel mentioned it to me.

Each morning and afternoon, I scatter a coffee can of sunflower seeds on the ground for the birds and squirrels. Squeaks' territory encompassed the area where I scatter the seeds, so she rarely gets out of sight of the feeding area. She usually gets to the new seeds first and eats her fill by the time her eight to twelve friends arrive. One of these friends is Pearl the Squirrel. Sometimes Pearl talks with me; most times she just eats and runs. Squeaks had pointed out that Pearl was off her feed. I watched and, sure enough, she ate just a few seeds and walked slowly over into the shade and lay down. Not only was she off her feed, she also no longer was her usual perky self. I asked Squeaks what ailed her.

"Don't know," she answered. "But I'm worried. Owes me six hickory nuts and two walnuts. If anything bad happens to her, I'll have to go to her nest of kin, and I don't know who they are. She's always walked a lot; maybe she's got very-gross veins. I'll go tell her and maybe that will jeer her up."

Squeaks hopped over to where Pearl lay and said, "Want to offer a digestion about your food. If you don't eat up, you're going to go down." Squeaks held one paw to Pearl's forehead and said, "Don't have a temperament. Must be the gollywogs."

Pearl responded in a low, halting voice. I could not hear what she said. Squeaks bounced back over to the porch where I was sitting, lay on the floor at my feet, spent several minutes scratching her back and sides, and then spoke up. "Got it all out of her," she said. "She needs one of those shy cologists, you know, the kind that shrinks your head when you've got a repression."

"Are you saying she's suffering from depression?" I asked.

"Swat I just said," answered Squeaks. "She's repressed because she doesn't know what to do. Told me all about it, all I ever wanted to know and lots more. Sure you want to hear it? Well, lets talk cats. That's right, cats. Not your Cleo Patrick cat or your thermos cat, but your neighbor's cat. The black beasty with the white patch on his fourheads. The one that's about six pounds long and weighs in at an even point zero zero seven three five tons. Think they call him Ali Kat. Well, he comes over here all the time when you're not looking. He's big on birds, hoptoads, wizzards, flybutters, and even squirrels. Doesn't always eat them. Just likes to bounce them around and put them down. Well, he wants to put Pearl down and that's why Pearl's repressed."

"You mean Pearl is afraid Ali Kat will kill her?" I asked.

"Oh, no!" answered Squeaks. "She can get away from him easy. But last week she went and got religion. It's her religion that's got her down. Says there's something called the golden ruler that's causing her trouble. This golden ruler says something about undoing others before they can undo you. Pearl is all down in the mouth about not knowing how to reply the golden ruler in the case of Ali the Kat. Pearl says if she were in Kat's place she would want the squirrel type to come down and get chomped on. So, if she follows the golden ruler, that swat she'd have to do. But, if she does that, she will be deaded down and won't be able to go to prayer meeting on Wednesday night. Now, how is that for a moral de-lemon? No wonder she's repressed!"

"Is she really as wacko as all that?" I asked. "Well, I think she has it all wrong. I should go talk to her, but she's so shy. She seems to think I'm going to tie a knot in her tail or something. Maybe you ought to talk to her, because she has the rule all wrong. The golden rule does NOT say do to others the way you think they want you to do. It says to behave toward them the way you want them to behave toward you. Does Pearl want Ali Kat to lie down and let Pearl eat him alive? Of course she doesn't. So, she doesn't have to offer herself up as a sacrifice to Ali. How does Pearl wish Ali would behave toward her? I think

Pearl would like for Ali to be friendly, kind, compassionate and, certainly, safe to be around. So, that is the way Pearl should try to behave toward Ali. Why don't you go tell that to Pearl? And, keep in touch. I want to know how this turns out."

65

Several days passed. They had been busy days for me. I had been leaving home shortly after daylight and not returning until almost dark. Other than the few minutes required to feed the animals, I had had no time to spend in the yard. But, finally, I had an hour free to sit and read and think. I hardly had time to settle into my porch chair and find my place in my book before Squeaks bounced onto the porch. She was singing,

"Food time, feed time.
Good old happy seed time.
Sunflowers, cashews, and walnuts, too.
Those are the things that I want from you.
Snack time, lunch time.
Good old happy munch time."

"Cut that out!" I said. "You know you've already been fed."
"Well!" Squeaks replied. "Gollywinkles! Can't a guy even sing around this place?" She pounced over to her usual spot on the porch, sat on her haunches, and quietly began her morning preening.

I turned to my book, read a few pages, and pretty much forgot about Squeaks. I read something in the book about religion, and then I remembered that Squeaks was still sitting there. "I thought you were going to tell me about your friend Pearl the Squirrel," I said. "What ever happened to her?"

"Well, it's like I told you yesterday," she answered. "Well, like I would have told you, except you weren't out here. Anyway, like I told you yesterday, she is really in a bad way. Worst recession I've ever seen. Don't think she's going to make it. Pretty sure she's a goner."

"You mean she's still in a depression?" I asked. "I thought you were going to talk to her and help her get her ideas straightened out. All you had to do was tell her exactly what I told you to tell her."

"Did!" declared Squeaks. "Laid on her the exact same identical words you told me. Except I forgot most of what you said and I had to sort of ad-lip. But, anyway, she got the message. That's why she's got the deep concession. You same as did her in, you know. If she doesn't make it—and there's not much chance she will—it will be just like you did to Sam the Serpent. Might just have well chopped Pearl in half and gotten it over with."

I maturely maintained my composure, resisted the urge to deliver several choice expletives, and said in a low, controlled voice, "This, by the way, is the one day of the week when I'm responsible for fixing dinner. How would you like to help me cook up some squirrel stew?"

Squeaks is clever. She ignored my question and proceeded to tell me about Pearl the Squirrel. "The way you did her in was to tell her she had to behave the way she wished others to behave. She's a gullible type so she did what you said. Didn't work! All the animals took advantage of her. She had nuts stored up to last all winter or fifty years. Other squirrels asked for them and she had to dish them out to follow her new corn... uh... concept of what the golden ruler really means. Now she's broke, bankruptured, and hungry. Suppose I could give her some of mine—I just 'cumulated an additional two or three tons of 'em the last few days—but, if I gave 'em back to her, I wouldn't be following MY rule."

"So," I said, "you took all of poor Pearl's acorns. What IS this rule you're following? Doesn't sound to me like a very nice one."

"Well," said Squeaks, "I'm following the iron ruler. That's the ruler that says might makes right. That's the ruler most animals use. And that includes sapheads, too. Anyway, 'might' doesn't just include having big teeth. It also includes being shrewd and clever. I laid a shrewd clever on ole' Pearl and now I've got a mountain of nuts and she's got nutting. How are you going to beat that?"

"Easy to beat that," I said.

Leaning against one wall of my workshop was a large scrap of plywood that had been left over from my last birdhouse building project. I had not yet had time to put it away in the attic of the workshop where I usually keep my scrap lumber. I walked out to it, lifted it and, just as I had suspected, found a pile of acorns. I gathered them up by the handsful, walked over to the edge of the woods, and scattered them on the ground. The other squirrels came running and hauled off the acorns almost as fast as I could throw them out. Squeaks was hysterical. "You can't do that," she screamed. "Those are all mine. Stole them fair and square, I did. Can't treat me that way. Illegal! Immoral! Inethical! Iniquitous! Inscrupulous!" She dashed over to where I was throwing the acorns and tried to fight off the other squirrels. Several of them were bigger than she and several others were faster. She ended up retrieving only two acorns, but suffered a chewed ear, scuffed nose, bruised tail, and lumped leg.

She limped back over to the porch, lay back in her spot on the floor, looked up at me with sad eyes, and asked, "Why for did you do that to me? Thought we were friends. When did I ever take anything away from YOU? Uh, let me dephrase that. When did I ever take anything away from you that I didn't want?"

"Just following your iron ruler," I answered. "It's really not a good rule. It's really a lose-lose proposition because lots of animals lose what rightfully belongs to them, and the top dog who takes away has to live in fear that something bigger than he will come along and take everything he has. Actually, though, I wasn't using your rule. Probably was using a rule called the bronze rule. That's the rule that says do unto others as they do unto you. I was just doing to you as you had done to Pearl."

"Is that the ruler," asked Squeaks, "that says an eye for an eye and a tooth for a toenail? Well, that seems like a fair ruler to me. I will commit... uh, remit... uh, admit that the iron ruler is not a very good ruler for a little fellow like me. I guess I got my just beserks getting done in by this here bronze ruler. I got about what I preserved. Lucky for me, YOU didn't get what I preserved—you didn't find most of my stash. It's still under your little storage building where you keep your... oops! Uh oh! Look at that cloud up there! Looks like a white pumpkin, doesn't it? See the one I'm talking about there? Speaking of pumpkins, it will soon be Halloween, so we better enjoy these nice, warm days while we can. Right? Aren't these nice warm days nice? Just feel the nice warm air."

For a minute or so, Squeaks stared intently at me and swished her tail violently as she does when she is tense over something. Finally, she spoke again. "Come to think of it," she said, "some of the animals I know use that ear-for-an-ear and tooth-for-a-tongue ruler all the time. Want to hear about it?"

"Sure," I said. "Why not?"

"Give you one zample," said Squeaks. "I'll tell about the McCoons and the Hatfields. They have been having a flue... a few... a feud for six months or nine hundred years. Started when old Rack McCoon accidently stepped on the hat of old Field Mouse. Field Mouse dealt out justice by dropping a rock on McCoon's head. Was the closest he could come to getting even, since McCoon never wore a hat. McCoon said wasn't fair because he stomped down the hat by axeldent and got knotted on the head on purpose. So he applied the old bronze ruler to Field Mouse's head in the form of a good whack with a stick. To get back even Mouse sold McCoon's den to a skunk type for forty pieces of silver. Because of this outrage, McCoon planted dynamite in Mouse's underground burrow. So, Mouse hired a hit man to... well, this could go on all day. But that's the way it's been and I don't know how it will ever stop so long as both of them are following that eye-for-a-pie and goose-for-a-moose ruler."

"I think you have just admitted," I said, "that the iron rule leads to tyranny and the bronze rule leads to unending vendettas. I think you are about to run out of rules here. Maybe you should go back and do some rethinking about the golden rule. I still say the golden rule is a wonderful rule that always turns out well. I think your problem is that you still don't understand how the rule works. Think for a minute what is really meant by 'as you would have them do to you.' Would you REALLY want others to give you things they couldn't afford to give? Would you REALLY want others to reward you for your deliberate misdeeds? Would you REALLY want others to be gullible and let you take advantage of them? Of course you wouldn't"

"Why not?" said Squeaks. "Sounds good to me. Don't try to sprain things to me that I already understand. I've got this golden ruler thing down real good and I think it's a great ruler for Pearl and other dimwits. But it sure ain't for me. I've got too much smarts for anything like that. Poor Pearl the Squirrel tried it out just like you told her to, and it didn't work at all. Might swell admit that it doesn't work. No use trying things that don't work. Well, got to go. Going over to ole' Pearl's place and see if I can con... uh, convince her out of some more acorns. If not, I will swack her with a stick. I bet, then, she will cough 'em up."

66

I went inside and sat for a while with Cleopatra the Cat. I told her what had happened.

"The trouble with you," she said, "is that you seem to think all animals are created equal. The golden rule is the perfect rule, IF you have any intelligence. You no doubt have noticed that I have followed it with great success for many years. Your little squirrely friends are all tail and no smarts. They cannot see that, when you treat others poorly, others will become more inclined to treat you poorly and, thus, you will be more inclined to treat them even more poorly, which will result in their treating.... Anyway, if someone does not take the initiative in breaking this vicious cycle, all creatures eventually will be at war with each other and all will be losers. Your squirrely friends could never understand the long-term advantages of making peace in the world by using a rule of conduct that sometimes sacrifices short-term gains. They have no understanding of the power of forgiveness and reconciliation. Such words as love, care, trust, and compassion are not in their simple vocabularies. Do you understand what I am talking about?"

I was honest with her and told her she was not telling me anything I didn't already know. I assured her that I was just passing the time of day with her and was merely relating to her what had just happened out in the yard.

She ignored my response and continued. "Do you think your squirrely little friend knows anything about love? Does she know anything about hate? Of course not! That is why things like the golden rule are not applicable to creatures like her. Let me tell you something about how love fits into the scheme of things. Love is one of those funny words that means almost anything. You love hot dogs. But that is not what I am talking about. To many, love means sex, dependency, or respect. There is nothing wrong with those, but they are not what I am talking about

234

either. Love means knowing, understanding, accepting, caring, and relating. It means sharing who and what you really are. Love is the one thing that makes it possible to see life as it really is. Love is the one thing that makes the world make sense. Love holds everything together by making order out of chaos, good out of greed, and belonging out of alienation. Love is a most wondrous thing. Hate is the flip side of love. Love and hate are very close together; their opposite is indifference. The ability to love and value ourselves and others comes from being loved and valued, and from having a sense of belonging. Hate comes from being unloved, devalued, and rejected by those from whom we expect love, valuing, and acceptance. Indifference comes from being so alienated from others that there are no expectations.

"So, what can you do about those who hate or are indifferent? Returning hate and indifference certainly will not accomplish anything positive. And, if you are able to return love, you do not necessarily need the golden rule. But your golden rule IS a good way of describing your behavior toward others when you are able to love."

Cleopatra stopped to catch her breath, and I thought—and hoped—she had finished her discourse. Well, she was almost finished, but not quite.

"Simple-minded creatures like your squirrely little friend have to follow simple-minded rules, even if the rules work to their disadvantage most of the time. However, she did, quite by accident, I assure you, raise an important question. How can we convince others that following the golden rule will make their lives better? We cannot do it directly. So we might just as well not waste any time trying. Instead, be contagious! Did you not say, last week, that you had gotten a distemper shot at the hospital? Or was that a flu shot? Anyway, as you know, some things are contagious. There is indifference, uncaring, mistrust, and enmity all over, if you look for them and focus on them. But love, care, trust, and compassion are even more contagious. So, go ahead. Spread them around.

XV. The Walled-In Pond Experiment

I want my chips, I want my beer,
And twelve vacations every year.
Indulge me as befits a king,
But don't ask me to do a thing.
Just call me when the work's all done,
And I'll come back and we'll have fun.

67

Rosie the Raccoon was late. During the summer, she usually comes in between two and three o'clock. I was lying on pillows propped against one end of the swing that hangs at the side of the walkway between the porch and the carports. I had just finished reading a book. I laid it aside, checked my watch, and noted that it was almost four o'clock. I could lie there another hour if I wished. The shade was soft and the faint breeze was warm.

I relaxed and daydreamed a bit. Ideas from the book I had just read drifted through my mind with sufficient impact to keep me awake but with detail so sketchy I was not inclined to draw any strong conclusions. The book provided a not-too-brilliant discussion of the relative merits of communism versus capitalism. Since I had always considered "cooperation" to be superior to "every-man-for-himself," I half-heartedly puzzled over the relative merits of the two systems. Was it possible for creatures to live together cooperatively and still maintain their freedom, dignity, and enthusiasm for life? It must be possible, but I was puzzled that so many cooperative efforts had ended in tyranny, apathy, and poverty. How could it be that what is best for the individual NOT be best for society, or what is best for society NOT be best for the individual? I lost my train of thought as I began drifting into sleep. I vaguely wondered why I was so sleepy. I seemed to have a blurry memory of my sleep being interrupted the previous night. Just then, something bumped the swing and caused it to move enough for the chains to squeak. I raised my head from my pillows and looked down to see what was there. It was Rosie the Raccoon. She had nudged the swing with her nose to get my attention.

"You're late," I said. "What happened?"

"I stopped by to look over your neighbor's new puppy," she said. "Raccoons and dog types are natural enemies, you know. Hate each other on sight or sound. Certainly is a cute little fellow. Wonderfully curious, and innocent as a lamb. Would like to have one myself. Your neighbor is going to have trouble though. If I am not badly mistaken, the puppy is one of those golden deceivers. It has your neighbor thinking it will always be a puppy, but that little thing will grow to be about the size of an elephant. Anyway, that's why I'm late. Did I miss dinner? Is it too late for maybe a little snack?"

I told her food was down—her usual can of dry dog food plus some potato peels soaked in margarine left over from my lunch. She went over to her usual place to chow down. I lay back and continued daydreaming. Rosie ate her fill, climbed the small tree beside the walkway, and made a short jump over to the roof over my head. She lay down with her head hanging over the edge so she could look me in the face.

"I suppose you heard what happened here last night," I said.

"Heard Jimmie's version," answered Rosie, "but have not yet heard yours. Reason I just made myself comfortable is I think I am about to hear your version which, when adjusted to accommodate the exaggerations, probably will be considerably closer to the truth than the version I heard earlier from Jimmie."

So, I told Rosie the Raccoon the following story of what had occurred the previous night.

68

"Our sound sleep was interrupted by noises coming from the direction of the porch. 'It's either a burglar, one of your friendly raccoons, or the sky falling in,' said my wife. 'If it's a burglar, tell him we don't have anything. If it's one of your friendly beasties, tell him we have a shotgun. If it's the sky falling in, I don't want to know about it.' She turned over and went back to sleep.

"I turned on the bedside lamp, stuck an arm into one sleeve of my robe, failed to find the other sleeve, gave up and draped the edge of the robe over my shoulder, and headed for the back door. I switched on the outdoor floodlights and the porch light and peeked through the peep hole in the door to see if there was anything as big as a bear moving on the porch. I didn't see a thing. I opened the door and stepped out. And there she was!

"Jimmie the Racketycoon sat in the middle of what was left of the barbecue grill. One grill lay on the floor and the other one leaned at an odd angle against the wall. The lava rocks were scattered all over. Jimmie had her head down and was eagerly scraping grease from the bottom of the grill. She was stuffing part of it into her mouth and the balance into the little bag she always wears around her neck. She heard me open the door, removed her sooty, grease-covered paw from her mouth, and stared at me with innocent eyes. I noticed that her ears twitched as she talked.

" 'You may think this is me,' she said, 'but it's not. Just looks like me. Actually, I am back at my den fast asleep and don't know anything at all about this mess. If you don't believe me, just ask me, and I will tell you the absolute, undisputable, indubitable, unequivocal truth. Besides, I just woke up a few minutes ago and just happened to come across this mess. I was going to ring your doorbell—except I can't reach it—and ask you what was going on here. Must have been a gas explosion 'cause things are all over. Fortunately for you, I was here when it happened and managed to get everything under control. Bet you want to know exactly what happened here so you can pass it on to your insurance company. Well, it was this big duckbill platypus. You know how they root around in the water trying to find shellfish and things. Well, you didn't have much water here for it to root around in, so it snorfed around in your grill instead. If I hadn't been here to scare it off, probably would have rooted down your whole house.'

"Jimmie stopped to catch her breath, and I said, 'The platypus lives in Australia and Tasmania. You will have to think up a better story than that.'

"Jimmie looked surprised and said, 'Australia and Tasmania, of course! Like I said, it came all the way from Australia and Tasmania—on a bus. I could tell by the travel stickers on his luggage. He would have gotten here yesterday but took him a long time to get here from Australia and Tasmania. Had to get a passport and shots and all kinds of things. Then, the bus ran late and he almost didn't get here at all. Bus ran into a tower in Pisa. Or was that the Eyeful Tower in Paris? Anyway, now that you are here to look after things, I will go find him and make sure his immigration papers are in order. If you need anything more from me, you can phone me at home. I don't have a telephone, so I left your number. So, if I get a call, let me know next time I come by.' And Jimmie the Raccoon was gone."

69

"Interestingly enough," said Rosie, "that is exactly the same story I heard from Jimmie. Some things in life are inexplicable, incomprehensible, unfathomable, and baffling, and she is one of them."

"She seems simple enough to me," I said. "She is simply a simple thief and liar. If you REALLY want to think about the inexplicable, think about communism versus capitalism."

"I don't know much, mostly just the stories I have heard," replied Rosie. "But I think I may know more about communism versus capitalism than you know about Jimmie the Raccoon."

I was surprised. I was sure Rosie would agree with me about Jimmie. And, how could she possibly know anything about communism or capitalism? There was only one way for me to find out what she knew. "I'm listening," I said.

Rosie stretched out further on the roof with her head and the front half of her body hanging over the side. At first, I thought she might slip and come crashing down on me, but she seemed to find a fine balance that kept her in place, so I readjusted my pillows, lay back, relaxed, and listened.

"Well," said Rosie, "this all started about four years ago, when Jimmie was barely out of her infanthood. Most of the animals know bits and pieces of this, but I think I am the only one to whom Jimmie has ever confided the whole story. She dropped in at about ten one morning, on a Tuesday if my memory serves me right, for tea and ginger cakes. While she was there, she told me the whole thing. I know what you are thinking. You are thinking that, if Jimmie told it, how could I possibly think it is true. Well, I know because I know Jimmie.

239

She always tells the truth unless she has reason not to. And there was nothing for her to gain that morning by telling me something that was not true. Also, by looking at her ears, you can tell when she is not telling the truth. When she is not telling the truth, her ears twitch. Lots of animals twitch their ears when they are not telling the truth. Also some animals only twitch them when they ARE telling the truth. So you have to be careful when you make assumptions about truth based on twitched or untwitched ears. For example, I had this uncle once, who had big ears. At least, my aunt said he had big ears. But I never did much like that particular aunt. She and my mother had... hmm. What was it we were talking about here?"

I reminded her that we were talking about Jimmie. She got back on track and told me the following story.

70

"When Jimmie the Raccoon was born, she was the youngest, by about three seconds, of the three. Her brother and sister apparently lived their lives in obscurity; there are no known existing records, either written or oral, that provide any insight into their living or passing. Raccoons are that way sometimes. Jimmie's mother, so I understand, was a librarian and her father was a senator from North Carolina. Such parentage presumably contributed to Jimmie's growing up to be both well educated and worldly wise. However, as often happens to creatures like Jimmie who are born into luxury, she gained an early disdain for material goods and developed what might be considered a distorted consideration for the plight of the less fortunate. Also, Jimmie was what I think you might call gregarious. She seemed to relate well to everyone she met.

"A strong influence on young Jimmie was her closest friend, Louie the Loof. I have no idea how loofs fit into the animal kingdom but I did hear Jimmie state emphatically that Louie was aloof. Louie the Loof was from a resource-disadvantaged family. The family members were so poor they would have had to strike it rich just to work themselves up to the poverty level. When Jimmie first met Louie the Loof, she was intrigued by this creature who was so withdrawn, reserved, remote, and detached. Jimmie soon realized that Louie was a loof because of his poverty. Since Louie saw no hope for a better future, he simply crawled into his shell and slammed the door shut—that is, with everyone except Jimmie. Because Jimmie is such a gregarious creature, she and Louie developed an immediate camaraderie. Louie pointed out to Jimmie the social and economic forces that kept him and his family in poverty. They were born with neither wealth, social position, skills, nor competitive instincts. They were too soft hearted to compete and too tough minded to beg. Also, so Jimmie reluctantly confided, they were not overly industrious, creative, or risk taking. They avoided conflict whenever possible and valued security over all other things, probably because they had so little of it.

"This relationship between Jimmie and Louie had a profound effect on Jimmie. She decided to devote her life to developing a compassionate society where all animals could live together cooperatively without the wastes and disruptions caused by competition and without the grinding poverty that seemed to be the inevitable lot of many in a competitive society. Jimmie dreamed dreams of a society where the idea of climbing the ladder of success, usually over the bodies of the defeated, would be replaced by the realization of a giant circle that included all living creatures joined paw to paw and marching together into a future that recognized the equality of all, not only in opportunity, but also in outcome. In this new society, all would share equally in reaping the rewards of their labors, and all would contribute equally according to individual capabilities. Those who had much would contribute much; those who had little would contribute what they could. Rules of behavior would simply be those rules that insisted that each creature behave in ways that were most beneficial to the total society. Because all creatures would have total security—which was the only thing any creature could ever need—the idea of individual freedom would be considered no longer valid .

"Jimmie established her new society on the far side of the woods by the nice little pond next to the state park. She built a high wall around it with only a single gate through which the new citizens could enter. The wall was intended to prevent the members from being contaminated by outside influences. After taking a good look at the completed wall and the nice little pond, Jimmie named the place WALLED-IN POND. She found a smooth plank, etched the name on one side of it, and nailed the sign to a tree next to the pond. After the first two days, there were three hundred and fifty-five animals inside the wall. At this point, Jimmie closed the gate and nailed it shut. She used her considerable personal wealth to provide the immediate necessities for the poor and disillusioned who had flocked to the new settlement. She selected a Committee of Twelve who were responsible for distribution of food and other necessities and for uniting the citizens into small communes. Each commune was assigned a particular part of the work necessary to making and keeping the village self sufficient.

"Everyone started to work with a will. Everyone was cheerful and happy. There was music everywhere and, in the evenings, the animals gathered together around a huge bonfire where they sang, danced, and partied. Meals were served in a large dining hall where food was provided in quantities and types to suit the differing tastes. A nursery was provided to take care of the little ones while the parents worked. There were free education, medical service, and flea picking. Every animal worked to the limit of his or her physical, mental, and emotional capabilities. No animal was forced to do anything it didn't really want to do. Tasks, such as latrine duty and floor moping, that might have been considered objectionable, were made acceptable by reducing the work minutes for those willing to undertake such tasks.

"The Committee of Twelve settled the few minor disputes that arose, made work plans, and provided general oversight. Membership on the Committee was considered the most prestigious position in the society. Most of the early bickering was between animals who wanted to be on the Committee. To resolve this difficulty, Jimmie made each of the current Twelve a member for life. Upon the demise of a member, his or her position would be taken by a new member selected by the survivors. This action seemed to cover all the problem areas and provide the leadership needed to ensure the survival and prosperity of the society. The outcome was a village of pleased, happy, comfortable, contented, satisfied animals—for about two weeks!

"The first thing to go wrong was disagreement among the members of the Committee of Twelve. Jimmie, who also was one of the Committee members, was a strong believer in law and order. She was not so much concerned about the exact nature of the laws as she was that everyone be held to the same set of laws. One of the other members, Jimmie's bosom buddy Louie the Loof, had no respect for laws. Actually, what he did not respect was the idea of everyone being held to the same set of laws. He thought the members of the Committee should have special privileges. He argued that there had been strict laws for everyone where they came from, but that the laws did little to prevent ordinary citizens from challenging those who were in power. He noted that, already, some of the society animals were grumbling about some of the Committee's planning. He recommended, as a means of shaping the thinking of the citizens, the institution of indoctrination programs in the schools and town meetings. He also suggested punishment or banishment of any animal who refused to obey the will of the Committee.

"Jimmie was horrified at these ideas. As she and a few other Committee members upheld the idea of equal treatment for all, her friendship with Louie cooled considerably. However, as time passed, Jimmie also grew concerned about the increasing number of animals who refused to perform their assigned tasks. These animals asserted that they had come to WALLED-IN POND primarily because they had been among the oppressed and that they certainly had no intention of permitting themselves to be oppressed here. Even the more industrious animals stopped working as hard when they saw their extra labors were gaining them no advantage. Jimmie's influence began to wane. Idealist that she was, she simply could not accept the ruthlessness that was becoming increasingly necessary to keep the society functioning. She eventually resigned from the Committee and, with her fortune now completely depleted, retired to a dark corner of the village and came out only to do her assigned work and eat the few scraps that soon were all that was available to most of the citizens.

"Other dramatic changes occurred in quick order. The village newspaper was placed under censorship, and the Committee appointed block wardens to spy on their neighbors and report on any citizens who under performed, over consumed, or spoke out against the Committee. Prisons were constructed for malfeasants, and citizens were accused, tried, and condemned by the Committee or its delegates. Louie the Loof, as he rose in the power structure, grew more ruthless and aggressive. He soon declared himself emperor for life and ruled the Committee and the society with an iron paw. Less and less real work was done, and poverty became rampant. Only Committee members were well fed and lived in luxury.

"Several of the more courageous animals decided to take action to return the society to its initial glory. They marched together to the next Committee meeting and demanded immediate change. They were never heard from again. Whether they were banished to a dungeon or were put to death was never known for sure. For Jimmie, this was the straw that broke the raccoon's back. She decided to leave. In secret, she and a few trustworthy friends slipped through the darkness of the night to the nailed up gate. Jimmie found the rock she had used to nail the gate shut and used the same rock to knock the gate down. She and her few friends rushed out to freedom and soon returned to their former homes on this side of the woods. When the sun rose, other animals who were trapped inside the wall spotted the broken gate. They, too, rushed out to freedom. Soon the entire village was aroused and, in spite of strong efforts by the Committee of Twelve, a flood of disenchanted citizens poured through the gate. The village soon was empty. Even several members of the Committee made their way through the gate to freedom. Finally, only Louie the Loof and several of his accomplices were left. They shut the gate again, nailed it tight, and declared WALLED-IN POND off limits for all but Loofs and Loons. Louie the Loof again crawled into his shell and became withdrawn, reserved, remote, and detached."

71

Rosie the Raccoon, from the place where she was lying on the roof over my head, yawned mightily and shook her head vigorously from side to side in a seeming attempt to shift her mind back to the present. I thought she might be finished with her story. I sat up in the swing and stretched. Rosie said, "Not finished yet!" So, I lay back on my pillow and listened.

"Jimmie the Raccoon accepted full responsibility for the failure of the WALLED-IN POND experiment," continued Rosie. "Jimmie acknowledged that she had overestimated animal nature and underestimated the danger of pushing animals beyond

244

their capabilities. She admitted she now accepts that we simply do not know enough about animal engineering to create a society that is both fair and noncompetitive. Jimmie recognized she had expected of the animals a level of intelligence and insight they simply do not possess. She says she still thinks the basic concept of WALLED-IN POND is sound, but not for this world as it is now. Maybe never in this world, and certainly not until the wheels of evolution turn a few more times. Maybe in another time and place, another universe, another realm, or another dimension.

"But the end of the WALLED-IN POND experiment was not the end of Jimmie. She was sufficiently shrewd to learn from her mistakes. She soon founded a new village of a sort. She sneaked back to WALLED-IN POND, stole the sign from the tree by the pond, and brought it back to her new village. She scratched out parts of the old name and etched in the new one, WALLED OUT. Said she named it that to remind herself that it is virtually impossible to wall out without also walling in.

"Her new village is a simple one. It is mostly a school for animals who have no other place to learn. She has a library filled with well-used books, and she has several teachers who make their own way in the world but who come to the new village in the evenings to teach. WALLED OUT serves simple meals to those willing to work for their food. Those who work much eat much and those who work little eat little. Those who study in the school are encouraged to live in the real world with all its evils, discouragement, hopes, dreams, and possibilities. The students are taught to look out for themselves but to do so in an intelligent manner. They are taught that we all are in this world together and that what really is good for one is good for all. They are taught that, if they truly do what is in their own best long-term interest, they also will be doing what is best for society as a whole. They are taught that a little love and compassion go a long way toward making this a better world, that compassion must not be confused with pity and that, while tough love works wonders, a soft, mushy love likely will do more harm than good. Most of the animals do not quite understand these concepts and many mistakes are made. But Jimmie claims to be more interested in small evolutionary steps than in giant revolutionary ones."

"So, you think Jimmie the Raccoon is a thief and a liar," continued Rosie. "By your definitions, you probably are right. She will not deny it. But, why do you think she always wears that little bag around her neck? You didn't think she ate all that food herself, did you? Where do you think those simple meals at WALLED OUT come from? Ask her about the way she abuses you and she will tell you she is playing with you by the same rules you use with her. You do not particularly treat her with dignity and respect. To you, she is just another toy to play with. She will tell you she knows you get great pleasure out of her mischief and thievery. She knows your life would be a little less interesting without her nightly raids and tall tales. She thinks she is being more than fair with you, and I tend to agree with her."

Rosie got up from where she had been lying, climbed down the tree beside the swing, and stood on the walkway beside me. She motioned toward the porch and asked, "What is that thing over there where your barbecue grill used to be?"

"That's the same grill," I confessed. "It really wasn't hurt much. I just had to put the rocks back in and put the grills back on. Actually, the whole thing needed cleaning anyway. No real harm done."

"Hmm. All that fussing, and now you say 'no real harm done!'" exclaimed Rosie. "Sapheads are strange and unpredictable creatures, that's for sure. What would you do if you ever had any REAL trouble?"

I did not answer. I'm not sure I know the answer.

XVI. The Bickering Flickers

He tries so hard to win at everything!
She strives for closeness and a wedding ring.
His independence, he will fight to hold.
Her bonds with friends, she finds as dear as gold.
Who's right? Who's wrong? Let's set a precedent
And just accept the truth: They're DIFFERENT!

72

My wife and I had been out with friends the evening before and had been up far past our usual bedtime. So, it was one of the rare mornings when we slept late. The sun must have been well up because, when I partially opened one eye, light was showing at the window through the crack where the drapes meet. I lay there with sleepy eyes half opened resenting whatever had awakened me. Maybe it would go away and I could go back to sleep. But it didn't, and I couldn't! When I closed my eyes and began to drift back into sleep, I heard again the noise that must have awakened me the first time. Something was going "bang, bang, bang, bang" on the side of the house.

I got up, stretched mightily, slipped on my robe and slippers, groped my way down the hall to the back door, opened it, went out into the cool morning air, stepped from the porch into the yard, and looked around to see what was making the noise. At first, I saw and heard nothing. And then there it was again, "bang, bang, bang, bang" on the side of the house. I turned a corner, looked up, and there he was on the wall just under the roof overhang. It was Floyd the Flicker, apparently attempting to tear a hole in the cedar siding that forms the exterior of the house.

"Stop that!" I screamed. "Just what do you think you're doing?"

Floyd stopped his banging long enough to peer down at me and answer in a grumpy, angry voice. "What does it look like

I'm doing," he asked, "digging a hole to China? And what business is it of yours? Can't you see I'm digging for bugs? That's what woodpeckers do, you know."

"It's my business because it's my house," I answered. "And what makes you think there are bugs in the wall of my house?"

"We'll never know, will we," he answered, "if I don't tunnel in there and find out? And, if I don't find them and peck them out, the whole house will come tumbling down. Just a matter of time, you know. Would serve you right, with your attitude."

"Don't do that!" I said. "Just don't do that. Just leave my house alone! Let me worry about whether or not I have bugs."

"Well, you don't have to yell," he said. "Sound just like my mate, you know. If you didn't want me debugging here, all you had to do was tell me. Or you could have put up a sign or something, you know."

"Well, now you know, you know," I said with a voice perhaps tinged with sarcasm.

"Oh," Floyd moaned in a teary voice, "I hate it so when I get fussed at. Why can't everybody just be reasonable? Why can't everybody just calmly and logically address issues as they arise, seek mutually-agreeable solutions to problems, and get on with orderly, well-planned lives? Why do some have to talk, talk, talk, about anything and everything, without any purpose, order, or logic? And, then, when you try to apply your problem-solving skills to what they are saying, you know, they just fuss at you something awful and tell you you just don't understand."

"Hmm," I thought, "this is a difficult fellow to fuss up. Might be better off just to let him peck my house down." And I was about right. Floyd seemed to be feeling quite angry, fragile, and vulnerable. Something big obviously was troubling him.

"Why don't you go out to the suet feeder and eat some breakfast?" I asked. "That should make you feel better, and then maybe you can tell me what's bothering you."

He blew his nose and wiped his slightly misty eyes with his wing. "What suet?" he asked. "Wire basket is all empty right now, you know."

"I'll put in a suet refill," I said. "Would you prefer raisin mix, peanut delight, high-energy nut combo, or millet mix?"

"Yes! Definitely! Those will suet me fine." he answered.

I went into the workshop, pulled down a package of peanut delight, took it out of its wrapper, walked out to the clearing next to the woods where I usually feed the animals, and stuffed the suet into the wire basket that hangs from the limb of an oak tree. Floyd flew over, hung upside down on the basket, and began eating. I went back in the house, noticed that Cleopatra the Cat was up, opened a can of chunked chicken for her breakfast, got myself a cup of decaf, came back out, and sat in a lawn chair to wait while Floyd finished eating. I had just settled down when I heard Cleopatra demanding to be let out of the house. I let her out and sat back down in the lawn chair to drink my now luke-warm decaf. Cleopatra sat at my feet and washed her face. Once finished with her clean-up job, she curled up on a stepping stone and watched Floyd as he ripped off big chunks of suet and wolfed them down. Floyd finally finished his breakfast, wiped down his beak, hopped over, and perched on the back of another lawn chair between where I sat and where Cleopatra lay. And then, to my dismay, he began sobbing.

"I'm not really crying," he choked. "I think I just got something in my eye, that's all. I hope you won't tell anybody about this. They might get the wrong impression, you know."

"I don't see anything wrong with crying," I said. "Besides, you really must be having a rough time right now."

"She's left me," he sobbed. "Packed her bags and went over to the next tree to stay with her mother until I get myself straightened out, whatever that means. Won't even tell me what the problem is so we can methodically and logically get at the issues and come up with whatever is wrong with her. She says we can't communicate, you know."

"DO you have trouble communicating?" I asked.

"I don't, but she does," he answered. "She just runs on and on and on. Doesn't make much sense most of the time. But I don't say anything, you know. I keep my beak shut to let her know I think she's running on too much. When she finally slows down, I tell her we should get logical and talk sense. I tell her it's the male's place to be strong and fix things. I tell her, if she will just tell me what needs fixing, I will get right on it. We'd communicate fine if she'd just listen to reason, you know."

We were not going to solve this in one sitting. Besides, I had not had breakfast, I was not dressed, and the trash had to be put out before the trash truck came. "Why don't you come back this afternoon and we'll talk about this some more," I suggested.

"All the way over here?" Floyd asked. "That's a long way, you know."

"Oh, come on!" I said. "You live in that tree just over there. I can hit a golf ball that far. With my putter, yet!"

"Oh," he said, "that's right. I forgot I lived just over there. Everything is a blur since she left me and I don't have anybody to do stuff for me and tell me what to do. I'll be here from one to seven. With no mate, don't have anything else to do, you know." And he flew off to do whatever woodpeckers do when they are not knocking my house full of holes.

Cleopatra the Cat raised her head and said, "I see you are, again, in need of my professional assistance. Fortunately I used to teach communications and animal relations at the university. Do not grovel. I am willing to assist you out of this difficulty you have gotten yourself into. Just never, never give me any more of that awful chunked chicken. It is the worst thing I have ever tasted in my entire life. From now on, serve only deluxe cracked crab or lake trout lite."

I thought, "We shall see what we shall see." I went back into the house and got on with my day's work.

73

The flicker, or *Colaptes auratus*, is a member of the woodpecker family, the *Picidae*. The flicker is a large, beautiful bird that may be found in southern Canada and the eastern United States. It is about ten inches long and has brown plumage with black markings underneath. Its head is mostly ash-colored, and it has red streaks on top of its head and on each cheek. The underside of its tail and wings is a rich golden-yellow. It has a long, slender chisel-like beak which it uses to bang holes in trees in its search for worms, bugs, beetles, and other insects. It also eats berries and is particularly fond of ants. It also is quite fond of suet. Its toes are arranged to facilitate its clinging to trees while it pecks. Its tail feathers also provide support and keep the flicker from falling over backwards from the force of the hammering blows of its powerful beak.

While the flicker is equally at home in a tree or on the ground, it always nests in a large hole it drills in a tree, usually a dead tree. It lines its nest with some of the wood chips that are produced by its hole-drilling operation. The female lays five to ten glossy white eggs. The young are hatched completely bare of feathers or down. Once the little ones feather out, grow larger, and learn to fly, the mother apparently has trouble letting go and letting be, so the family tends to stay together for a short time before each member goes its separate way. The flicker is loud-voiced but rather shy. Our birds generally acknowledge my presence by calling from their perch in the trees. They seem to be calling "treeee, treeee."

74

I looked out the kitchen window shortly after noon and saw Floyd the Flicker clinging patiently to the side of the tall pine tree just to the left of the suet feeder. I looked again at two o'clock and again at four o'clock. He had not moved.

Cleopatra the Cat awoke shortly after three o'clock from the last of her several afternoon naps. She asked to be let out. I opened the back door for her and noticed her purposeful walk into the edge of the woods. I suspected she had something in mind, probably something that had to do with Floyd the Flicker. I was not wrong. When I looked out the window again shortly after four o'clock, Floyd was still clinging to his spot on the pine tree, Cleopatra was sitting on a stepping stone near the suet feeder, and Flora the Flicker, Floyd's mate, was clinging to another pine tree just to the right of the feeder. Cleopatra obviously had sought out Flora and coaxed her into coming over. I went out, pulled a lawn chair up close, and sat where I could either participate in or just observe whatever was about to take place.

Cleopatra was the first to speak. She turned to Floyd and said, "You were saying your mate left you."

Floyd looked furtively around and whispered his response. "Let's kind of keep it down. I don't have a problem. There is really nothing wrong. My mate is, maybe, perhaps, having one of those little spells that females have sometimes, you know. She has this little difficulty communicating. Can't focus on the issues and come up with logical solutions. Doesn't recognize that I can fix things if I know what's wrong. Says she wants us to be close and equal. Can't do that, you know. I have to maintain my individuality and independence. But we ARE equal. Always have been. I'm good about that. It's share the work and share the responsibility, you know. I let her be responsible for all the things I think she can handle and I worry about all the hard stuff. Like, I let her be senior executor of all the nest work while I decide when to build a new nest and how to invest our savings. I take my commitments and responsibilities VERY seriously. She's MY mate, and I'm committed to taking care of things that are mine. Promised her parents, when I asked for her wing in matrimony, that I would take good care of her. Can't let ANYBODY, even her, get in the way of my taking good care of her, you know. I get very upset, you know, when she gets all bossy and won't let me take good care of her. So, if she would just tell me what's wrong, what needs to be fixed, I would hop right to it, come up with a logical solution, and fix it for her, you know."

This was a long speech for a woodpecker. I was impressed. I hoped Cleopatra would encourage him to keep talking or, at least, let him know she heard what he said. She did the latter. She stared Floyd straight in the eye and said, "You are saying Flora is the one who has the problem, that she has difficulty communicating in that she does not focus on the issues so you can come up with logical solutions."

"Whew!" said Floyd, in a more subdued voice. "It surely feels good to know somebody understands, you know."

Cleopatra turned to Flora and asked, "I am wondering what you think about what Floyd has been saying."

"Oh, goodness, gracious," Flora answered. "He's not telling it the way it is! Well, some of it, he is. But not all of it. I don't have any trouble communicating. I communicate with all kinds all the time. Actually, he's good at communicating, too. At least he used to be. He used to be better than I was. And he's right about being good at solving problems. Even when there are no problems to be solved. He ALWAYS has a logical solution to everything. But he doesn't have a logical solution to the little problem of my being THOROUGHLY SICK of his logical solutions to every problem! And he's right about being VERY good at fixing things. I mean, he fixes EVERYTHING! I just wish sometimes we could just talk, just be close, just be able to tell each other things instead of always having to FIX things. And did I hear him say he took his commitments seriously? Ha! Ask him about his little fling with Flicker Flirty down at the Cathouse Cafe!"

"Aw, that's not fair," interrupted Floyd. "That was just one of those little, insignificant things all males do from time to time. Nothing to it. And what's wrong with having lunch with an old friend and, maybe, smacking around a little? Besides, it was all your fault. If you'd stayed at work the way you were supposed to instead of going past the cafe to shop on your lunch hour, you'd never have known anything about it. And, then, there would have been no problem, you know."

Cleopatra ignored Floyd and, in her best facilitating style, spoke to Flora. "What I think I hear you saying is that Floyd is focusing on getting things done and preserving his independence while you are focusing on preserving intimacy and togetherness."

"Huh?" Flora responded. "I'm not sure what that means. It's more like, well, last week, I had picked up the little ones at the sitter's on the way home from work and, when I got home, I still had all the nest work to do. I had a bad headache from pounding on a tree trying to get supper in, the little ones were all fretful, the nest down had to be dusted, and feathers had to be unruffled. I was feeling threatened and pressured. I needed him to love me and help me. But he came in and just sat down without saying a word. I asked him if he would please take out the garbage. He didn't answer. Just sat there reading the newspaper. I asked, if he were not too busy and didn't mind, would he PLEASE take out the garbage. He didn't answer. I asked him again or, maybe, fifteen or twenty more times, in every way I could think of, if he would PLEASE, PLEASE take out the garbage. He never said a word. Just sat there with his beak glued to that newspaper. THAT'S when I dumped the trash in his lap and pulled the trash can down over his head."

"I think I hear you saying," said Cleopatra, "when you need him to love you and help you, he ignores you."

"Just a darned minute here," shrieked Floyd. "I do not ignore her. But I'd been out working like a slave all day. I was tired, you know. I just tried to sit down for a minute and rest my weary beak and read the newspaper a little bit, and what do I get? Take out the garbage! Take out the garbage! Nag, nag, nag. That's what I get. If she had just piped down, I would have done the stupid garbage in my own good time, you know. Besides, at work, everybody is always telling me what to do, and I have to do what they say. Home is the only place where I don't have to have somebody always telling me what to do. Besides, I didn't say I WOULDN'T take the garbage out. She should have known I would do it when I had time, you know."

"How could I know he would do it?" Flora peeped in anger. "I'm not a mind reader. And why do we always have to do things HIS way. Why can't we do things MY way sometimes?"

Cleopatra said, "Floyd, I think I hear you saying you expect to be in charge around the nest and that you do not like Flora telling you what to do. Flora, you seem to be saying you have as much right to be in charge as Floyd has."

"Well, not really," said Flora. "I don't see why either one of us has to be in charge. Why can't we be equals? I do some things well, and he does some things well. So why can't each of us just do the thing we do best without arguing over who gets his way. You may know that I'm an anesthesiologist in the Wing wing down at the hospital. We treat broken wings, sprained wings, weak wings, tired wings, and wing dings. What I'm saying is that I work hard, too. So why can't he help out around the nest sometimes?"

"So you think you contribute in many ways to the nesthold", said Cleopatra, "and you think Floyd doesn't do much."

"Well, he does a lot, but I think he could do more. But, actually, that's not the real problem. I would like for my mate also to be my friend. I would like for us to be close and talk to each other. I don't mean talk about how to fix things, but just talk about... well, talk about US. And I don't like to have to GUESS what is going on with him; I didn't want to have to GUESS what he was going to do about the garbage. I want him to TELL me what is going on with him."

"You mean you just wanted me to TELL you I was going to take the garbage out? You mean you wanted me to TELL you I was tired but that I would do it in a few minutes?" asked Floyd, with some of the anger seemingly gone from his voice. His problem-solving skills seemed to be coming into play. "You mean if I had just, you know, TOLD you I would take out the garbage in a few minutes when I got a little rested, it would have saved me from having all that nagging laid on me?"

Flora was still quite angry. She shouted to Cleopatra, "Tell him I was not nagging!" And, then she half turned toward Floyd and said in a soft, pleading voice. "I just wanted him to hear me. I want so much for him just to hear what I say and to show a little tenderness."

Floyd was puzzled. "Do you really not know I hear you?" he said. "I thought you knew there is nothing wrong with my hearing. I have VERY good hearing, you know."

"He used to listen, and he used to talk," said Flora. "It was wonderful. I wish he were that way again."

"But, I tell you everything I think you need to know, you know," Floyd responded. "I try to be a good mate, you know."

I could tell from the way Cleopatra's ears were perking up and her tail was swishing that she was listening intently to every word. Apparently she thought both Floyd and Flora were trying and were making progress but that they now had reached an impasse. Since their anger seemed to have abated, she decided to try to intervene with some of her wisdom.

"Perhaps," she said, staring first at one and then the other of the bickering flickers, "you have not been able to understand each other because you are not talking the same language. You both seem to value your relationship highly, but you seem to want different things from the relationship. Perhaps you would find it helpful in understanding each other if each of you would tell exactly what you want from the other."

Flora began speaking almost before Cleopatra finished her last sentence. "Togetherness is what I want from him," she answered between sobs. "I just want us to be close the way we once were. Before we mated, he WORSHIPPED and ADORED me. I felt like a little princess, and he was my knight in shining armor! I want those times back. I want him to show me he likes me. I want to know what goes on with him and I want him to know what goes on with me. Not just THINGS, but all the FEELINGS we have. I want to know he hears what I say, and I want to know how he feels about what I say. I want to be respected. I don't like having to act subservient and like a little girl just to please him. I want us to be equal. He almost always has to have his way. And, when he does let me have my way about some little something, he makes it seem like he's doing me a big favor. I don't want to have to FIGHT with him to get my way. I have to do enough FIGHTING at work—I have to fight to be successful. At home I... I... well, I want to be cherished, and... and protected. Feeling cherished and protected is... is what keeps the chemistry right between us. And being mated just... just doesn't work if the chemistry is not right."

There was silence for a minute or so, except for Flora's soft sobbing. Cleopatra stared at Flora with what seemed to be a puzzled look in her eyes. "Let me see if I am hearing you correctly," she said. "You want to be worshipped, adored, cherished, and protected—treated like a little princess. AND you want to be equal."

"Yes! Yes! That's it!" replied Flora with considerable enthusiasm.

Cleopatra turned to Floyd and said, "Well, what do you want?"

Floyd hesitated as though thinking deep thoughts and finally answered, "Well, mostly, I just want some respect here, you know. I want to know that she knows I'm strong, competent, and dependable. I want to know she knows I'm a winner, and I want her to... to... uh, love me. I'm a good architect, you know. Design good nests, ant hills, gopher holes, and things like that, you know. And, sometimes, I build things, like holes in houses. I just want her to know how hard I have to work at staying at the top of my profession, maintaining my status in the world, and staying up high in the pecking order, you know. And, if I do say so myself, I do a pretty good job of that. I rank third out of twenty-seven in my line of work. And I'll move up another notch if I can win the mole tunnel contract away from old Flicker Flanahan, you know. But I don't think she knows it, because she's never said anything about it. I want her to be happy. And I try to make her happy, you know. And... and... well, I heard what she said just now. And I DO protect her. And I WANT to adore and cherish her, but that's hard to do when she nags all the time. But, be EQUAL? I'm not sure I can protect and cherish and still think of her as EQUAL! In this world, you're either above or below. You either give orders or you take orders. If we were equal, there would be no one to make the decisions when we can't agree?"

I took a close look at Cleopatra and was surprised to see again what appeared to be a bit of confusion showing in her eyes. However, she recovered quickly, turned to Floyd, and said, "As I mentioned earlier, you want to dominate. You see your world as a competitive place and you see that, in a competitive world, there is no such thing as equality. At the same time, you want Flora to recognize your successes and be happy because you are a winner. You seem to have two sets of needs: to dominate in the relationship and to have someone understand how hard you try and how scared you get sometimes.

"And you, Flora, want to be adored as the little princess and also treated as an equal.

"From my superior position, I see that each of you have needs that are incompatible. The question here is how you can improve your relationship by managing these conflicting needs. Well, the first giant step is for you to understand fully the conflict within yourself and within the relationship. I see your conflicting desires as somewhat classic for males and females. I wonder if this male need for dominance and female need for intimacy and companionship are carryovers from back in the beginning when the females stayed near the den with the little ones and enjoyed close companionship with each other while the big, strong males went out and hunted bear. So, from that early beginning, the..."

Here, Floyd stopped Cleopatra in mid sentence. I was surprised. Cleopatra rarely is interrupted by anyone. Floyd spoke up in a clear, authoritative voice. "All wrong," he said. "Flickers NEVER hunt bare. When flickers go out to hunt, they always go out in full feather, you know."

Cleopatra fumed but did not respond to Floyd. Instead, she said, "Anyway, your understanding of your conflicting desires should make you more tolerant of each other. And, hopefully, as you mature, you, Flora, will have less need to be a little princess, and you, Floyd, will have less need to dominate. And perhaps, as society matures, values will change to the point that self-respect, accepting responsibility, and valuing relationships will become more important than materialism.

"But now we have an immediate problem that needs to be resolved. You will never understand each other if you don't talk to each other."

Flora had stopped crying by now. She said, addressing Floyd directly for the first time, "I didn't know we were so different. I didn't know you would have difficulty trying to be both protective and equal. Maybe I can be more patient with you and try to teach you how to... uh... hmm... well, maybe, teach you when to do one and when to do the other. And maybe, once or twice a week, we could just hang out and talk about who we really are and what is going on with us, without your trying to fix anything."

"Sure I can do that," promised Floyd. "Can do most anything if I really put my mind to it, you know. Yes! We can get together once or twice a week for no purpose other than to talk about what is going on with us. I can tell you all about what I'm doing in the stock market and, maybe, explain to you how I clean a carburetor and reset spark plugs. I know all about things like that, you know."

"Maybe you could just talk about how you feel about things and what is going on with you," suggested Flora.

"Hmm," said Floyd, "not sure HOW I feel about the stock market, carburetors, and spark plugs. But, if you could help me along a little, I bet I could get the hang of it, you know."

Flora seemed to be puzzled over something. "I don't understand," she said. "You... you sound like you have difficulty talking about personal things? When you talk with your friends, do you talk about personal things? What DO you talk about?"

"What do I talk about with my friends? Why, personal things, you know," answered Floyd. "Personal things, like which team I think will win the series and who they think is the best long ball hitter. Personal things like that. Can't talk about myself, you know. Might show a weakness that they'd use against me. Got to defend my position, you know. And, besides, talking with you is different. You're... you're my MATE, not my friend!"

"Talking to you is hard work, you know," Floyd continued. "I have to struggle hard to keep thinking of interesting, useful things to say."

"But, I get so tired of hearing interesting, useful things," said Flora. "You don't have to do that with me. Instead, just tell me what you've done all day and how you feel about what you've done."

"Really?" said Floyd. "But... but... how will you ever learn things if I don't tell you interesting, useful things all the time?"

"Maybe the only interesting, useful thing I need to know is what you like best about me," offered Flora.

"Really?" said Floyd. "I never thought of that, you know. But... but... how would I get respect?"

"You already HAVE my respect," said Flora. I like you because you are YOU, not because of what you can DO."

Flora turned to Cleopatra and said, "I think just our realizing our differences, just our understanding more about why we have trouble, will help us get along better."

Floyd chirped in, "I'll, uh, admit we probably would get along better if we knew more about each other, and, and, and, well if each knew more about how the other... uh, well, uh, FELT about things."

I thought they were doing quite well, but suddenly there was an unexpected interruption. Squeaks the Squirrel came in from the woods to search for a few stray sunflower seeds and to see if she could con me out of a hickory nut or two. She noticed immediately that something was going on that was absolutely no business of hers so she entered into it with great enthusiasm.

She looked straight at Floyd and yelled, "I have a nuncle on my father's side who knows all about snuff like this, and I know what he would say. He'd say don't let her rederange your whole life. She wants you to stop being so repetitive and to start being remissive; to stop being tough and be gender. But, as my nuncle on my father's side would say, if you want to be a ninny, go ahead and whimper down like she wants you to. But you better get two sets of feathers, one to wear at work and one to swear at home. 'Cause, if you mush up out there, you will get tromped right down to the bottom stomp of the ladder of recess. And that's an honest subscription of the facts as they really are out there in the real swirl. THAT'S what my nuncle on my father's side would say! And he knows all about competition and all about females 'cause he's got a zillion dollars and has a new mate every time I see him!"

Cleopatra jumped up, grabbed poor Squeaks by the scuff of the neck, shook her a few times, and shouted, "GO!" Squeaks went. I debated whether or not to go with her. I decided against my loyalties and stayed where the action was.

"I think that squirrel type has a point there," Floyd said.

Cleopatra scowled at him, but he continued. "If I'm going to keep on bringing in the big bugs at work, you know, I can't let anybody know about this 'feelings' stuff. Can't let down my guard for a single second out there, you know. I feel like no one knows that I have to take orders all day and I have to do things that I don't really know how to do. Sometimes, I just can't stand it any more. No one—sob, sob—knows how hard I try to be somebody and how scared I get sometimes, and—sob, sob—how hard it is not to have anybody in the whole wide world I can talk to about how rough life is for me sometimes."

Flora left her perch, flew over to where Floyd was clinging to the pine tree, and murmured, "I'm so sorry if I haven't been understanding. It's all right to cry if you want to. Takes a very brave and tender man to cry. I think you are wonderful."

Cleopatra turned her head, yawned mightily, looked back at the pair, and asked, "Well Flora, does that mean it is all right for him to be the boss and for you to be the chief flunky?"

"Oh," Flora replied, "I don't think that is the issue here. I think what's important is that Floyd has a rougher time than I realized. But now, at least he has me to talk with about it. What's important is that he is going to share his feelings with me and I am going to take more time to listen and be supportive when he is having a hard time at work."

Cleopatra gave another toothy yawn and said to the two of them, "Communicating well is so new to you you might find it easier to start by just letting the other know you heard and that you understand the words. If you have noticed, that is exactly what I have so cleverly been doing with you today. Now, if you had looked to HIM for guidance," she said, looking my way, "all he would have done is lay a lot of 'shoulds' on you. But the two of you will notice that all I did was cleverly paraphrase what each of you said and play it back to you. And that small amount of my letting you know I heard and understood turned your whole relationship around and set it on a course of mutually satisfactory companionship and living happily ever after, for all eternity."

Cleopatra walked over to the tree where Floyd was perched. "Go," she commanded. "Get her luggage in before she changes her mind."

Floyd jumped to the ground, held one wing up to his beak, and whispered into Cleopatra's ear, "How long do you think it will take her to get off this 'equality' kick?" And, then, seemingly in a daze, he flew off in the wrong direction, realized his mistake, turned, flew straight into a tree, recovered, got his directions straight, and was off.

Cleopatra eased over to the tree where Flora still clung, and spoke softly to her. "Be patient with him. I may not be around next time to help."

Flora held one wing up to her beak and whispered into Cleopatra's ear, "You don't think he's going to start crying all the time, do you? I can't STAND it when a grown male cries!"

Cleopatra did not respond. She waved goodbye to Flora, walked slowly over to the chair where I was sitting, stood in front of me, glared at me, and said, "Fortunately for you, I was available to straighten out the mess you made. Let that be a lesson to you never to meddle in things that are none of your business and about which you know absolutely nothing. If you were not so finicky about those old cedar boards on your house, this never would have happened. Now it's my meal time, if you please!"

I got up, headed for the door, and thought to myself, "Yes! I do believe there is at least one more forty-eight-can case of that chunked chicken."

XVII. The Quackenduckers

Rushing, rushing little one,
Why, I wonder, do you run?
Why the hurry, why the pace?
What ambition do you chase?
If you find it, can you stop?
Or will you run until you drop?

75

It was mid-afternoon on Friday and, as I eased the car out of the hospital parking lot onto the road and in the general direction of home, I felt weariness washing over me. I was close to physical and emotional exhaustion from months of pushing myself beyond what seemed to be my limit. My schedule of activities filled every available minute plus some minutes that simply were not available. In addition to the multitude of small tasks on my schedule, each day had its own special, major activities. Monday was golf day. Tuesday was spent grocery shopping, reading newspapers and journals at the local library, and working out at the fitness center. Wednesday was for making any needed repairs around the house and, usually, having lunch with a few friends. Also Wednesday was the one day of the week when my wife "permitted" me to prepare our evening meal. Thursday was set aside for yard work and another trip to the fitness center. Friday was the day I work as a volunteer in the emergency room of the local hospital. Also, on Friday evenings, my wife and I usually went out to dinner with friends or had friends over. Saturday was for doing my long list of household chores and, if I was not too tired, another trip to the fitness center. Sunday was for Sunday school, church and, at last, a few hours to read the newspaper and, maybe, a few pages of a book. And then there seemed to be fifty million unexpected things that had to be squeezed in somewhere. I wondered how I possibly could have managed in previous years when I also worked forty to sixty hours each week in an office. There was no doubt I was feeling somewhat stressed out from trying to do too many things or from worrying too much about whether or not I would get them all done to my satisfaction.

As I eased the car through the intersection onto the highway, I realized I had some conflicting feelings. A strong feeling of not having enough time hung over my head like a dark cloud. I had an ever-present, nagging feeling I was getting further and further behind with my scheduled activities which included only the bare minimum of what I should be doing. I was troubled about my priorities, concerned that I might be using some of my time for inconsequential things. How was I going to live a full and meaningful life if I did not have my priorities straight and could not find time to do the things I considered important? Also, I strongly suspected that part of living a full, meaningful life was avoiding the very stresses I was feeling. But how could I avoid the stresses? By not being so busy? By changing some of my priorities? By staying busy but changing some of my attitudes? I did not know the answers. Mixed with these emotions was the feeling that, in spite of the stress, this had been a good day, a tiring but rewarding experience. While I doubt I will ever learn how to be around people who are hurting without hurting with them, I also doubt I will ever fail to be amazed at the calmness, courage, and courtesy displayed by most of the sick and injured. I also am somewhat in awe of the kindness and competency of most of the hospital professional staff. I felt some pleasure in being able to contribute, even if only in a small way, to the healing, mending process.

As I continued down the highway toward home, my thinking was interrupted by a noise behind me. I saw in the rear view mirror a police car, lights flashing, siren howling, speeding down the highway toward me. I quickly slowed down and steered to the extreme right side of the road to give the police person plenty of room to pass. The speeding car zipped past and quickly disappeared over a rise in the highway. Somebody, somewhere obviously was in some kind of trouble. Whoever it was, I wished them well. So many bad things happen to people every day, I thought. Before leaving for work that morning, I had noted that the headlines of the morning newspaper reported eight people murdered in our city in the past eleven days. I also noticed the newspaper made no mention of the approximately 298,992 who had NOT been murdered. Bad news sells! But there IS good news out there, too, I thought. I recently heard someone say there is goodness all around us and that it will have its day. I believe this to be true. I had seen much goodness during the day. The light of this goodness was sufficient to illumine my way even when the clouds of anxiety, doubt, and fear cast their gloom.

I was almost home. I looked forward to sharing some of my experiences of the day and some of my muddled, disjointed thoughts with my wife. I made the last turn off the highway and onto the road that goes past Lake Splash. As I approached the pond, I looked out over the water at the ripples of light reflecting the bright afternoon sun. I noted the deep green of the newly-mowed grass and the shrubs that line the banks of the pond. I had not intended to stop, but I saw something at the edge of the water that just didn't look right. It appeared to be... but, no! It couldn't be! Goslings? I had talked with the goosenganders just recently and no one had said anything about expecting goslings. I parked by the side of the road and walked toward the spot where I was sure I had seen several small somethings in the water. Directly in my path were two goosenganders standing in the long grass between the pond and the low shrub-covered area by the stream that feeds into the pond. They were caught up in some kind of activity and completely ignored me. I stopped to see what they, Socs and Glory, were doing. The two of them were fooling around with some kind of weird looking instrument. I asked Socs what was going on.

"Trying to teach her how to use my electron microscope," he replied. "She is not particularly mechanically minded but she keeps insisting that, if I will be patient, she will pick it up eventually."

A third goosengander showed her head from behind a nearby shrub and called out, "I could have mastered it hours ago. But do you think anybody around here ever tries to teach me anything? She and her clever ways! I think she's snuggling too close to my mate, that's what I think."

Eden seemed to have her feathers more than a little ruffled. I asked her why Glory wanted to use Soc's microscope.

"I know why she SAYS she wants to," replied Eden. "Says she's got to be doctrinally correct and; therefore, has to find out for sure precisely how many angels are on the head of a pin. That's a pin she's holding with her other wing. Keeps dropping it in the grass and leaning on my mate while she tries to find it. And he's so proud somebody is interested in that stupid microscope he built that he doesn't even know it's past lunch time."

I nodded to acknowledge that I heard and then moved toward the strange objects I had seen in the water. I approached the bank, peered over the high weeds that grew from the shallow water at the pond's edge, and there they were! I was looking straight into the eyes of a pair of mallard quackenduckers.

76

The quackenduckers seemed as surprised to see me as I was to see them. For some reason, there are no resident quackenduckers at the pond. This pair obviously were strangers to these parts. They had something unfolded between them that looked like a road map. One of them, whom I later learned was Millard the Mallard, looked up at me and said, "I suppose you are one of the denizens of this locale, so I suppose you know where you are. This IS eastern Long Island, isn't it?"

"Afraid not," I answered. "This is more like central North Carolina."

The other one, whom I later learned was Mildred the Mallard, threw up her wings and shrieked, "I told you so! I told you to hang a left off the I-95 interchange onto 495 east. I told you to stop at a gas station and ask for directions. But, 'NO!' you said, 'A real man never asks for directions. I'll find it; no problem,' you kept saying. 'Straight ahead on Interstate 95 and then right on 40 will get us there in thirty minutes,' you said. And, now, we're north of—what was it you said?" she asked, looking up at me.

"North Carolina," I answered.

"Oh," she moaned. "We've got to meet relatives at Lake Montauk. Do you mean this is not Lake Montauk?" she asked as she looked out over our little neighborhood pond. "We were supposed to get there Tuesday. This IS Tuesday, isn't it?"

I answered as gently as I could. "I'm afraid this is a little over five hundred miles, as the crow... uh, as the duck flies, from your intended destination. And, this is Friday. You are either three days late or four days early."

Millard flapped his wings in preparation for take off and said, "If we're already three days late getting there, we've got to get a move on if we're going to get there on time."

Mildred held out her wings and said, "Wait up, Buster! I'm tired. Let 'em wait! I don't have time to waste on your dumb in-laws anyway."

"MY in-laws?" asked Millard. "I thought they were YOUR in-laws."

They glared at each other for a short spell and then Millard's head turned slowly toward the water and he took a long, careful look at the pond. "Nice little pond you have here," he said wistfully, as he turned back toward me. "A quiet, bucolic setting."

"I thought quackenduckers always traveled in large flocks," I said. "Are there just the two of you?"

The pair climbed onto the bank, waddled over to where I was standing, and introduced themselves. I sat down on the grass beside them. "We used to do those tour group things," said Mildred, "but we got tired of always being slowed down by somebody else's schedule. Now, we like to plan our own itinerary so we can crowd in as much as possible. We are straining to live full, meaningful lives, you know, so we wish to see the whole world at least three times over. Now, because he can't keep his directions straight, we are a long way behind schedule. Is this really Friday already? We're invited to a pool party in Schenectady this afternoon. We'll never make it! And, then, there's the clambake in Poughkeepsie on Saturday. And here we are way down in North... what was it you called this place? Don't know what we're going to do. We're so far behind, we'll never catch up. And my wings are so tired I could just hunker down and die."

Millard flapped his wings a few more times to keep them from going stiff on him and said, "Could be worse, I guess. We were going to join that wing dance crowd at upper Chincotasgue Bay on Sunday afternoon anyway. We can do this part of the country this afternoon and tomorrow and fly up to Delaware on Sunday morning. Then we'll be all rested by Monday morning and wing on over to Cleveland for the Labor Day celebration.

Only problem is we have all of a day an a half down here. How are we going to kill time after we get through looking over the Carolinas and Georgia?"

I was impressed. I said, "My gracious, you do get around, don't you."

Mildred, responded with, "How do we get around, did you ask? Well, most times we fly point-to-point, sometimes we travel the interstates, sometimes we take Amtrack, sometimes we do rivers, and sometimes we just go out for an afternoon flight and simply keep going in whichever direction we happen to be headed. We most always end up somewhere and, when we don't, we end up someplace like this. By the way, how are the accommodations around here? Any sushi bars? How's the opera schedule? Any museums? What do you do around here in the culture, education, self-improvement, and entertainment departments? Let's see. If we do North—what did you call it, again?—Carolina today, South Carolina by ten tomorrow, and a quick once over Georgia, we can... yes, it should work out quite well. Doesn't take long if you just hit the high spots. Don't have time for any details. Got to go, go, go if you're going to have a full, happy, meaningful life. Don't you agree?"

I thought I knew the answer, but I kept quiet. Something here was bothering me a bit. But I was not sure if THEY were bothering me or if I was bothering me. My troubling thoughts were interrupted by a noise from the edge of the pond just behind the quackenduckers. A huge figure emerged from the water, causing the water level to drop several inches. It was Fun City the Goosengander. "Don't go to the museum," he said. "Food's terrible! Do the Chowder Pot! Takes about all day, service is so slow. But food's good and lots of it. Anything you want to know about doing fun things, just ask me. I'm the expert around here when it comes to fun and pleasure. And, since you asked, I'll tell you. First thing you've got to do is slow down some. Can't do three big states in a day and a half. Takes three days at least. You've got to slow down and smell the muck if you are going to live to a fun-filled old age. Just settle down in this little ole' piddle puddle for a few weeks or a month and I will show you how to relax hard and get it over with so you'll be all rested up for having fun, fun, fun."

"I was afraid of something like this," Mildred said to Millard. "Boston or Philadelphia this certainly is NOT! No culture, no elegance, no learning, no world vision, no nothing. Much, much too provincial for members of the jet set like us. Let's get out of this place before we get contaminated."

"Sure," agreed Millard with a sigh. "So on we go to Cleveland and then to the games in Toronto, the opera in Ottawa, then down to the sing-in at Woodstock and the seminar at Bangor!" "Yes!" said Mildred. "And then a long flight. Quick stops at James Bay, Lake Winnipeg, and that little place at Coeur D'Alene, and on to Puget Sound and Klamath Falls. Then two days to do California, Nevada, and Arizona."

The two quackenduckers rose heavily into the late afternoon air. They were just beginning to gain altitude as they flew across the road. Millard followed in Mildred's airstream while he took a last careful look at the road map. He did not intend to get lost again. A truck was coming from the other direction. Millard glanced up from his map and saw the truck almost in time. He swerved wildly in an attempt to clear it. Almost made it, but not quite! He bounced off the top of the cab, and was flipped off-course and upside down by the impact. He struggled to regained his balance and partially succeeded before making a crash landing back at the shore of the pond. Mildred made a tight circle and flew back to join him. The four goosenganders rushed over to assist the downed flyer. Fun City rushed too fast, could not stop in time and collided with the injured one with almost as much force as the truck collision.

Millard was surprisingly calm; Mildred was surprisingly rattled. "Oh, my poor mate," she screamed. "They've killed him! He's gone! Oh, why wasn't I more careful? Why didn't I take better care? Why didn't I watch where he was going? Why did I fuss at him for getting us off track by a mere five million miles? What does it matter where we fly so long as we fly together? Do something somebody! Don't let him die! Save him! Please, save him!"

Millard reached up, patted her on the head with his good wing, and murmured in a soft voice, "I think it's going to be all right. Well, almost, maybe. It's just a wing, I think. Lost lots of feathers. Seems to be bleeding all over, but not much. Probably broken but possibly not. Maybe just a bad bruise or a super fracture. With superb medical attention, a long bed rest, and appropriate physical therapy, I might be able to try flying again in a few months or fifty years."

The goosenganders took over at this point. Glory gently stretched out the injured wing, Eden plucked a feather from her breast and wiped away the blood, and Socs gave the wing a careful examination. Fun City did his part by walking around in a tight circle and shouting advice. In no time at all, the cuts were treated, two broken feathers were removed, and the bruised wing was strapped down to prevent further injury. Our wounded hero was helped to a quiet recess in the reeds beside the pond. Socs stood guard while Glory and Eden rushed off to make soup for the patient and his mate. Fun City cheered up the wounded one with tales of how he had seen the same thing happen to fifteen others, had attended the funerals of fourteen of them, and had seen the one miraculous survivor live out the remainder of his life as a crippled beggar selling pencils from a sidewalk stand downtown on the corner of Hillsborough and Salisbury Streets. Mildred was so overwrought by the recent events that she lay in a daze snuggled up against her injured mate.

77

The mallard, or *Anas platyrhynchos* of the family *Anatidae*, is a wild duck found nearly everywhere in Eurasia and North America. However, while it may be found nearly everywhere, it will not necessarily be the same duck every time. The mallard drake (male), is a beautiful bird. He has an iridescent green head and a chestnut breast. The female is pretty enough, but not particularly beautiful. She is a modest speckled brown. Each wing has white bars on each side of a patch of blue. The mallard is about twenty inches long. The drake is slightly larger than the female.

The mallard can be a noisy bird. Sometimes, the female quacks and quacks and quacks. The drake does not give a quack but, rather, communicates with a reedy note of his own. The mallard prefers to live by still waters such as lakes and ponds. Sometimes it has to settle for a river or stream. It may migrate every year or it may decide to settle in a single locale. The mallard usually is seasonally monogamous, selecting a new mate each year. The drake selects the nesting place, after which the female builds the nest. The nest usually is on the ground in a reedy area and is lined with leaves and twigs and covered with a layer of down. The female incubates the nine to thirteen eggs for twenty-two to twenty-six days. For the first few days of the incubation period, the faithful drake stands by ready to provide a vigorous defense of the nest should any enemy approach. Then, after about a week, he forces himself to gain some relief from this irksome responsibility by flying off with the other males, presumably to shoot pool and drink beer while awaiting the arrival of his offspring.

The mallard eats seeds, plant shoots, and grass. It also collects food from the surface of the water. It is not a diving bird and does not go underwater for food. Annually, after it molts, it cannot fly until it grows new feathers, which takes about a month.

While many mallards die from disease and parasites, man is the major enemy. Hunters' shotguns kill millions of ducks each year. Then, for each duck the hunters carry away, they leave behind an estimated one thousand, four hundred shotgun pellets. Lead pellets in particular are deadly to ducks. A single lead pellet, swallowed with food or taken as grit and ground in the duck's gizzard, can introduce sufficient lead into the bloodstream to cause the duck's death. While steel pellets can be used for hunting, these not only have some ballistic disadvantages but also can cause serious wear on the shotgun barrel. Other major man-made causes of death to ducks are pesticides, mercury from pesticides, and oil from spills.

78

I planned to stop by the pond again Monday afternoon on my way home from golf. I expected the two mallards to be gone by then. Or, if they were still around, I expected them to have the whole pond population frantically busy with some kind of cultural, educational, or other activity in an attempt to ensure full, meaningful, happy lives. I was wrong on both counts. By the time I came that way again, the quiet pond setting and the intelligence and common sense of the goosenganders had begun to work their magic on the two busy, busy mallards.

It was three o'clock in the afternoon by the time I finished my twenty-seven holes of golf and drove back through town and out to the pond. I parked the car and quietly walked over to the spot where the quackenduckers and goosenganders were gathered. Several of them seemed to see my approach but were too occupied to pay much attention. I sat in the grass between where the males were clustered in one group and the females in another. The bandages were off Millard's wing and he was flexing it gingerly every few minutes to help work the stiffness out of it. Fun City was standing over Millard and Socs. He was talking and yawning at the same time. "Been a good day," he said. "Planned to do nothing all day. Got up bright and early and got right at it. And here it is only mid-afternoon and, already, I've mostly got it done."

Millard was in a deep conversation with Socs. "You agree, of course," he said, "that happiness is what it's all about. If you don't have happiness, you don't have anything!"

After a minute of silence, Socs said, "I think I hear you saying you absolutely must be happy, you will be most unhappy if you fail to achieve happiness, nothing else matters except that you be happy, you owe it to yourself and others to be happy, to be happy is your born duty, to be happy is your primary responsibility, you cannot afford to let down the whole animal kingdom by failing to be happy, and you will be happy even if it kills you. So, hmm... how can I tell you this. The truth, as I see it, is that happiness is vastly overrated. And I can tell you emphatically you don't have to be happy if you don't want to! It is perfectly alright with me if you put your webbed foot down and just flat refuse to be happy."

"Hmm! Well! Uh! Like I said," responded Millard, "while you don't have to be happy if you don't want to, happiness still is the most desirable thing. And, if you don't try real hard and work at it every second, how are you ever going to find true happiness?"

Socs did not give a direct answer. Instead he murmured, "I wonder if it is possible that happiness is like a cool rain on a hot summer day and is most inclined to drop down on you unexpectedly when you are completely involved with something else?"

"Uh! Hmm! Yes." replied Millard. "Well, maybe you just have to work hard at happiness part of the time or, maybe most of the time. There is so much in this world waiting to interfere with your happiness, too many unfortunate and unfair things to

271

just let them creep up on you. If you don't keep on the move and never look back, the bad things will catch up with you and you will never be happy. You agree with that of course."

"What you are suggesting sounds to me more like running from reality and not accepting that the world IS the way it IS and that life is not always the way we think we want it to be," offered Socs. "Running from reality is not nearly as scary as facing up to it."

Millard thought for a minute and replied, "You think I am running from reality while I think YOU are the one who is refusing to accept the truth about what the world is like. Remember, I travel all over. I know what the world is REALLY like. I see a great deal of hate and crime in the world?"

"I see," responded Socs, "a great deal of love and virtue in the world."

"Moreover," continued Millard, "there is selfishness and greed all over."

"There is magnanimity and generosity all over," said Socs.

"Also," sighed Millard, "animals just don't get along with each other. Even most matings end in divorce."

"There is a great deal of peace and good will among animals. A great many matings last forever, and matings that don't work can be dissolved so that each of the pair can make a new start," added Socs.

"And, everywhere, there's competitiveness that leads to stress and strain," said Millard.

"There is competition that often motivates, encourages creativity, and leads to better products and services at lower prices," added Socs. "And, also, there is a great deal of cooperation that enhances productivity and tranquility."

"Furthermore," continued Millard, "for most of us, there simply is not enough time in the day to do all the things we need to do."

"We all have exactly the same amount of time every day. And we almost always can find the time to do the things we really want to do," countered Socs.

"Too," moaned Millard, "all of us suffer most of the time from injuries or disease."

"Most of us are in good health most of the time," whispered Socs. "And, sometimes, even injury and disease can have a positive side. Maybe, sometimes, that is the only thing that causes us to slow down and get our priorities straight."

"Additionally," mumbled Millard, "there is poverty and pain all over."

"There is the kind of poverty that keeps us from what we want and the kind that keeps us from what we need," murmured Socs. "There also is charity, support, caring, and opportunity. Though there is physical pain, there also is healing for wounded bodies. Though there is emotional pain, there also is balm for wounded spirits."

"And then after that," grumbled Millard, "there is old age. All of us, if we are among the lucky ones, are going to grow old and feeble and not be able to take care of ourselves."

"Life is a cycle," said Socs. "Fortunately, we don't have to stay young forever. We can grow into wise old age. Most of us can slow down in our old age and focus more on the things we really want to do. And this growing old presents opportunities for us to accept caring assistance from others with the things we no longer can to do for ourselves. Growing old may have its disadvantages, but would any of us seriously wish to be half our age again?"

"Worst of all," groaned Millard, "is the cold, hard fact that all of us are doomed! We all are going to go down one of these days and never get up again!"

"Fortunately," answered Socs, "we do not have to live forever. Before this life has a chance to become too boring, we can put it all aside and go on to the time/place/realm where we can use the wisdom we have gained in this life."

"Time/place/realm?" asked Millard. "Surely you're not serious! Where do you get such far out ideas?" He was quiet for a minute and then sighed, "I think what bothers me most of all is that others are so busy doing their own thing they never have time to pay attention to anybody else. Animals just aren't interested in each other any more. They don't have time for friends. They... they don't have time to be friends with ME."

"I agree with you that friends are important," said Socs. "Friends probably are the one thing most of us want the most. And, like most things that are valuable, we have to work to have friends. Friendship is sharing and caring. I'm glad I have you for a friend."

There was a soft sob from Millard and then silence. I shifted my position to get more comfortable. Finally, Millard spoke up again in a softer voice. "Sometimes I get so tired of flying all over. But, when I try to settle in somewhere for a while, I just don't seem to fit in. All the others seem to have their own friends and routines. They just don't seem to have time for me. I don't know, maybe if I stayed at one place long enough, I might fit in." And, then his voice rose, and he practically shouted, "One thing I know for sure and that's that your thinking is all scrambled up. I emphatically, ardently, zealously, vehemently, and most strongly disagree with you about everything in the world being so perfect. I think you just have your head in the sand."

"Perhaps," murmured Socs. "I didn't mean to give the impression that I think everything is perfect. I agree with your list of negatives. It's just that I think these negatives are only one side of the picture. I simply was trying to point out that there also is a brighter side. I think we would both agree that looking only at the bright side would leave us in a vulnerable position. Some bad thing could come along at any moment and knock the props from under us. But I also think there must be a reason why some of us look only at the dark side. Perhaps if we limit our focus to the negative aspects of life, we don't have any hope. And, if we don't have any hope, we don't have to try very hard. We can just keep on running and never let life catch up with us. I think, maybe, reality is seeing the positive AND the negative and, somehow, coming to terms with both. Did you ever really like something and find you could have as much of it as you wanted?"

"Well, yes. I think so," replied Millard. "Why in the world did you ask that? I used to like tamales. Would have loved to eat them morning, noon, and night. I liked them so much I bought half interest in a tamale shop. Ate tamales until I could blow fire out my ears. Ate so many the shop went broke. Just in time, too. Because I hate tamales. Hope I never see one of them again as long as I live."

"Are you saying," asked Socs, "if we have all of something we want, it becomes less dear to us? Are you saying positive things in life seem good to us only when contrasted with the negative? Is it possible that we like rain only because we have experienced drought, enjoy food only because we have experienced hunger, savor life only because we are aware of death, and appreciate a strong wing only when we have had an injured one?"

"Well," answered Millard, "I think I understand most of what we are saying here, even though I don't understand most of it. Hmm. I mean I do and I don't, if you know what I mean. I still think I do a pretty good job of seeing and accepting reality. My mate and I simply are trying to whack reality into line here and there where it doesn't quite fit the way we think it should. We do that by going all over and telling others they need to stay busy doing lots of educational and cultural stuff. Nothing wrong with that of course. Right?"

Socs did not answer. "Do you think it possible," he asked, "that the reason you are trying to change others is because you really have not accepted that they are the way they are?"

"Hmm," answered Millard, "This time, you are REALLY wrong. If you just accept others the way they are, they will never get any better. Main thing wrong with the world is that most just take things the way they are and never try to change things they don't like."

"I suppose," said Socs, "you have changed lots of things for the better. I would love to hear about all the things you have been able to change to make the world a better place in which to live. That is, if you don't mind sharing some of those experiences."

"Well, sure! Lots of things. Don't know quite where to begin. Well, one of the real biggies was... hmm. Wait, are you being sarcastic here? I can't tell you all the facts because I've always left and gone someplace else before I had a chance to see how things I started had a chance to work themselves out. But... but... but at least I have traveled far and I have come here and shared my travel experiences with you. And I'll bet you can't look me straight in the eye and tell me you are not at least a little bit changed by it."

"Well said!" exclaimed Socs. "And, you are right! Your short stay has been a peaceful but challenging time for me. We differed about many things, but you have been gracious in your disagreement. You helped me to see some things from a different perspective. You introduced me to places and ways that were strange to me. But I think most of all you reinforced my belief that friends are wonderful things."

Socs paused for a moment and then continued on another subject. "Do you think it's possible," he asked, "to accept the conditions around you the way they are and, at the same time, try to change them some? That way, you could get satisfaction if you succeed OR if you fail. That way, your happiness would be based more on your awareness of reality than on your accomplishments. In fact, maybe happiness is not dependent on accomplishments at all."

"Well, I don't know about that," said Millard. "I suppose you could be right. Perhaps happiness is based more on what you know or learn. Perhaps as soon as I learn everything there is to know, I'll be completely happy. Got any books or stuff around here that I can start studying?"

Socs again was quiet for a minute and then said, "Have you ever heard of anyone who knew everything? Neither have I. So, if we have to be all-knowing to be happy, might we not just as well forget about happiness? It seems to me most of the things we learn are simply details that we could look up somewhere if we really needed to know them. What really helps is to have a broad framework of knowledge and wisdom built on a solid foundation. That's all we really need. The details will fall into place if we just keep our wits about us. I think perhaps this solid foundation consists primarily of understanding that the world the Creator made is basically good, the forces She put into motion are positive ones, and life, even with all of its troubles and sorrows, is good."

"That's what I guess I said," puzzled Millard. "But I don't know what button you push to understand things you just don't understand."

"Neither do I," admitted Socs.

"See," said Millard, "you admit there are lots of things you don't know. I think you get stale from never going anywhere and just staying around this little pond. I admit, though, I think it's a very NICE little pond."

Millard moved over and lay on the grass next to Socs. Fun City yawned again, moved in close, lay next to Millard, and soon was fast asleep. The three were comfortable with each other. They had become fast friends.

When the three males settled into their quietness, I turned my attention to the gaggle of females. It appeared that all three were talking at once, apparently on at least three completely different topics. Mildred was talking about finances. "We were so rich," she said, "we spent all our time just counting our money. Never had time to go anywhere or spend any of the money. Interest and dividends came in faster than we could count them. Then we got lucky. Lost almost all of it in the stock market. Used to own outright about nine zillion cows, pigs, and sheep. But when the stock market goes, it goes. Almost overnight, all we had left was milking rights to one cow. And I think we bought that one on margin. When we gave up being rich, that's when we got into the meaningful, happy life business. If you can't be rich, you just have to do the next best thing, which is to be happy. One thing that can be said about...."

Glory was talking about her Sunday services. "Started the whole thing all by myself," she said. "Was just I and a few half-drowned mice. Started it up only about five years ago. And, as you were able to see for yourself this past Sunday morning, the congregation has almost doubled its attendance. Would have been even more there if the weather had not been so wet and rainy. Lovely days like that, as you know, are when sinners like to puddle around and...."

And Eden told about contamination in the pond area. "Just this past week," she said, "cars on that road threw out six aluminum cans, two glass bottles, three sandwich wrappers, eleven cigarette butts, and lots of other things that I don't know what they are. And look at the population increase just here at this little pond. At the beginning of last week, there were four of us waterfowl. By the end of the week, there were six. That's a fifty percent increase. At that rate, in only one year, if my mathematics are correct, the waterfowl population in this little insignificant pond will be five billion, seven hundred and thirty-eight million, five hundred and ninety thousand, and eight hundred. So, it should be clear to any thinking citizen that...."

The three of them had no difficulty following the intent of the conversations. As with the three males, they were comfortable with each other. They, too, had become fast friends. Both Millard and Mildred had gained a new perspective from their contact with the goosenganders. This quiet time at the pond was actually the first REAL vacation the quackenduckers had ever had, and they were enjoying it to the fullest. But, more importantly, this was the first time they had enjoyed close friendships, and friendships help provide the security that permits exploration of new ideas. The goosenganders, also, were gaining something from their contact with the quackenduckers. They were beginning to understand more of what the world is like outside of their limited domain. But, more importantly for all the waterfowl, they had given of themselves. Needed aid had been extended and graciously accepted. Information and ideas had been exchanged, considered, and discussed. Lives had, perhaps, been changed.

79

I did not see the quackenduckers again. Several weeks passed before I had a chance to stop again at the pond. It was then that Socs told me what happened. Millard's wing healed nicely and he and his mate spent long hours talking with each other and with their friends, the goosenganders, about their future. They decided to forsake their desperate struggle for meaningful, happy lives, accept the goodness of life wherever they found it, treat others as they themselves wished to be treated, spend more time being aware of reality and less time running from truth, and slow down and smell the muck. Well, that was their plan, but they did not exactly stick to it. One does not change overnight. That would be like jumping out of one's feathers.

In their last few days at the pond, the two quackenduckers became increasingly despondent. They were accustomed to constant activity and stress, and the quietness and serenity of the pond was beginning to leave them feeling that life was passing them by. They were beginning to think long thoughts, and long thoughts can be ever so scary. They had gained a dim vision of a different way of life, a more peaceful life, a more hopeful life. But visions and hopes must coexist with doubts and fears. They felt a strong urge to escape the doubts and fears by going everywhere and doing everything as quickly as possible. Alaska, Mexico, Greenland, and Florida beckoned. They bought a new video camera to tape the whole world; they would review the tape on stormy nights when they were forced to hole up in some obscure inn or busy airport waiting room. The whole world beckoned to them and they felt forced to respond. They said their last farewells, promised to write often and visit at least once each year, took a good look at their well-worn road map BEFORE flight time, made a smooth take-off from the surface of the pond, flew straight into the setting sun, and disappeared into the evening sky.

I said my "goodbye, for today" to Socs, waved to the other goosenganders, and drove back home. I had plans for the afternoon. I would lie in the hammock with my head propped comfortably on a pillow, listen to the birds sing, and watch the grass grow.

XVIII. On the Campaign Trail

I'll vote for sure, if it doesn't rain,
For Smith, or Jones, or What's His Name,
Who promised stuff and things for all,
Or something; I just don't recall.
With such support from folks like me,
Pray tell, what can the reason be
For so much mediocrity?

80

It was one of the last hot days of summer. The raccoons, opossums, and squirrels were fat from the abundant summer harvest; the deer were sleek from feasting in the green park; the box turtles, toads, lizards, woodpeckers, and wrens were stuffed from the ample supply of bugs and beetles; and the chickadees, titmice, nuthatches, and other birds were in full form from the more-than-adequate supply of seeds. All was at peace. There was time yet before the frantic activities of fall and the slowing down and deep sleep of winter, time yet before the days would grow shorter and the evening shadows lengthen. It was that between-season pause when life can be so pleasant there is danger of downright boredom. Some excitement was due, and the animals were up to the challenge. Tuesday of the following week, in early September, would be election day, the day when the next Mayor of the Woods would be elected!

The candidates for Mayor of the Woods had announced their intentions, platforms replete with weasel words were being prepared, issues were being invented, strategies for clouding the issues were being devised, deceptive ploys were being planned, and votes were being bought and paid for. It was to be a typical, knock-down-drag-out, no-holds-barred, don't-bother-me-with-the-truth political campaign.

The announced candidates were Devious the Deer, Windy the Wren, Rascal the Rabbit, and Pete the 'Possum. It was my fortune—or misfortune—to have the opportunity to talk with each of them regarding his or her political position. During the warm days of late August, each candidate had, at one time or another, stopped me in the yard to solicit my vote, ask for a donation to their campaign treasury, or request permission to nail political announcements to the trees in the back yard.

81

Devious the Deer was the first to approach me. It was early evening, the time deer usually come in to take a bit of seed from the bare spot on the ground where I feed the doves, or to trash a few azaleas or a bed of ivy. But Devious did not come for food; she was on the campaign trail. She danced into the yard and got directly to the point. "I'm sure you will be wanting lots of things from the mayor's office," she said. "And, remember, I will be there to do the will of the citizens. Whatever you want, that's what you will get. All I ask from you is your vote. Well, and maybe any cash you might have to spare for a super worthy cause that's sure to pay you back handsomely. Don't put yourself out any here, but if you happen to feel the need to support reduced government interference; strong zoning regulations; limitations on big business; a humane minimum wage; enforced improvements in workplace environments; price controls; tariffs on foreign goods; and a dedicated effort to ensure mother's milk, apple pie, prayer in the schools, and salutes to the flag, you may wish to make a small donation to support my campaign to make sure the sniveling cowards who are my opponents are defeated in their attempt to bamboozle, flimflam, and otherwise hoodwink the fair citizens of this fair community."

"Wait! Hold on a minute," I said. "Let's get serious here. What specifically do you intend doing if you are elected?"

"Glad you asked that," she replied. "Makes my heart glad to hear a concerned simpleton... uh, citizen ask such discerning, perceptive, judicious, sagacious, and ludicrous... uh, logical questions. What am I going to do, you ask. Why, I am going to do the will of the citizens. That's what democracy is all about. I will represent the animals who voted for me. In a democracy like ours, what the majority want the majority get. If the majority want lemonade in every water fountain, that's what they get. If they want taxes abolished and a guaranteed annual income, that's what they get."

"Now, wait a minute," I said. "You are saying two things that are incongruous. You said you were going to do what the voters want AND what is good for the voters. As you well know, what the voters say they want usually is not good for them. They can't have it both ways and neither can you. So, make up your mind. Which is it going to be?"

"Glad you asked that," she said. "Shows that you are an asinine... uh, astute citizen. The answer to this, as you will see spelled out clearly and in great detail in my official platform statement and, as the no-good scum who are my opponents either have failed to address or have distorted because they refuse to listen to the will of the citizens.... Now, issues, that's what we have to address. No mud slinging or character assassination here. Just force the slimy slobs who are my opponents to stick with the issues. Now you, as a concerned citizen, want to know if I intend doing the will of the voters. Of course I do. I am firmly dedicated to the principle of doing the will of the voters."

Here, Devious stopped talking, looked around to see if anyone else was listening, and asked, "You're not with the press are you? Do you actually want to know if I intend doing the will of the voters instead of doing what makes sense? Well, just between the two of us, I really do. The way I figure it, that's the only way to get elected and stay elected. If I don't do what the rabble... uh, citizens want, they'll throw me right out of the mayor's seat. And then what will happen to my chances to be the next state senator? If I wanted to do what makes sense, I would be a corporate executive, plumber, or dentist. A politician who makes sense? The very idea! So I stand firm in my commitment to the will of the mob... uh, multitude. You can quote me on that but, if you do, I will be forced to deny it and will have to reconsider your appointment as chairperson of the mayor's blue-ribbon stuff-and-things committee."

82

My next encounter with a candidate came the next morning when I went out to feed the birds. One of the birds who was out early was candidate Windy the Wren. She saw me coming and perched on top of the sunflower seed feeder where she was sure

I would notice her. "Glad to start the day off," she sang, "getting better acquainted with a strong supporter of the candidate who vows to do what's right no matter what. Uh, you are a strong supporter of good government and doing what's right no matter what, aren't you? Thought so. I could tell right off by the gleam in your eye, the spring in your step, the rosy glow on your cheeks, and the feathers or whatever on your chin that you are an astute, discerning citizen. Mind if I paste these billboards on the side of your house to let everybody know you are a strong proponent of good government and a firm backer of the candidate who vows to do what's right no matter what?"

"Nope," I said, "Rather you didn't do that."

"Astute choice!" peeped Windy. "Keep them guessing, that's a shrewd move. Anyway, I can hang these old signs any place. Confidentially, what I really need is your financial support. It won't hurt you to give if you give 'til it hurts. A sizeable donation will be cheerfully accepted. While I strongly affirm my position as the candidate who absolutely cannot be bought, it's perfectly all right for you to try. But, whether you contribute a lot or contribute your all, I still will stand tall as the candidate who promises to do what's right no matter what!"

"Just exactly what do you mean by doing what's right no matter what?" I asked.

"Ah," she replied, "one of those who likes to look beyond personalities and get right to the issues. Shrewd! Shrewd! I see that no one is going to fool you with a bunch of typical political palaver. Asking questions and demanding answers! That's the way to force those politicians to stop wooley-whooping, lollygagging, and pussy footing around and get right to the issues. That's the way to make sure you get good, solid, honest, competent, creatures in public places. That's the way to make sure you get someone who always does what's right no matter what. Uh, did that answer you question?"

"No," I answered.

"Glad I could fully address your concerns," said Windy. Always glad to... uh, did you say, 'no?' Hmm. Are you sure? Well, what was the question again?"

"I asked you what you mean by doing what's right no matter what," I repeated.

"Hmm," she said. "That's what I thought you asked. Maybe I'd better just perch down here and think while you rush in and get your checkbook. Unless, of course, you prefer cash."

"Well," I said, holding out my hand, "actually, I do prefer cash."

"Thought so," she said, as she reached into her purse, pulled out her wallet, and counted out two tens. "Wait!" she shrieked, catching herself at the last moment, "You are supposed to be giving ME money!"

"Why?" I asked.

"Why?" she answered. "Because I'm the candidate, the one who is going to do what's right no matter what!"

"Just exactly what do you mean by doing what's right no matter what?" I asked.

Windy blinked her eyes, wiggled her wings, scratched her head, and drooped a bit lower on her limb. "Means I'm my own bird," she said. "Means I have my own reasons for messing things up. Means I'm not one of those who messes things up just so those nitwit voters will vote me back into office. Means I don't give a feather what the voters want. Ask one hundred voters what they want and you'll find they want one hundred different things. Well, looking at it another way, they all want exactly the same thing. They all want something for nothing. I think an elected official ought to be a bird of character and convictions. She should not yield to the multitude and do what she knows is stupid just because the multitude thinks it will line their pockets. Instead, she should give some thought to her own pockets! Now, does that answer your question?"

"Pretty good answer," I said. "Do you really think you will get elected, with ideas like that?"

"Sure," Windy answered. "No doubt about it. Doesn't it sound noble, honorable, ethical, upstanding, and responsible? Think for a minute like one of the melon-headed voters when he hears my opponents talk about doing the will of the citizens. Does this particular citizen want the CITIZENS to get what they want? Of course not. He doesn't care a peep what the CITIZENS want. He just wants what HE wants! Does he consider himself to be noble, honorable, ethical, upstanding, and responsible? Of course he does. So, he's sure that I, as the candidate who pledges to do what's right no matter what, have in mind doing exactly the things he wants done. Can't fail. A cinch. Just have to go through the motions. Well, you think it over and I will drop back by tomorrow after you have had more time to decide how much you wish to contribute to a campaign for the candidate who pledges to do what's right no matter what!"

83

I tried mostly staying in the house for a couple of days. I had had about enough of politics. But, the lawn needed mowing, and I could not stay in forever anyway. I got out early to get the lawn mower ready. Fortunately for me, Devious and Windy apparently were politicking elsewhere. However, there were other candidates. Rascal the Rabbit came hoppity skip up to where I was putting gasoline into the lawn mower. "Fine machine you have there," he said. "Always a pleasure to see industrious citizens like you out in their yards getting ready to mow down the weeds so the grass and clover will grow high so as to provide food for our hungry children and support the elderly and give comfort to the sick and maimed and ensure a glorious future for our neighborhood and our country."

"Huh! Come again?" I asked.

He stuck out a paw that was still damp from the morning dew and said, "Shake paws with the next Mayor of the Woods."

"So," I said, "you really think you will win out over the other three?"

"Sure," said Rascal. "No problem there at all. They are rank amateurs while I am a rank professional. Besides, with my soapbox... uh, platform, I can't lose."

"What is your platform?" I asked.

"Increased services, reduced taxes, and prison reform," he answered.

"What kind of prison reform do you have in mind?" I asked.

"Oh, nothing in particular," he replied. "Just more privileges and less restrictions on the inmates. Just trying to look out for my in-laws."

"Do you plan to do what the voters want, or do you plan to do what you think is right no matter what?" I asked

"Exactly!" replied Rascal.

"Well, now, you can't do both," I said.

"Doesn't matter what I do," he said. "It's what they THINK I do that counts."

"You mean you would deliberately deceive them?" I asked. "Seems to me you don't have any real convictions."

"Not so!" he cried. "I've been convicted lots of times. Luckily though, I've never had to serve time."

"You mean you've just barely managed to stay out of jail?" I asked.

"Of course," he answered. "How else could I be such an expert on prison reform? And, now, before you decide how much to donate to my campaign, let me tell you about my plans to increase services and cut taxes."

"Sure," I said. "I would like to hear how you are going to do that." I pushed the lawn mower aside and made myself as comfortable as possible on the concrete floor of the carport.

Rascal squatted down opposite me and continued. "Well, it's really very simple. I'll figure out some little something that most of the citizens want and I'll give it to them. And, when it gets close to tax time, I'll simply cut taxes twenty-five percent."

"But you can't do that," I protested. "If you cut taxes, how will you pay for the increased services?"

"Simple," said Rascal. "Ever heard of deficit spending? Didn't think so. Takes a rank professional to think of things like that. Deficit spending is simply spending now and paying later."

"But, won't the ones who will have to pay complain about it?" I asked.

"Can't complain," he answered. "Not born yet."

Rascal stopped to give his ears a good scratching and then continued. "Give the voters lots of goodies, cut their taxes and, if anybody ever notices the deficit—and they probably won't— simply blame it on Japanese imports or those politicians up in Washington. That's the way to keep everybody, especially me, docile and contented."

I told him he sounded, and smelled, to me like a well-seasoned politician, and that I had to admit he sounded like a winner. I, however, declined his suggestion that my campaign contribution be deposited in his Swiss bank account. He thanked me kindly for being such a strong supporter and took his leave.

84

It was almost dark the same day when I looked out the window and saw Pete the 'Possum carrying a sign and walking slowly out of the woods toward the clear spot where I swing my hammock. He seemed weary, as though he had walked a long way. I had been surprised to hear he was running for office in our neighborhood. I always thought he lived clear across the park in a different district and, thus, was not eligible to vote or run for office here. Well, probably he had moved. I went outside and sat in the hammock to wait for him. As he drew near, I called to him, "Ah, the dark horse candidate has arrived!"

Pete stopped, put down his sign, scratched his sides, looked up at me, and grunted, "Not dark horse! I, Pete."

"Well," I apologized, "I didn't mean literally a dark horse. That is just a term that means one who is considered to have only an outside chance to win an election."

"I win!" declared Pete. He picked up his sign and showed it to me. Someone apparently had used a crayon to scrawl in crude letters "A vote for Pete's a vote for eats."

"What is that supposed to mean?" I asked.

"Don't know. Didn't write. He wrote," said Pete, nodding in the direction of the edge of the woods.

I looked in the indicated direction and saw what seemed to be Mugger the Mole lurking in the shadows with field glasses pressed against his weak eyes. He was peering in our direction. "Campaign manager," clarified Pete.

I hoped it was not so. Mugger was thought by many to have strong underworld connections. Surely the underworld element would not become involved in this relatively unimportant local election! "Why are you running for public office?" I asked.

"Graft," replied Pete.

"Well, I can't believe this," I said. "You may be sure you will get no support from me!"

"You support," said Pete. "Or else!"

"Or else, what?" I asked indignantly.

"Or else I get no graft," answered Pete.

"I don't like to be threatened and I don't think you will make a good mayor," I said. "Why don't you just leave!"

"Don't hurt me," pleaded Pete. "I leave. I hungry. Just want graft. I VERY hungry. Please."

He had me there. I went into the workshop, scooped up a coffee can full of graft... uh, dog food, brought it out, and fed Pete the 'Possum. He ate his fill, picked up his tattered sign, and disappeared into the woods. The sinister Mugger the Mole followed closely behind.

85

It was the evening before the election and the animals were gathering in the back yard for an open meeting at which the four candidates for mayor were to debate the issues. The time and place for the debate had been a hot topic for weeks. While our local elections seldom followed party lines, disagreements between the two major factions were bound to occur. The "day" animals, those who work during the day and sleep at night, wanted the meeting to be held in the civic center at high noon; the "night" animals, those who carouse by night and sleep by day, did not want to meet at all. Early evening in my back yard was the best compromise on time and location that could be hammered out.

I decided to sit on my porch and listen to the debates. Squeaks the Squirrel bounced in from the woods and joined me. The candidates had not yet arrived; there was time, yet, for me to find out what Squeaks thought of the election. This would give me insight into how the typical voter was reacting to the campaign. "Who gets your vote for Mayor of the Woods?" I asked.

"Thomas Turkey, for sure," she responded with considerable enthusiasm.

"Why would you vote for him," I asked.

"Well, I think I might have known somebody who knew somebody who might have known him," she answered.

"You can't vote for him," I said. "He's not running for mayor. He's the republican candidate for the state senate."

"Oh!" said Squeaks. "Well, anyway, I feel angry and betrayed 'cause of the untangable tax. So I'm voting for big change. Everything's a mess and we've got to get somebody in there who'll brush it out straight."

"The intangible tax is a state tax," I said. "There's nothing the Mayor can do about it."

"Well," she replied, "I don't like it anyway, so I'm going to vote the rascals out."

"Why not vote for Devious the Deer?" I asked. "She's for doing whatever the voters want."

"Ohhh, no," sighed Squeaks. "I'm 'gainst her. I know those voter types and, if they get what they want, they'll get my stuff for sure. We need somebody in there who'll clean up the mess, not go changing things 'round."

"Well," I said, "maybe you will go for Windy the Wren who promises to do what's right no matter what."

"Ohhh, no," groaned Squeaks. "Last time I went right, it mattered 'cause I got left. And I don't know what's left when right's wrong?"

"What about Rascal, then," I asked. "He's the one who's for increased services, decreased taxes, and prison reform. Is that what you want?"

"Ohhh, no," moaned Squeaks. "I'm 'gainst him. Don't want 'em increasing my service; I work too hard now. And, if they decrease Texas, ought to shrink Alaska too. I'll remit, though, that most prisoners could use some reform."

Squeaks put her paws over her eyes and moaned for a good two minutes and then asked, "Ohhh, what am I gonna do?"

"Why don't you do the sensible thing and study what the different candidates represent and make an informed decision?" I asked.

"Can't do that," she answered. "They must all go to school to study up on how to tell whoppers with a straight face. The only REAL issue is which one's telling the biggest whopper. Ohhh, I know what I'm going to do. I'm voting 'gainst all of 'em. Voting for that 'what's-his-name' who nobody knows nothing about. He's not a whopper teller!"

"What makes you think Pete tells the truth?" I asked.

"Didn't say that," insisted Squeaks. "Said he lays out less whoppers. Can't lie as much 'cause he don't talk as much. He's got my votes, all six of 'em. That'll show those polly... uh, polly... uh, those who are running from office that they better not fool around with smart voters like me."

I probably would have questioned her further, but the crowd gathering in the yard quieted down as three of the four candidates assembled at the opening in front of the trees. At the last moment, Pete the 'Possum crept in. He seemed to be weary, as though he had walked a long way. A mole with field glasses around his neck followed furtively behind Pete and settled down at the edge of the woods. The candidates drew straws to see who would speak first, and Devious the Deer rose to speak. Her speech consumed most of two hours and will not be repeated here. Her primary points, however, were the following:

She said one of her opponents blatantly acknowledged having no intention of doing what the voters wanted. Rather, this opponent scandalously admitted running for office with the full intention of using the office to follow her own misguided agenda. This opponent, according to Devious, completely failed to understand the constitutional right of the voters—whose minds typically were completely uncontaminated by any knowledge of what good government was all about—to be able to use government at any time to support any foolishness whatsoever that happened to cross their minds.

Another opponent, according to Devious, claimed he would increase services and reduce taxes. He claimed, for example, he would reduce the cost of medical services while extending such services to all animals regardless of their ability to pay. How could he reduce the cost when not a single one of the animals currently paid a cent? How could he extend services that currently were nonexistent? And then there was his prison reform plans. Why would he, as he promised, put two television sets in every cell. Would this not constitute cruel and inhumane punishment?

And the third opponent, according to Devious, promised only food. What about shelter? What about dust ruffles? What about mobile telephones? Does he have no concern for all these things that add so much to the quality of life? Devious repeated her promise that she would do what the voters wanted. She reiterated her position that the voters did not want their elected officials to do what was intelligent; they wanted them to do as they were told. When she was elected, she assured them, it would be all for one and one for all!

Windy the Wren was next. She spoke for only three hours. Here is the gist of what she said:

Her female opponent, said Windy, was devious and sly. She claimed she would do the will of the voters, well, which voters?

The ones who voted for her, of course. But what about the other voters? Were they not important too? And why was she going to do the will of the voters? Because she refused to accept responsibility, that's why. But the voters, Windy claimed, have no way to know what they want. That is why they elect officials of dogmatic convictions, biased beliefs, and well-developed, half-baked ideas.

Another opponent, said Windy, was part of the old political establishment that wanted to make sure nothing changed from the good old days when politicians lived the life of kings while the poor voters suffered. These old politicians were so behind the times that they thought the voters were naive enough to support their outmoded plans to increase services while decreasing taxes. But this is a new day of enlightened citizenry who would support a new way of doing business. Windy, therefore, announced her intentions to increase taxes and decrease services. That was the wave of the future and it was high time to bring this neighborhood into the nineteenth century.

Of her other opponent, Windy spoke only for an hour or so. What did he REALLY stand for? What kind of eats did he have in mind? Never trust a politician who refused to tell you what's for lunch! Instead, cast your votes for the candidate who promises to do what's right no matter what!

Rascal the Rabbit spoke next. Since it now was almost midnight and half of the audience was asleep, he cut his speech in half and spoke for only four hours. Mostly, what he said was as follows:

One opponent, who was promising to do the will of the voters, had spuriously spoken out against Rascal's plan to provide better medical service at lower cost. Rascal insisted that, of course, his plan would work. Cutting costs was simply a matter of getting bids from competing groups of service providers. Using the competitive process would guarantee the lowest possible price, which would, of course, represent a great savings when compared with paying a great deal more. This plan also ensured free choice: Any animal would have complete freedom either to take it or leave it. And, as for the quality of medical service, the plan called for comprehensive cradle-to-grave coverage that included diaper-rash powder, band aides, and tombstones (but not much else).

As for the other candidate who promised to do what was right no matter what, Rascal had only one thing to say (and, he took only an hour to say it). First, doing what is right completely ignores the needs of what is LEFT. It only does half the job and does not do it well. Second, his opponent didn't have the RIGHT to do what's right. It's never been done in the history of our fair community; it's undemocratic, unethical and, probably, illegal. Third, what does she mean by no matter what? What a cynical attitude for one who hopes to serve the voters! Does she have no conscience, no caring, no cause other than her own welfare? Apparently not. And, fourth....

As for the final candidate, Rascal mentioned only that he had eaten with him once and Pete's eats were not fit to talk about in public much less share with the voters for four years. He summarized by repeating seven variations of his promise to increase services and reduce taxes.

At last, it was Pete the 'Possum's turn. He stood up, walked to center stage, looked up at his sign to refresh his memory, and said "A vote for Pete's a vote for eats," and sat down. He received a standing ovation. The aroused crowd cheered and cheered and lifted Pete to their shoulders and carried him four times around the spot where Mugger the Mole stood bowing and scraping and peering around with his beady little eyes. Two minutes later, the yard was deserted. The debate was over and tomorrow would bring the results of the hard fought campaigns.

86

The woods animals voted from sun up to sun down, most of them several times. Just as the sun set, the ballots were tallied and the results announced. Fourteen votes for Devious the Deer, fourteen votes for Windy the Wren, fourteen votes for Rascal the Rabbit, and one hundred and twenty-seven votes for Pete the 'Possum. Pete appeared to be the winner by a large margin.

As the crowd around the ballot box began to disperse, and the winner and losers accepted congratulations and condolences, I decided to satisfy my curiosity. I eased up behind the winner and whispered in his ear. "Why," I asked, "didn't you vote?"

"Can't," said Pete. "Don't live here."

XIX. Dreams

"Big Bang" they call the incident
That hurled the stars through time and space.
Was this a mindless accident,
Or mindful, caring, planned event?
If mountains, trees, and oceans grew
From that primeval residue,
Were thoughts and dreams and love and grace
Inherent in the "Big Bang" too?

87

I was checking the oil in our automobiles. Darkness was creeping in on me, and I was using a flashlight to see to put one of the dipsticks back in. I felt something push against my leg. I finished with the dipstick and looked down to see what was there. It was Rosie the Raccoon. I was surprised that she would be on the carport; her food was down, and she should have been eating. "What's up, Doc?" I asked.

"Who?" she asked. "Don't know any 'Doc'. I think this is just I. Anyway, I wanted you to shine that flashlight over there and tell me what's going on."

Actually, she was not altogether telling the truth. She didn't need my flashlight to see. It wasn't THAT dark. I followed her to the feeding area and shined the light at the spot where she pointed. There was nothing there. Well, almost nothing. Squeaks the Squirrel sitting on a limb holding an acorn in her paws was all. "What's the deal?" I asked Rosie.

"Ask him what he's doing," Rosie demanded.

"Why don't you ask him yourself?" I replied. "Besides, he's a she, not a he."

"Don't know his name," said Rosie. "And you have to be careful talking to strangers when you are out this time of night all by yourself."

"Rosie the Raccoon, meet Squeaks the Squirrel," I said.

"Squeaks, what are you trying to do with that acorn?" asked Rosie.

"Studying," answered Squeaks.

"Studying WHAT"

"Studying this here acorn," said Squeaks. "Chewed a hole in one end of it. See, right there. That's where I chewed the hole in it. That's so I can see inside and see if I can find 'em."

"Find what?"

"Well," said Squeaks, I buried forty-eleven thousand of these acorns last year and trees came up. Hickory nut trees, noke trees, mable trees, popular trees, peanut trees, sunflower seed trees, dandy lion trees, and watermelon trees. So, I'm looking in here to see if I can find the trees."

"What makes you think there are trees inside that little 'ole acorn?" asked Rosie.

"Well, if you plant them and trees come out, got to be trees stuck away in there somewhere. I want to find the watermelon trees and pull 'em out and see if they've got hickory nuts hanging all over."

"You can't get hickory nuts from a watermelon tree. And you absolutely, positively, definitely are not going to get any hickory nuts out of that acorn," declared Rosie.

"Why not?"

"Because it's an acorn, that's why. You can only get out of something what's been there all the time. OAK trees come from acorns. That's because acorns come from oak trees. The oak tree puts all those little baby oak trees right in the acorns and, then, drops them on the ground for you to bury so all the little baby oak trees can come out. If you want hickory nut trees, you've got to look inside a hickory nut and, if you want watermelon trees, you've got to look in a watermelon. Anyway, you can't get nuts off the trees inside that acorn until the trees have had time to grow up and make baby nuts."

"Oh, then I'll just sit here and wait. Uh, how long does it take?"

"Years and years. Longer than you're ever going to live," answered Rosie.

"Oh," said Squeaks, "no nuts inside this nut, huh? And I had my mind all set on eating a nut. Guess I'll just have to suffer this-appointment."

"Why don't you just eat the acorn?"

"Huh! Say! You're right! Golly willigins, I'm glad you came along. Sure. Of course. Why didn't I think of that. I'll just neat the acorn."

And, she did.

88

I live right next to a large state park and often go walking in the park on Sunday afternoons. Sometimes my wife goes with me; sometimes I go alone. This time I went alone. I took a bottle of water and a couple of sandwiches in case I got thirsty or hungry. We rarely enter the park through the regular entrance; usually we just go in at the point nearest our house. That's what I did this time; I walked along the edge of our neighbor's lot and straight into the park. There is not much of a path there but, particularly in the early fall, the woods are clear enough to get through without any trouble. I walked several miles, climbed down a steep bluff to the creek, spent fifteen or twenty minutes feeding bread crumbs from the crust of my sandwich bread to the minnows, and then headed into the woods on the other side of the bluff.

I reached the outcropping of rocks where, as best I can tell, most of our resident raccoons spend their time when they are not out foraging. Here, I sat in a clear spot, leaned against a friendly tree, and ate my sandwiches. I might have gone to sleep; possibly I dreamed; I'm not sure.

89

I heard a clackity, clackity, clack, clack, ding; clackity, clackity, clack, clack, ding sound coming from over behind one of the larger rocks. I floated over to the rock to see what was making the noise. I peered over the top of the rock and saw, in a clear spot under the trees next to a small brook, a most unusual thing. Well, actually, to call it "unusual" is a masterpiece of understatement. It was perhaps the most extraordinary thing I have seen in my entire life. What I saw was a monkey sitting at a crude log desk pounding away at a typewriter. There were reams of paper all over, most of it with typing on both sides. The desk was partially shaded by a single large poplar tree. The tree trunk was covered with short marks of some kind. Rosie the

Raccoon was standing beside the tree using a pocket knife, the one I had lost a few months earlier, to carve another mark into the bark of the tree. When she finished the mark, she walked purposefully over to the typing monkey, stopped him, and handed him a banana.

"Rosie! Rosie! Rosie!" I said. "What in the world is going on here?"

"I don't have the foggiest," she answered.

"You mean you don't know why the monkey is here, and why he is pounding on a typewriter, and why you are carving notches in the tree, and why you are stuffing a banana down the monkey's throat?"

"I don't have the foggiest," she insisted. "Just doing what my mate told me to do. He hadn't slept for five days, or maybe forty years. Finally had to take a short nap. Told me to watch the funny looking one and to make a mark and stuff a banana every time he got close to finishing off another ream of paper. Don't have the foggiest why. What kind of key did you call the funny looking one? Oh. A mon-key."

"So," I said, "this is all your mate's doings. Who's he?"

"Don't know his name," she said. "Only been mated two years and didn't want to get too personal too soon. Anyway, you can ask him. He just woke up."

From behind another rock emerged a sleepy-eyed, tousle-haired, male raccoon. He apparently had heard us talking. He stuck out his paw and said, "Names Remington the Raccoon."

I told him I was pleased to make his acquaintance and would he kindly tell me what was going on here.

"Nothing much," he said.

"But," I insisted, "one does not, as a rule, have a monkey banging away at a typewriter."

"But," he insisted back to me, "I'm pretty sure there is a firm, absolute, unequivocal rule that says there is an exception to every rule."

With that, he stopped, scratched his ears, stared at me, pointed toward the typewriter, and asked, "What did you call the gismo?"

"Why," I said, "looks like an ordinary typewriter to me. Where did you get it?"

"Why, I built it," he answered in surprise. "Out of scraps of this and that."

"Why didn't you just go down to Walmart and buy one?" I asked. "Surely would have been easier than building one."

"Thought I invented it myself," he said. "Didn't know there was another one in the whole wide world and South Dakota."

"Where did you get the monkey?" I asked.

"Oh," he answered, "bought him down at Walmart."

"What is he trying to do?"

"Nothing. He's just banging away. That's the whole idea. I'm a scientist. Trying to check out one of my theories. Been working on it for five months or seven hundred years. According to my theory, if you set a monkey to banging away at a type-writer in his usual random fashion, and if you continue it for eleven zillion jillion reams of paper, he eventually will, just by sheer chance, turn out an exact copy of one of Shakespeare's dramas."

"Really!" I said. "You mean you are REALLY trying to do that?"

"And you are in luck," said Remington as he checked out the marks on the tree and did some quick calculating. "When he finishes this ream of paper—and he only has two sheets left in the ream—it will be the eleven zillion jillionth one. So, it's now or never. And we shall see what we shall see."

The monkey swallowed the remainder of the banana, started back up with his random banging on the typewriter, and quickly finished the last two pages of the ream. Remington went over, took the monkey by the paw, led him over to Rosie, and said, "Stash him away somewhere until tomorrow. Then take him back to Walmart. They are good about returns. Just tell them I don't need him any more."

Rosie handed the monkey the last banana, lead him away, stashed him somewhere, and came back to see what would happen next.

Remington gathered up the last ream of paper, peered carefully at each sheet, did a great deal of grunting and mutter-ing and, finally, jumped to his feet and shrieked, "Eureka!"

"What happened?" I asked. "What do you have?"

"Shakespeare's 'All's Well That Ends Well'!" he answered. "Word for word!"

I floated over to the shade of an oak, settled down on a small, flat rock, and watched as Remington, not able to contain his excitement, danced around in a tight circle screaming "eureka!" He eventually tired and sat on the ground in front of me to catch his breath.

"Now that you have proved your theory," I asked, "what are you going to do with it? What does it really mean? What difference will it make to anybody?"

"What? Isn't it obvious?" asked Remington. "Why, it's the greatest discovery since the beginning of time. It proves that, without a doubt, all of creation is a sheer accident. It proves there is no meaning or purpose to anything. It proves that, if you allow random events enough time, anything you can possibly imagine will come to pass. Mostly, it means you can make something out of nothing if you just try enough times!"

Rosie walked up and said to Remington, "You're sitting in my place. Move over." Remington moved over a few feet and Rosie sat in the spot where he had been. "Do you mean," she asked, "that Squeaks the Squirrel really could have found hickory nuts inside of that acorn if he had just stared at it long enough?"

"Well, no. Not exactly," replied Remington. "But, if he had looked inside enough acorns, he eventually could have found a hickory tree or most anything else he wanted to find."

"You absolutely, positively are wrong," said Rosie. "Squeaks is not a 'he;' he is a 'she.' And besides, he could NEVER get a hickory nut out of an acorn. Every acorn has eleven zillion jillion oak trees in it. That is just the way it is and chance has nothing to do with it."

"Eleven zillion jillion trees in one acorn?" I interrupted. "No, I don't think so. You can plant it and find out. You only get ONE tree per acorn."

"Not so," said Rosie. "Sure, there's only one tree, but that tree has zillions of nuts built into it. And each of those nuts has a tree in it. And each of those trees has a zillion nuts, each of which has a tree in it. And each of those trees has a zillion nuts, each of which... well, anyway, it all adds up to precisely eleven zillion jillion trees."

"Doesn't make any difference," said Remington. I just proved acorns and oak tree are the result of random chance. The first oak tree certainly didn't come from an acorn because there was no oak tree to make the acorn. And, besides, don't bother me. I'm busy thinking what else I'm going to make out of nothing. Gold, maybe a mountain of gold. Or what about pearls, or diamonds, or maybe twenty dollar bills, or half a chicken?"

"Can't make those out of nothing," declared Rosie.

"Can so too," insisted Remington. "Didn't I just prove I could make one of Shakespeare's dramas out of nothing? And, if I can make that out of nothing, why can't I make ANYTHING out of nothing?"

"Didn't make it out of nothing. All the pieces were there all the time. You just put them together a certain way."

"What? Are you trying to say I didn't just prove I can make anything I want any time I want it?" roared Remington.

"Right," said Rosie. "All you proved is that maybe you can take what already is and reorganize it some."

"But... but... what about that acorn and oak tree? The first one HAD to come from NOTHING. Only way it could have gotten here." insisted Remington.

"Didn't either. Don't know where it came from, but it had to come from something that had the POTENTIAL for producing an acorn or an oak tree. It had to come from...."

That was when we were interrupted by the mysterious flying object.

90

From the shadow it cast, it appeared to be a rather large bird. But was I dreaming, or did it really have four legs? I held my hand over my eyes to shade them from the afternoon sun and watched as the object turned and flew back in our direction. It skimmed just over the tops of the low trees at the edge of the clearing, stretched its leading edges for a landing, glided skillfully between a gap in the rocks, and landed smoothly at our feet. I stared in astonishment at the creature. I knew it couldn't possibly be, but it looked exactly like Squeaks the Squirrel.

"How'd you like that four-paw landing?" asked Squeaks as she removed the large pot from her head and flung her back pack to the ground. "Notice how I slimmed over those trees, sneered between those rocks, and landed without a single ounce? But now, back off. I've got work to do."

"What... what are you going to do?" I asked.

"Flew out here where I can have some privacy," she answered. "Going to make up a new batch of baby squirrels. Going to do something different this time. I'm going to make green ones with long ears." She turned the pot right side up, opened her back pack and begin to pull out bags and cans of something or other.

"Wait up!" I cried. "You can't make green squirrels with long ears. And what are you doing with that pot? You can't make babies that way!"

"Can so too," said Squeaks. "Going to make these from scratch." She opened one bag, pored the contents into the pot, and began to stir with a long stick.

"What's that?" I asked.

"Scratch," she said. "Told you I was going to start from scratch with these. Now don't bother. Got to be very cheerful here and not make any mystiques."

"Now let's see," she continued as she checked off the ingredients from the recipe in her recipe book, opened bags, boxes, and cans, and poured their contents into the pot. "One box of selected inanimate materials; two bags of suitable environment; one bottle of gaseous atmosphere containing hydrogen, ammonia, and methane; six jugs of water; six candles to burn up all the oxygen—can't have any oxygen here, not yet, anyway; a pint or two of cosmic radiation; two cups of radioactivity; a pinch of chlorophyll to make 'em turn green; a pinch of chloroform so they'll sleep nights; two drops of essence of rabbit to make their ears run long; and a dash or two of this and that just for good measure. Now, got to use this spray can to whomp down the ozone layer 'cause got to have lots of ultra-violent rays from the sun. And, here, go plug this detention cord in somewhere. Got to have lots of electric discharges. Now there, it's all finished."

"Where are the long-eared, green babies?" I asked with a touch of sarcasm in my voice.

"Oh, it takes time," Squeaks said as she stirred away on the contents of the pot. Let's see. Says right here in my receipt book that you have to wait precisely eleven zillion jillion years."

"Does it really take all that to make a squirrel?" I asked.

"Beats me," said Squeaks. "I don't think about things like that. I just follow directions."

"Yes it does," interrupted Rosie. "If you make them from scratch, that is. That's the way ALL life got started, way back there so far I barely can remember it. Weren't any living things in the whole wide world. Just some scratch and stuff like he just put in that pot. And since you can only get out what you put in, every living thing in the whole wide world is right there in that pot."

"Wait a minute!" I said. "I thought she was making squirrels. There are lots of living things in the world besides green, long-eared squirrels."

"But," said Squeaks, "it says right here in my receipt book that, when you make up a batch squirrels from scratch, you can't help getting lots of other things too. It says, if anything comes out big and ugly, to swack it down with the stick." Squeaks took a hard look at me and continued, "Somebody back there somewhere must have gotten careless."

"I don't like this," muttered Remington. "I just don't like any of this. You've got to have monkeys and—what did you call that gismo—typewriters to get things started. I just proved that. You can so make things from nothing. If you couldn't, we would run out of stuff, because everybody knows we use up things all the time and things die all the time."

"Not so!" snorted Rosie. "We don't get rid of anything, just change it around a little. And 'die' is a relative term. Nothing ever dies in the sense that is stops being. It dies in the sense that it changes from one thing into another. See that tree over there in the corner that died fifty years ago? You don't? Well, I don't either. But all of the atoms are still around. There's still a slight rise in the ground and, if you dig down deep, you will find parts of it yet. And you could find all of it if you had the right equipment and were smart enough. It's still around. You just don't recognize it."

"I think she's right," I said. "I don't think there's actually anything new in the universe. Things just change as time passes. We can change things around a lot, but everything that exists has to have been here in some form from the beginning. Everything that exists had to be inherent in the original source that created the universe."

"Really?" asked Squeaks. "You mean EVERYTHING? You mean this here original force was chuck full of things like trees and nuts and heat and cold and caring and unconcern?"

"Well, almost," I answered. "Actually, I think trees and nuts are the same thing. Just at different stages of maturity. And there really aren't any such things as cold and unconcern. There is heat. But cold is merely the absence of heat. And there is caring. But unconcern is merely the absence of caring."

"Brrr!" shuddered Squeaks.

"What's that all about," I asked.

"Sun's going down and I'm suffering from the absence of heat," answered Squeaks, handing me her stirring stick. "Here. You stir. I'm not going to stray around here and wait. Never could stand being around baby squirrels. Got no hair or anything hardly. Ugly! Ugly! Ugly! Now move over. Got to have plenty of room for a smooth takeoff."

"Wait up!" I said. "You can't do that. Squirrels can't fly!"

"What?" said Squeaks. "You never heard of a flying squirrel?"

"But you're not a flying squirrel," I said. "You're a gray squirrel."

Squeaks turned her head and did her best to look over her shoulder at her pelt. She reached, pulled her tail under her, and took a look at the end of it. Then she took a good look at her paws. "Gee, willikins, gosh!" she said. "You're right. I'm a—what did you call it—gray squirrel all right, and you say everybody knows gray squirrels can't fry? Ohhh! What am I going to do? How'll I ever get home? I'll NEVER be able to walk all that far."

"I'll get you home," interrupted Rosie. "Got to go that way tomorrow anyway to take that mon-key back to Walmart. You'll have to stay the night though. I have a bag of marshmallows, and we will build a bonfire and toast marshmallows."

"Ohhh, that will be fun," said Squeaks. I always did love toasted muskmelons."

Remington walked over with a worried look on his face. He was mumbling something that sounded like, "Yes. I proved you can change things around plenty if you just give it enough time. I think that's what I proved. Anyway, I'm sure I proved SOMETHING."

He turned to me and asked in a low, hesitant voice, "Did you, by any chance, know this Willy Shakespeare fellow first hand? I mean, he WAS an Italian, wasn't he? The original 'All's Well That Ends Well' WAS written in Latin, wasn't it?"

"Of course not," I answered. "He was very English and he, of course, wrote everything in English."

"Uh oh!" muttered Remington. "Afraid of that."

This was all too much for me. I walked back over to my nice tree, sat on the ground, leaned back against the tree, and, possibly, dropped off to sleep. When I awoke, I was alone, and darkness was creeping in. I got up and went home.

91

I had a busy schedule the next day and gave little thought to what I was sure had been a weird dream caused, no doubt, by bad peanut butter or jelly in the sandwich I had eaten. It was almost dark before I had a chance to put down food for the animals. It seemed strange that no animals were around. Squeaks was usually there in the evening. And one or more raccoons were almost always there. I stood for a moment and listened to the quiet of the evening. Not a creature was stirring.

And then I seemed to hear the faint sound of something moving through the shadows of the woods. I took a close look but, in the gathering darkness, I could not be sure. And, of course, I had to be mistaken. I saw what appeared to be Rosie the Raccoon carrying a squirrel on her back and leading a monkey by a leash. They seemed to fade into the shadows and disappear into the night.

XX. Fly-Away Day

From time to time in every life,
The summer yields to winter's strife.
Two paths are open to us then.
One leads to mourning what has been.
The other to a welcoming
Of new adventures in the spring.

92

The first cool days of fall moved in. The air was clear and pungent with the faint smells of burning leaves. For the first time since spring, the foliage on the trees had cleared out enough for me to see the houses of our three closest neighbors and the cars traveling along the road behind our woods. I was out early doing the things I usually do in the mornings. The squirrels and birds were fed, the bird bath was hosed down and refilled, and the newspaper was fetched. I flipped my hammock upside down and dumped the leaves that had piled up on it during the night. I wondered how many more days I would be able to use it before winter set in. The air was still, the sky was clear, and the sun was just beginning to peep over the horizon. I watched the doves as they fluttered down into the feeding area for their morning snack.

It was a quiet and beautiful morning, my favorite time of year. The hot, humid days of summer were gone, but there was still time for tranquility and rest before facing the cold, challenging winds of winter. I stood and gazed into the cloudless blue of the heavens. All was at peace.

I was about to turn and go back into the house when my ears picked up what seemed to be a faint signal from beyond the woods. I wasn't sure at first, but then the sound grew louder and clearer. It was coming from above the trees off toward the east and the rising sun—a discordant "Honk! Honk! Honk!" from at least a dozen sources. The honks grew closer, and their sources

became apparent. Twelve to fifteen goosenganders were flying just above the tree tops in a giant V-formation. Just as they approached the back edge of our woods, the main body veered to the right and headed northwest as they began to gain altitude. Two of them broke from the formation and headed straight to where I was standing. One of them landed heavily at my feet. The other miscalculated, overflew his intended landing spot, crashed into me, and almost bowled me over. This was the first time I had ever seen Socs and Fun City away from the pond.

"What's... what's going on?" I asked as soon as I got my breath and balance back.

"It's fly-away day," said Socs. "We're going on a trip. Wanted you to know so you wouldn't wonder what happened to us. We're coming back, of course. It's just a little vacation."

"Going all over," Fun City chimed in as he shifted his back pack into a more comfortable position. His back pack was bulging, and odd items such as a tennis racket, football helmet, and bowling shoes were lashed to the outside. "Going to go everywhere and see everything and do everything. Trip of a lifetime! Got reservations all over at the fanciest places you've ever heard of. Going to live it up. Going to see things and do things and eat things and gamble some in the casinos. Big doings! Had to come by and let you know so you can go green with envy and wish us bon voyage and tell us au revoir, hasta la vista, adios, auf Wiedersehen, and goodbye until we meet again."

"Are all four of you going?" I asked. "Where are you going? How long will you stay?"

"All four of us," answered Fun City. "Going all over. Won't be back until the week after New Year's 'cause we're going to do New Year's eve in New Orleans."

"Actually," said Socs, "He is partly right. We want to see some mountains and the ocean. And we are going to visit for a while with those two quackenduckers who visited us at the pond. They are not in New Orleans, but he thinks they are"

"I'm glad you stopped by, I hope you have a good trip, and I will miss you," I said. "How are you ever going to find Millard and Mildred the Mallards. Won't it be hard to catch up with them?"

"I meant to show you the last letter I got from them," said Socs. "But I don't know if I could ever find it in this back pack. Anyway, I remember exactly what they said. They said, 'We have decided to forsake our desperate struggle for meaningful, happy lives, accept the goodness of life wherever we find it, oppose injustice wherever it appears, treat others as we wish to be treated, spend more time being aware of reality and less time running from truth, and slow down and smell the muck.'"

"Also," continued Socs, "you might be interested in knowing they took their last resources and purchased a houseboat on the inland waterway over in the Pamlico Sound area. They intend to use it as their primary residence and the base for their planned survey of flood plains flora and fauna, a subject that has always intrigued them. They have been sending me rare plant specimens that I have been using to restore the upper end of our pond to the way it used to be."

Fun City flapped his wings and prepared to take off. He obviously was impatient to leave. "Time is wasting," he shouted. "Got to go, go, go!"

"Those quackenduckers have changed considerably since you knew them," said Socs, apparently oblivious to Fun City's urging. They are an interesting pair. I have learned a great deal from them. They are the primary reason we are making this trip. We wish to visit with them, and also they have convinced me I can learn something by getting out and seeing a bit more of the world. I suppose we should leave. Don't want to keep the others waiting too long, and I think he may be anxious to go. You might be surprised to know he has changed some too. You wouldn't know it from listening to him today because he is all excited and not quite his usual self. He, too, seems to be seeing life from a somewhat different perspective than he once did. He even reads a few of my books—has four or five of them in that bag of his. I actually am beginning to enjoy being around him. Well, have to go. See you around."

"How will you keep from getting lost?" I asked. "How will you find your way?"

"It's not difficult," answered Socs, "if you get your directions straight before you get too tired."

"Goodbye and other things that I can't remember," cried Fun City. "Off we go into the wild blue yonder and other stuff like that!"

The two taxied to the other end of the driveway, revved up their wings, sped down the driveway, lifted heavily from the surface, barely cleared the tree, rose into the still, cool, morning air, and disappeared over the tree tops.

I felt a sweet sorrow at seeing them leave. I would miss them and joyfully welcome them back once their adventures were over. I walked slowly back to the porch, sat in my favorite porch chair, and thought about the past, present, and future. With the departure of the gooseganders, a part of my life seemed to be ending and another part beginning.

Squeaks the Squirrel apparently had eaten her fill of the sunflower seeds I had put out for her. She hop-skipped over to the porch, stood up straight with her front paws folded across her chest, looked me in the eye, and asked," What are you so down in the mouse about?"

"I'm not down in the mouth," I answered. "Some of my good friends just left, and I'm sitting here thinking about them."

Squeaks looked surprised and said, "Good friends did you say? I thought I was your friend."

"Well, you are," I answered. "But so are they. You can have more than one good friend you know."

"Can't either," Squeaks insisted. "Can only have one friend at a time. You are my only friend. And will be as long as you keep putting seeds down for me whenever I want them. But, if you ever stop, you're a bummer."

"Then I suppose you are what I would call a fair-weather friend," I said. "You're only my friend when things are going well for you."

"Right," replied Squeak. "Fair-feathered friend is all I want. Don't need any bad-feathered ones. If weather's bad, I just stay holed up in that tree over there and go over my nut collection. Don't need any fiends again until the sun goes bright."

Squeaks skip-hopped back over to the feeding area to check for any seeds she might have missed the first time. She would stay the winter, of course. Much of the time she would be holed up with her nut collection and in no need of a friend. But, at least, on the good days, she would cheer me through the winter—unless my seed supply ran low. I really did not consider her to be merely a fair-weather friend. She had shared her feelings and thoughts with me. She had been honest with me. She really was my friend.

A scratch at the door indicated that Cleopatra the Cat had finished her shirred salmon and was ready to come outdoors for twenty or thirty seconds of exercise before nap time. I opened the door and watched her regal stroll across the porch to the spot where she usually stood to observe her domain and make sure all was right with her world. "Who were you talking to?" she asked.

I told her about the visit from Socs and Fun City and my conversation with Squeaks. "I'm glad it soon will be winter," she said. "Perhaps we can have a bit of peace and quiet around here. I've noticed already that the gold finches, cow birds, thrashers, mocking birds, robins, and blue jays have thinned out. I could do a number on some of those wrens, doves, chickadees, and flickers if it were not for getting feathers stuck in my mouth. When do those raccoons start coming in at dark instead of noon? Rabbits seem to have thinned out some. Did you ever get a permit to beat some of those deer off with a stick or something. I would not mind living in a zoo if animals would keep decent hours, call and make sure it is convenient before dropping in, and keep their visits short. But who ever cares what I want around this place? Anyway, I am glad to see that you have the firewood cut, split, and stacked. Winter definitely is on its way. Winter is a beautiful time. Winter is lying on the carpet in front of a roaring fire while everything outside is cold, forbidding, desolate, and barren. Winter is lapping warm milk when an ice storm rages outside your window. Winter is the bright indoors when all without is dreary, bleak, and dark. Winter is curling up in a warm and dependable lap and sleeping while the cold winds blow. But the most beautiful thing about winter is knowing that, as surely as the sun always rises, spring will come again."

Walking out on the porch was enough exercise for Cleopatra for one morning. She went back indoors for the first of her morning naps. She was right of course. Winter was not too far away. For me, this had been a meaningful spring and summer. Part of my journey from HERE to THERE was completed, and tomorrow would bring new adventures. While I still felt somewhat like a stranger passing through a strange land without a map or a compass, I now seemed to have some of my directions straight. I seemed to see a bit more of the entirety of life. I felt an increased sense of awe of life and a strong desire to live each moment to its fullest.

I looked up at the corner of the porch where the wrens had nested, and over at the barbecue grill Jimmie had wrecked. I looked forward to another spring with many of the animals back doing their familiar things and some new animals filling in for those who would not return. The cycle of life would continue, the mundane and negative would fade into nothingness; friendships, compassion, and love would endure.

This would be a long fall and winter. I would miss my friends. But some, both animal and human, would stay close. There would be bright and happy times. There would be times of darkness and despair. But there was a new wellspring of faith deep within my being that knew with steadfast certainty that there is meaning in both the bright and dark times. In the winter, I would be able to sense the spring. In the dark moments, I would remember that, when I have the courage to be aware, the will to work, and the patience to wait, the sun really does shine at midnight too.

About The Author

Dr. Cox lives near Umstead State Park on the outskirts of Raleigh, North Carolina, with his wife, Julie. He recently retired from the Research Triangle Institute after eighteen years as Senior Research Psychologist. While there, he served as project director or task leader on more than fifty national, state, and local research projects. During his lifetime, he has engaged in a variety of careers: engineer, theologian, therapist, and researcher. He currently is working on a sequel to *The Sun Shines At Midnight Too*.